An Introduction to
the Law of Obligations

An Introduction to the Law of Obligations

A. M. Tettenborn, MA, LLB
Fellow of Pembroke College, Cambridge
and Assistant Lecturer in Law at the
University of Cambridge

London
Butterworths
1984

England	Butterworth & Co (Publishers) Ltd 88 Kingsway, London WC2B 6AB
Australia	Butterworths Pty Ltd Sydney, Melbourne, Brisbane, Adelaide and Perth
Canada	Butterworth & Co (Canada) Ltd, Toronto Butterworth & Co (Western Canada) Ltd, Vancouver
New Zealand	Butterworth of New Zealand Ltd, Wellington
Singapore	Butterworth & Co (Asia) Pte Ltd, Singapore
South Africa	Butterworth Publishers (Pty) Ltd, Durban
USA	Butterworth Legal Publishers, Mason Division, St Paul, Minnesota Butterworth Legal Publishers, Seattle, Washington; Boston, Massachusetts; and Austin, Texas D & S Publishers, Clearwater, Florida

© Butterworth & Co (Publishers) Ltd 1984

British Library Cataloguing in Publication Data

Tettenborn, A. M.
    An introduction to the law of obligations.
    1. Obligations (Law)—England
    I. Title
· 344.206   KD703.02

    ISBN Hardcover 0 406 26067 2
        Softcover 0 406 26068 0

Typeset by Phoenix Photosetting, Chatham
Printed by Mackays of Chatham Ltd

Preface

This book is not a textbook in the normal sense; it is neither big enough nor exhaustive enough for that. It attempts instead to provide a thoughtful introduction to the law of obligations as a whole, bringing together the aspects of contracts, torts, trusts and property that go to make it up.

Now this is an unfamiliar idea in England, even though on the Continent the idea of a 'law of obligations' is commonplace. But why write (or read) a book about it? Three reasons come to mind.

First, clarity of thought when it comes to commenting on the law as it stands. Speculation as to *when* legal liability ought to exist, and *why* , is clearly something that can only be done properly from the point of view of the law of obligations as a whole, rather than a particular part of it.

Secondly, the development of common principles. The gulf between the rules applying to different heads of legal liability is often less wide than it might seem; there is much in common, for instance, between the law on extinction and modification of contractual and other obligations, or between the duty of care owed in tort and in equity.

Thirdly, there are the problems of the present system of classification. It is commonplace that the differences between liability classified as contractual and that classified as tortious are often arbitrary and illogical; the same equally goes on occasion for the distinction between contract and trusts and even that between contract and property. A coverage of the law of obligations as a whole does something to alleviate these problems.

The scheme of this book is fairly self-explanatory. Part I deals with the incidence of obligations, covering liability without fault, liability based on fault, liability for causing deliberate financial loss, liability to return unjustified enrichment and promissory liability as a matter of general principle. It also deals specifically with the protection of person, property and reputation. Part II deals with ancillary matters, for instance, factors negativing obligation, the transfer of obligations, and – perhaps most importantly – their enforcement. Some matters that might be considered relevant are left out for reasons of space: for example, limitation of actions (which in any case is well covered in Professor Lawson's *Remedies of English Law*, an introductory book in similar vein).

I am indebted to many. To Dr Patrick Elias of Pembroke College for help and encouragement and comments on parts of an earlier draft. To the other members of the Faculty of Law of Cambridge University for the more intangible encouragement resulting from exchanges of views in any learned organisation. And lastly to the Master and Fellows of Pembroke College for providing a congenial environment to write in and sufficient non-legal conversation to keep a sense of proportion.

Pembroke College, Cambridge   A.M.T.
December 1983

Contents

List of cases

Table of statutes

References in this Table to *Statutes* are to Halsbury's Statutes of England (Third Edition) showing the volume and page at which the annotated text of the Act will be found.

Chapter 1

The law of obligations

The law of obligations, like most other parts of the law, serves a variety of purposes. It protects wealth, and (through the law of contract) provides facilities for adding to it. By setting standards for commercial advisers, and those providing services generally, to reach, it provides a framework for business relationships. In providing compensation for personal injury it adds to State benefits already available in the field. Lastly, in protecting certain 'moral' interests in themselves, even where no loss is suffered (as with defamation, assault, trespass to land and other 'non-pecuniary' torts) it acts as a sort of social barometer; broadly, the more stringent the protection of an unmeasurable interest, the greater the social importance put on it. If any general theme runs through the law of obligations, as that of 'wealth' permeates the law of property, it can only be the very general (and rather inconsequential) one that it provides the fabric of legal control without which social life would be impossible.

1. The idea of obligation

'Obligation' suggests duty; something somebody has to do – or not do – which a court may tell him to do (as with specific relief, such as an injunction, or an action to recover a debt), or mulct him in damages if he does not. Now this is true of many duties. The seller can be made to convey the house he has agreed to sell, and to pay damages if he does not; similarly, I can be prevented by injunction from defaming you and if I do so am liable in damages.

But this view of obligation is incomplete for two reasons. First, many obligations involve not a duty to do something, but instead a responsibility that a state of affairs exists, or will exist. A seller of a car may warrant that it has covered only 20,000 miles (see Ch 11, below); a keeper of a dangerous animal is responsible for any damage it does (see Ch 5, below). Both may be liable in damages, if the car has covered more than 20,000 miles, or if the animal bites a passer-by; both are in breach of their obligation, even though neither has done, or failed to do, anything. Indeed, obligations to see that something is the case differ strongly at times from other obligations; for instance, impossibility is largely irrelevant to them, as also (for obvious reasons) are specific, rather than pecuniary, remedies.

Secondly, the idea of obligation just mentioned comports the idea of a *wrong*. Apart from the slightly peculiar exception of an action to recover a debt, pecuniary remedies exist to compensate a plaintiff for some breach of duty by the defendant; for some wrongful failure by him to do as his obligation demanded. But this equally is too narrow. If I pay you £100 by mistake you must return it, not because you did *wrong* in receiving it, but because you would be unjustifiably enriched by retaining it (see Ch 10). Again, it is possible for an act to be rightful and yet to carry a duty to pay compensation; the right of the Crown to seize property under the Royal Prerogative in an emergency, for instance, carries an obligation to compensate the owner.[1]

2. Parties to an obligation: rights and duties

Obligation in civil law implies two parties; an 'obligor', obliged or responsible as the case may be, and an 'obligee', for whose benefit the obligation exists, and who can enforce it. In other words, any obligation can be analysed into a right in the obligee and a duty in the obligor (duty being understood in the wide sense of comporting an obligation to see that something is the case, as well as an obligation to do something). The presence of an obligee, or someone who can enforce the obligation for his own benefit, is what partly marks off the law of obligations from the criminal law.

Normally, the benefit the obligee takes from the obligation is two-fold; he both benefits from performance of the obligation, and can choose to invoke the remedies available to enforce it. In some cases, though, those roles are separated, the clearest being contracts to benefit third parties. A contract by A with B to pay C £100 is for C's benefit but enforceable by B alone. Here usage is to refer to B, rather than C, as the obligee.

We refer to the breaking down of obligations into 'rights' and 'duties'. It has been argued that the idea of a 'right' is superfluous in this connection;[2] if a right in X connotes a duty in Y, why not limit consideration to the latter? The short answer to this argument is to ask why it is logically necessary to regard duties as paramount rather than rights. Certainly on occasion lawyers think the opposite way; positing a right to the protection of a certain interest, and then inferring a duty not to infringe it (the development of the 'neighbour principle' in negligence, that one must take care not to injure one's neighbour, is

---

1   *Burmah Oil Ltd v Lord Advocate*, [1965] AC 75 [1964] 2 All ER 348.
2   Eg by H. Kelsen in his *General Theory of Law and State*, Ch 6; more practically by W. I. Jennings in *The Law and the Constitution*, 2nd edn, 1938, 242.

perhaps the best example[3]). True, *some* legal rights can only be effectively thought of only in terms of the duties protecting them; the right to the preservation of one's financial interests from deliberate interference is one of them.[4] But it is surely unsound to assume that all legal thinking must logically follow the same pattern.

3. Obligations and remedies

An obligation is – at least in general – not the same as the remedies available to enforce it. The duty to convey a house one has contracted to sell is the obligation; the court's power to enforce specifically that duty, and the seller's liability to pay damages if he breaks it, are remedies available to enforce it.[5] If the purchaser of a house sues the vendor for damages for failure to convey it at all, the legal result of judgment for the purchaser is that the 'primary' obligation to convey the house is destroyed and replaced by a 'secondary', or remedial, duty to pay damages.[6] One might think this was an argument over nomenclature, but in fact it is more serious than that. Confusion between obligation and remedy has led to the paradoxical argument that, with obligations not enforceable specifically (such as contracts to sell generic goods), an obligor is not obliged to perform at all. He has a choice, whether to perform or pay damages.[7] There are two objections to this point of view. First, it counters common usage with respect to the concept of obligation. More importantly, the fact that an act is 'wrongful', albeit only in that the actor must pay damages, has other, indirect, legal consequences. It may, for instance, found an action for unjustified enrichment (see Ch 10), or liability for causing loss by unlawful means (see Ch 5).

4. The sources of obligations

Formally, legal obligations arise from many sources; contract, tort, the law of trusts, the emergent law of unjustified enrichment, and so on. Now some formal classification of obligations is necessary; in the nature of things, obligations dealing with different subject-matter

---

3 Ie the rule in *Donoghue v Stevenson* [1932] AC 562; see below, Ch 6.
4 See Ch 8, below.
5 Technically, the duty to pay damages for breach of an obligation is itself an obligation, subject to many of the rules affecting obligations in general. But this does not affect the point in the text, which is that remedial obligations are secondary to the obligations whose breach they remedy.
6 *Moschi v Lep Air Services Ltd* (sub nom) [1973] AC 331 at 350, [1972] 2 All ER 393 at 403, per Lord Diplock.
7 O. W. Holmes, *The Common Law*, 301, is the classical exponent of this view.

4 1 The law of obligations

ought to be subject to different rules. The law relating to the enforcement of promises should be treated differently from that relating to compensation for loss, or the protection of property. The difficulty with the formal sources mentioned at the beginning of this paragraph is that very often the differences between them are artificial. Indeed, one situation may often engender parallel obligations from the various different formal sources (for example, the hirer of a car who wrongfully sells it is liable to the owner both for breaking the contract of hire and also for unlawfully interfering with his property; that is, both in contract and tort. Similarly, it seems a bank giving negligent advice to its customer on his investments may be liable to the latter in damages in tort, contract and also for breach of 'fiduciary duty' in equity). The aim of this book is to draw together as many of the features of obligations emanating from different sources as deal with similar subject-matter as is possible; hence the headings of the various chapters may seem a little unfamiliar.

5. The law of obligations and other legal concepts

(a) CRIMINAL LAW

For the most part, the distinction between the law of obligations and the criminal law is fairly straightforward, though not surprisingly it is sometimes blurred at the edges. In some cases it cannot be said definitely which side of the line a given rule falls.

To begin with, there are procedural matters. Different courts in general try civil and criminal cases, according to different rules of evidence and other procedure,[8] and with appeal lying to different bodies.[9]

Secondly, with criminal duties there is no obligee; criminal duties may exist for the benefit of others, but they are not owed to them. One cannot obtain damages for the commission of a crime, or (unless one is the Attorney-General, who acts effectively for the Crown) an injunction to stop it;[10] fines, where enforced, go to the State and not to anyone else. The victim of a tort can release his aggressor; the victim of a crime cannot demand that the prosecution of the criminal stop. There are of course exceptions to these rules. In at least one case[11] an informer can

---

8   For instance, some of the harsher rules of evidence are relaxed by the Civil Evidence Act 1968, but only for civil proceedings; conversely, the judge's general power in criminal cases to suspend certain rules of evidence in favour of the defendant is clearly inappropriate in other sorts of proceedings.

9   Section 18(1) (a) of the Supreme Court Act 1981 and its predecessors, precluding appeal to the Court of Appeal (Civil Division) in 'any criminal cause or matter', have caused as many problems of classification as any other rule.

10   *Gouriet v Union of Post Office Workers* [1978] AC 435, [1977] 3 All ER 70.

11   See the House of Commons (Clergy Disqualification) Act 1801, s 2.

sue a criminal for a penalty for his own benefit. As a result of a useful power in the Powers of Criminal Courts Act 1973, s 35, a criminal court convicting a person can order him to compensate his victim as well, up to a statutory limit. Again, there are interesting powers in the State to initiate proceedings to secure the return of stolen property to the owner, or to obtain justice for the shareholders of a company against those who have defrauded it.[12] But the exceptions are, even in total, rather minor.

Thirdly, criminal obligations are generally enforced with a view to punishment of the defendant, while civil proceedings are brought to vindicate an interest (pecuniary or otherwise)[13] of the plaintiff. Damages reflect in general plaintiff's prejudice rather than defendant's culpability; indeed, as appears in Ch 17, one cannot even stipulate for penal damages in contract. Again there are exceptions; in certain cases of very blatant wrongdoing, a tortfeasor may be liable for punitive damages, for example; but once again, the exceptions are minor.

Lastly, there are some substantive points. Obligations may be negatived by consent; not so duties under the criminal law. The prize fighter cannot sue his opponent for hitting him,[14] but the latter is still guilty of assault.[14] Again, most obligations are destroyed by the obligor's bankruptcy; duties under the criminal law, such as the duty to pay a fine, are not.[15]

Some legal duties, not surprisingly, are hybrid; sharing characteristics from both the law of obligations and the criminal law. Normally this does not matter; it is sufficient to refer to the fact that such duties share characteristics from both sides. It becomes important only where, on rare occasions, a duty must be classified 'civil' or 'criminal' in an arbitrary way; where, for instance, it is in issue whether the civil or the criminal rules of evidence apply, or which court appeal lies to. Hence the courts can only do the best they can to see which characteristics seem to them most important; in any case whatever conclusion they reach will be somewhat arbitrary.[16]

There is little difference (and hence we have not tried to distinguish) between the *content* of criminal and other duties, as against their legal treatment.[17] Any attempt to limit criminal duties to acts somehow in themselves immoral,[18] or to deliberate wrongdoing, has been obsolete

---

12 See the Theft Act 1968, s 28; Companies Act 1980, s 75.
13 For an example of the vindication of a non-pecuniary interest, see the large damages available in defamation irrespective of proved financial loss; damages which are clearly compensatory, though, rather than punitive.
14 Compare *Murphy v Culhane* [1977] QB 94, [1976] 3 All ER 533, with *R v Donovan* [1934] 2 KB 498.
15 This is the result of the Bankruptcy Act 1914, ss 4 and 30.
16 For examples of such decisions (generally recondite and unimportant) see 11 Halsbury's Laws, (4th edn), para 2.
17 See on this point the argument of G. L. Williams, (1955) 8 CLP 107 at 123.
18 As apparently in C. K. Allen, *Legal Duties*, 233 f.

at least since the turn of the century. One reason is the rise of the regulatory offence carrying strict liability, conviction of which counts as misfortune rather than disgrace. Another possible reason is the increasing incidence of corporations as criminal defendants, who cannot in any real sense be said to act immorally anyway.

(b) OBLIGATIONS AND PROPERTY

The borrower of a thing is obliged to give it back to the owner; the seller, who has agreed to sell it, to hand it over to the buyer. These claims, superficially similar,[19] are not the same. The owner claims the thing by saying that it is his; the buyer by saying that it is not, but that he has a right to it.[20] This difference encapsulates the difference between obligation and property. Now, we do not deal in this book with the incidents of property as such – its means of creation, transfer and so on. Yet much of the law of property necessarily comes into it, for several reasons.

First, there is the obvious point that property creates, and is protected by, obligations; my obligation not to interfere with something belonging to you, and to give it up to you if I have it, for instance. This is the subject of Ch 2.

Secondly, the benefit of an obligation can be transferred; the rules relating to its transfer, as described in Ch 16, neatly straddle obligation and property.

Thirdly, the distinction between property and obligation that we have drawn is less neat than it seems. Many legal situations can be placed plausibly in either category. A declaration of trust, for example, can be regarded as either a transfer of equitable ownership (property) or – at least in practice – a form of enforceable gratuitous promise to transfer legal ownership (obligation).

Indeed, this book deals with several cases of rights that fit more happily into the law of obligations but are nevertheless regarded as part of the law of property. The reason for this tension is normally that it is desired to harness some aspect of the law of property that does not apply to the general law of obligations (such as the ability to prevail over third parties[1] or in an insolvency); or alternatively that there is simply a gap in the general law of obligations that ought to be filled. Examples of the latter are the use of property – here the constructive trust – to allow a promise to be enforced by a third party (as where A conveys land to B, who promises A to let C use it[2]); or to supplement

---

19   Both involve the same physical action; that is, handing over the thing concerned.
20   An instructive case on the difference between these two claims is *Franklin v Neate* (1844) 13 M & W 481.
 1   The law of property is harnessed, for instance, to allow a specifically enforceable contract for the sale of land to be enforced against third parties. See Ch 9, below.
 2   See *Binions v Evans* [1972] Ch 359, [1972] 2 All ER 70, below, Ch 9.

the law of unjustified enrichment (a thing transferred pursuant to a contract ineffective owing to mistake is recoverable by the transferor on the ground that it remains his, not that it represents the transferee's unjustified enrichment[3]). In short, the distinction between property and obligation, apart from being simply a tidy device of classification, is as often as not a device to achieve the right results with a minimum of doctrinal distortion.

---

3 See, eg *Hardman v Booth* (1863) 1 H & C 803; see below, Ch 10.

Part 1

Chapter 2

Protection of property

There would be little point in property as an institution unless others were under an obligation not to interfere with it. Imposing such an obligation, however, is not as simple as it looks, since interference with property is a very wide concept. Thus there are at least three substantial forms of interference with others' property; unauthorised use, unauthorised taking, and other forms of misdealing such as touching, destruction and damage. Property itself, moreover, exists in at least three forms. One is ordinary physical objects, such as a car, a candlestick or a cargo of sugar. The second is immovables: broadly, land and things, such as houses, attached to it. Thirdly there are intangibles, such as a debt, credit at a bank, shares in a company or a right under a trust. Now these kinds of property are protected in different ways, partly for historical reasons, more importantly because they are naturally prone to different sorts of interference. Land, for example, cannot be effectively stolen, whereas a diamond ring can. On the other hand, land, unlike other things, is likely to have its value and usefulness destroyed indirectly without being physically affected; by smells or noise, for example.

1. Unauthorised use of property

(a) UNAUTHORISED USE OF LAND

Most direct users of another's land, like the squatter or the walker taking an unauthorised short cut, are caught by the tort of trespass, which covers practically any physical interference with land. In fact, however, this is not a very important liability unless the landowner wants specific relief such as an injunction, or to exercise self-help by ejecting the trespasser.[1] Damages will be insubstantial unless the trespass caused damage, or was blatant or otherwise aggravated; and, at least where land is used as a short cut, apparently its owner does not even have a claim against the user for a reasonable fee for such use based on unjustified enrichment.[2] (An owner may, however, by suing

---

1 Note, however, that self-help to regain possession of land may on occasion be a criminal offence – Criminal Law Act 1977, s 6.
2 *Phillips v Homfray* (1883) 23 Ch D 439. The rule is tellingly criticised in R. Goff & G. Jones, *The Law of Restitution*, 2nd edn, 474 f.

for 'mesne profits', recover a reasonable rent from a squatter or unauthorised occupier whom he ejects.)

One can occasionally exploit someone else's land without physically interfering with it at all; a house owner next to Lord's, for instance, could let out space at his upper windows to let others watch the cricket without paying for admission.[3] Such conduct is not wrongful; nor even does it engender a claim based on unjustified enrichment. The exercise of property rights negatives either kind of claim.

(b) UNAUTHORISED USE OF PHYSICAL OBJECTS

Liability for use of physical objects is almost as general as that for use of land; provided there is some physical interference the user is normally liable, both for the tort of conversion, and (unless the thing used is already in his hands, for instance because he is a bailee) trespass to goods as well. Indeed the owner of a chattel is better protected than the landowner, because the user of a chattel is further liable on the basis of unjustified enrichment for a reasonable charge for the use he has made.[4] Furthermore, the torts of conversion and trespass to goods carry strict liability; a defendant may be liable in damages even though he did not know the property he was using belonged to another or intend to infringe another's rights by using it.

(c) INTANGIBLES

Fairly clearly, this form of misdealing does not apply to intangibles; one cannot 'use' a debt owed to another in the same way as one can borrow his bicycle without permission.

2. Unauthorised taking or keeping of property

(a) UNAUTHORISED TAKING, KEEPING OR DISPOSAL OF CHATTELS

A rational system of liability in this part of the law would be simple. A person finding himself in possession of someone else's thing would be obliged to return it to the true owner, or at least pay him its value; further, a person knowingly taking another's thing, or disposing of something (for instance by sale) which he knew belonged to another,

3   See the interesting Australian decision in *Victoria Park Racing & Recreation Grounds Ltd v Taylor* (1937) 58 CLR 479.
4   *Strand Electric and Engineering Co Ltd v Brisford Entertainments Ltd* [1952] 2 QB 246, [1952] 1 All ER 796. The result is apparently different, however, where property is kept and not used – *Brandeis Goldschmidt & Co Ltd v Western Transport Ltd* [1981] QB 864, [1982] 1 All ER 28.

would be liable to the owner for any loss suffered as a result. But English law is not rational here) and even when the Law reform Committee tried to make it so[5] only the worst anomalies were removed as a result. In particular, two historical oddities still plague this part of the law.

First, although the act of disposing of another's thing should be governed by just one tort, in fact a person doing so may commit any of three: conversion, trespass to goods, and a third, which in the absence of a better name we call reversionary injury. (There used to be a fourth, detinue; but that was abolished in 1977, by which time it was virtually co-terminous with conversion.) The interplay between these torts can be complex.

Secondly, there is failure to distinguish essentially different forms of interference. Disposing of another's thing to a third person is conceptually different from refusing to give it back to the true owner; yet English law subsumes both under the tort of conversion. As a result features appropriate only to the latter kind of interference are applied to all disposals of others' property. For instance, a person disposing of another's thing is strictly liable even though he had no reason to know it belonged to that other; moreover, he is liable not simply for the loss suffered by the owner, but ipso facto for the market value of the thing.

We deal first with liability for taking another's thing or disposing of it to a third party. The basic rule is simple: the defendant is liable in damages to the owner for the value of the thing concerned, provided he intended to act towards it as an owner would. A thief must pay the value of the goods he steals (although not the owner, he behaves as if he were); similarly an innocent purchaser, since his innocence is irrelevant and he, like the thief, has acted as owner. Indeed, the innocent purchaser remains liable to pay the owner the value of the goods even after he has himself disposed of them; in other words, an owner of stolen goods can recover their full value from anyone through whose hands they pass, however innocently. (Of course the owner cannot recover multiple compensation. Once he recovers the value of the goods he ceases to have any interest in the goods themselves. Effectively he has an election; he can either recover his property in specie[6] or recover its value, thus forcing the defendant to buy him out, but he cannot do both.)

The remedy thus given to the owner is drastic. Making the innocent purchaser pay the value of goods even though he has since disposed of them is hard; equally hard in practice, though theoretically leaving no-one out of pocket, is the owner's right to force any converter to buy

---

5 In its 18th Report, Cmnd 4774 (1971).
6 A remedy in the discretion of the courts – see now Torts (Interference with Goods) Act 1977, s 3(2).

him out by claiming the full value of his goods. It would be fairer in many cases, if the defendant still has the goods, to allow him to insist on the owner taking them back in specie. As a result the right to claim the full value of goods is mitigated in two ways. First, a defendant who still has goods he converted in good condition can mitigate any pecuniary claim by the plaintiff by tendering the goods back; if the goods are worth the same as when he converted them, this effectively reduces the plaintiff's claim to nil. Secondly, for a taking to be a conversion and thus allow the owner to claim the full value of the goods, it must be inconsistent with recognition of the true owner's rights; a rule that excludes many innocuous takings.[7] In one case,[8] for instance, the defendant, unloading timber from a ship, inadvertently stacked some timber belonging to the plaintiff with his own. The defendant failed in an action for conversion (and merely got his timber back) because by accepted stevedoring practice timber was sorted provisionally only, mistakes being rectified without question; hence the defendant's action was not inconsistent with recognition of the plaintiff's rights. Similarly, in the old case of *Fouldes v Willoughby*[9] it was held that wrongfully putting the plaintiff's horse off a Mersey ferry might be trespass to goods, but was not conversion since the defendant had not purported to act as owner.

A person may be liable for the full value of another's thing as much by disposing of it (for instance, selling it) as by taking it. A thief, for example, who steals goods and then sells them converts them twice, as does the innocent purchaser who later resells. The owner, in claiming damages of the value of the goods, may rely on whichever conversion took place when their value was higher. (However, where an innocent purchaser of goods improves them before reselling them in good faith, the owner may recover their improved value only if he gives credit for the cost of improvements.[10]) Moreover the person disposing of property is liable whether or not he had reason to know it belonged to someone else. This is hard; especially as, to add insult to injury, the owner's contributory negligence is irrelevant when he sues in conversion.[11] The owner may, by allowing his goods to be stolen, be 90% to blame for the goods having been handled by the innocent purchaser; nevertheless he can still claim their full value.

This liability, moreover, extends even to those, such as auctioneers,[12]

7   Though by no means all innocuous takings. It is submitted that the guest who mistakenly takes someone else's hat from the rack is technically guilty of conversion even if he puts it back immediately. Damages of course would be minimal; the return of the hat would mitigate them.
8   *Sanderson v Marsden* (1922) 10 LL L Rep 467.
9   (1841) 8 M & W 540.
10   Torts (Interference with Goods) Act 1977, s 6. This expands a similar rule at common law: *Greenwood v Bennett* [1973] QB 195, [1972] 3 All ER 586.
11   Torts (Interference with Goods) Act 1977, s 11(1).
12   *R H Willis & Son v British Car Auctions Ltd* [1978] 2 All ER 392, [1978] 1 WLR 438.

who help others to dispose of goods which happen not to belong to them; a liability difficult to defend, except in so far as auctioneers can insure against it and therefore in practice pass it on, through increased charges, to those who use their services. The Law Reform Committee in 1971 nevertheless recommended retaining this rule on the rather unconvincing ground that it was necessary to prevent dishonesty.[13]

In three cases, for reasons of obvious fairness, the strict liability normally attaching to those disposing of others' goods does not apply. One is where the defendant is a mere minion; the auctioneer who sells inadvertently a stolen picture is liable to the owner, the servant who holds it up in front of the bidders is not. Another is that an innocent bailee may safely give goods back to his bailor; it would be monstrous if, having borrowed my neighbour's lawnmower and returned it, I were liable for its full value if it turned out not to be my neighbour's at all.[14] Lastly an involuntary bailee (for instance a shopkeeper finding lost property in his shop) is not liable if he gives it up to a person he reasonably thinks is the true owner, even if he is wrong.[15]

So much for taking or disposing of another's goods. On the other hand, for *keeping* another's thing and refusing to return it to him, strict liability is entirely appropriate. An owner of a thing must be able to get it, or its value, back even from a bona fide possessor on demand. The only oddity of English law is that it reaches this result through the law of tort, arguing that the possessor does wrong by possessing the owner's thing and that damages for that tort are the value of the thing. More logical would be the approach of Roman law and most Continental systems, which regard the right of an owner to get his goods back as part of the law, not of obligations, but of property. Indeed, English law moves some way towards this solution in that by statute[16] a court may order the possessor of another's thing to return it in specie without the option of paying its value.[17]

Lastly, although we return to this subject later when discussing who can sue for interference with property, it should be noted that a person taking property in another's possession, most obviously the thief, may also be liable to the owner, or the possessor, of what he takes, in the tort of trespass to goods or reversionary injury. These torts, which – as we shall see – broadly cover any physical interference with goods owned or possessed by another, are however, not very important in this context

13 Cmnd 4774 (1971), para 14.
14 See *Alexander v Southey* (1821) 5 B & Ald 247; *Hollins v Fowler* (1875) LR 7 HL 757 at 767, per Blackburn J.
15 *Helson v McKenzies Ltd* [1950] NZLR 878; cf *Elvin & Powell Ltd v Plummer, Roddis Ltd* (1933) 50 TLR 158. (Contra, Burnett (1960) 76 LQR 364.)
16 Torts (Interference with Goods) Act 1977, s 3(2).
17 The power is generously exercised in many cases – see,eg, *Howard E Perry & Co Ltd v British Railways Board* [1980] 2 All ER 579, [1980] 1 WLR 1375.

since it will normally be more profitable for the owner or possessor to sue in conversion.

(b) UNAUTHORISED DEALINGS WITH INTANGIBLE PROPERTY

The torts we have mentioned as protecting chattels – conversion, trespass and reversionary injury – do not protect intangibles; nor indeed does any other tort specifically do so. Logically this lack of protection seems odd; in fact, however, pragmatic considerations mean it makes practically no difference. To begin with, few intangibles are not represented by something tangible, such as a piece of paper; and a promissory note or share certificate, for instance, being tangible, can be converted as much as anything else. Moreover, the measure of damages in conversion is, as we have seen, the value of what is converted; and where a piece of paper (such as a cheque) evidencing an obligation is converted, by a fiction, its value is deemed to be the value of the obligation itself. In other words a cheque for £100 is deemed to be worth £100.[18]

In any case it is very difficult to deprive the owner of an intangible of the benefit of it. One cannot walk off with a debt in the same way as one can walk off with someone's watch. If A owes B £10 he continues to even though C obtains £10 from him by impersonating B; again, a shareholder in a company retains his right to be registered as such even though a thief steals his share certificate, forges a transfer and dupes the company into registering him instead. Of course, it is theoretically possible to deprive another of the benefit of an obligation. A may contract to pay B £100 on terms that the debt is discharged if A pays someone he reasonably thinks is B. If C then obtains £100 from A by impersonating B, he deprives B of his rights. But this is hardly a common problem; and even here B might have a remedy against C for the tort, mentioned in Chapter 8, of causing loss by unlawful means.

In this connection, however, equitable interests, such as interests arising under a trust, are exceptional. They are intangible and common law remedies are unavailable to protect them;[19] nevertheless, equitable remedies protect them very effectively. Obviously a trustee making away with trust property is liable to compensate the beneficiary; more to the point, a third person co-operating with a trustee committing a breach of trust (for instance by misappropriating trust property) is liable with the trustee as a joint wrongdoer. So a solicitor must compensate a beneficiary when he concurs in the payment of trust money to the wrong person;[20] more recently, a trade union official was

---

18 *Bavins Junr and Sims v London and South Western Bank Ltd* [1900] 1 QB 270.
19 Except in one case, justified pragmatically. Where A holds property for B absolutely on trust, B's equitable right to possess the goods as against A apparently suffices to allow him to sue third persons for conversion; *Healey v Healey* [1915] 1 KB 938.
20 *Lee v Sankey* (1872) LR 15 Eq 204.

prevented from encouraging insurance agents holding money on trust for their principals to refuse to hand it over.[1] A third person, moreover, who receives trust property otherwise than as a bona fide purchaser, is bound by the terms of the trust and can be sued for certain breaches of it in the same way that a trustee can. Furthermore, although a trust beneficiary does not have common law remedies for interference with property, the trustee does; and he can be forced by the beneficiary to use those remedies against anyone interfering with the trust property who would be liable at common law.

3. Other unjustified interference with property

(a) CHATTELS

After the obligation not to take or dispose of another's thing, not to use it without the author's permission and to return it to its owner on demand, there remains the obligation not to interfere with it in lesser ways; in particular, damaging, moving or touching it. This is the province of the torts of conversion and trespass to chattels, among others. The boundaries of these torts are important; English law recognises no general wrong of interfering with another's property, so interference as such is not actionable provided it amounts to no specific tort. Thus in the Australian case of *Penfolds Wines Pty Ltd v Elliott*[2] the plaintiff sold wine to customers in returnable bottles that remained his property throughout; yet he failed to stop the defendant shopkeeper refilling those bottles with his own wine when customers brought them to him. The bottles were indubitably the plaintiff's, but the defendant committed no tort in interfering with them. Again, a possessor of another's goods must let that other have them back on demand, but need not send them to him; if the owner fails to collect them the possessor can apparently hold on to them for as long as he likes.[3]

As for interferences that are actionable, we begin with destroying property (or, what comes to the same thing, turning it into something else).[4] This amounts to the tort of conversion; it is an act clearly inconsistent with recognising the plaintiff's ownership, in which terms the tort is defined. This liability in conversion is important, because it means the plaintiff can sue for the entire value of what was destroyed or transmuted (abandoning his interest in the result, if any, to the defendant), and is not limited to claiming his actual loss.

This drastic remedy, however, does not apply to damage short of

---

1 *Prudential Assurance Co Ltd v Lorenz* (1971) 11 KIR 78.
2 (1946) 74 CLR 204.
3 See *Capital Finance Co Ltd v Bray* [1964] 1 All ER 603, [1964] 1 WLR 323.
4 As with watering wine in the old case of *Richardson v Atkinson* (1723) 1 Stra 576.

destruction, nor to other interference; this is the province of trespass to goods, where liability is for actual loss suffered. The ambit of this tort is wide: deliberately damaging, taking or moving another's thing is rendered wrongful by it, as (it appears) is even deliberately touching it.[5] (This latter is uncertain; but it would accord with the rule on trespass to land, and would sometimes provide a necessary remedy – for instance against repeated touching of a museum exhibit.) Liability, as with conversion, is independent of whether the defendant knew the property he was interfering with was the plaintiff's.

The main limit on liability for trespass is that it lies only where property interfered with was in the possession of another, and moreover is excluded if the person who *was* in possession (even if not the owner) consented to what was done. Thus a person borrowing a car without the owner's consent for a 'joy-ride' commits trespass, but not the person who, having lawfully borrowed a car for one purpose, uses it for a different one;[6] nor does the person who buys property from a thief; nor (as we have seen from *Penfolds Wines Pty Ltd v Elliott*) the shop-keeper who fills up bottles brought to him by customers which happen to belong to third parties.

(b) INTANGIBLES

This sort of interference is effectively inapplicable to intangibles such as debts; as regards interests under a trust, the reader is referred to pp. 16–17, above.

(c) LAND

(i) Direct interference
Interference with land divides into direct interference, physically impinging on land itself and a matter of the tort of trespass to land, and indirect interference not affecting the land itself, but still reducing its value or utility; this is governed largely by the law of nuisance.

With trespass to land, the obligation is starkly simple: one must not go on land without the owner's consent, nor put anything (such as rubbish) on it; not even lean anything, such as a ladder, against a building. Rights above and below land, as might be expected, raise a few problems. Anything in airspace a few feet above land, such as an overhanging bill-board, is clearly a trespass;[7] but not an aircraft – at least if flying at a reasonable height (which in any case is protected from liability by statute). The correct criterion seems to be that of Griffiths J

---

5   But not apparently brushing against it – cf *Everitt v Martin* [1953] NZLR 298.
6   See N. E. Palmer, *Bailment*, 123.
7   *Kelsen v Imperial Tobacco Co Ltd* [1957] 2 QB 334, [1957] 2 All ER 343.

in *Baron Bernstein of Leigh v Skyviews & General Ltd*,[8] that above a few feet infringement is trespassory at common law only if it unreasonably inhibits the amenity or value of the land. This corresponds with the test of liability for indirect affection of land, a clearly sensible solution since at any substantial height direct interference shades into indirect anyway. Below land the problem is one of mining and a few other activities; and with mining the problem is largely academic since most of it is done under statutory powers excluding common law remedies. Authority suggests, however, an absolute right in a landowner to control what goes on under his land; hence the opinion of an American court that conducting sightseers round a cave below another's land could be prevented as a trespass.[9] Moreover, the criticism that this is 'dog in the manger' law is misplaced. True, there is something unattractive about a landowner being able to prevent activities that harm him not in the slightest. But that a non-landowner should be able, for profit, to exploit attractions under someone else's land without paying for the privilege is equally unattractive. Since one suspects most landowners would come to some arrangement with those wishing to conduct operations under their land, the present law seems to have merely the beneficial effect of making sure the exploiter can be made to pay for the privilege.

Befitting a law attaching much weight to property rights, liability for trespass to land is strict in at least three senses. The defendant's knowledge is irrelevant. Moreover, practically no excuses are tolerated; even duress is no defence to trespass, or so a seventeenth-century case decides.[10] These cases are in fact more symbolic than relevant; limited damages for technical trespasses and the removal of differences between lawful and unlawful visitors (for example, to a large extent in the duty of care owed by the landowner to them[11]) make sure of that. More significantly, merits and motive are largely out of account, as is the triviality of the plaintiff's complaint. One may thus force removal of a hoarding projecting only four inches above one's property merely in order to have a free hand in later selling the space it occupied to the highest bidder.[12] On occasion, however, the force accorded property rights is such that, whereas the plaintiff's illegitimate motive will not deprive him of the right to prevent a trespass, the defendant's motive will deprive him of an excuse he would otherwise have had. One may use a footpath across another's land without being a trespasser; but one becomes a trespasser, and may thus – for instance – be thrown off the land, if one uses the path for a wrong motive. A famous example is

---

 8 [1978] QB 479, [1977] 2 All ER 902.
 9 *Edwards v Sims* 232 Ky 791, 24 SW 2d 619 (1929).
10 *Smith v Stone* (1647) Aleyn 65.
11 See now the Occupiers' Liability Act 1984: Ch 6, below.
12 *Kelsen v Imperial Tobacco Co Ltd*, note 7, above.

that of the enemy of the landowner walking across his land only in order to spoil his shooting.[13]

(ii) Indirect interference

Trespass leaves untouched two sorts of interference: factors such as noise or smell, that reduce the value of land without actually impinging on it, and damage done indirectly, as where factory fumes kill roses or propagated weeds infest a farmer's field. Activities affecting others' land in this way are governed largely by the law of nuisance.

The obligation involved here can be broadly, if slightly uninformatively, stated. One cannot carry on activity on land or elsewhere that unreasonably damages other land (or buildings or things on it), or that unreasonably impairs its amenity. So householders can complain of anything from smell from a pig-farm, to noise from water-sports, smuts from a petroleum-works, earth in the garden from an unstable mound next door, or tree roots undermining their foundations. Similarly in commerce: a doctor's surgery cannot be rendered unusable by vibration from a workshop, or a butcher's shop by dust from a coal-mine.

Not that matters are as simple as that. Activities are, and must be, carried on that do affect others' land, and they must be accommodated somehow. English law could have dealt with the problem in several ways. It could have exonerated entirely defendants who acted reasonably, or meritoriously, or who fulfilled social need by carrying on vital industries; but, despite Lord Denning MR's famous attempt to use this means to justify playing cricket even where it damaged neighbouring property,[14] it never did. On the contrary; very essential activities have been prevented as nuisances because damage to others' interests resulted, such as electricity generation and sewage disposal.[15] Nor did it admit that meritorious activity was wrongful but limit those prejudiced by it to damages, thus allowing a sort of compulsory purchase of their rights. Despite this being common American practice,[16] it was rejected; property rights should be sacrosanct, and acts, it was felt, should be either rightful or wrongful and not something peculiar in between.

Instead the law looks to the damage to the plaintiff's land; it must be unreasonable – or, as a Scottish judge put it, *'plus quam tolerabile'*.[17] Now this rule has two aspects. First the interest the plaintiff seeks to protect must not be too sensitive;[18] an amateur astronomer with a delicate

13 *Harrison v Duke of Rutland* [1893] 1 QB 142.
14 *Miller v Jackson* [1977] QB 966, [1977] 3 All ER 338.
15 See, eg, *Shelfer v City of London Electric Co* [1895] 1 Ch 287.
16 Prosser, *Torts*, 4th edn, 603–604, advocates this trend; *Boomer v Atlantic Cement Co* 257 NE 2d 870 (1970) exemplifies it.
17 *Watt v Jamieson* (1954) SC 56 at 58, per Lord President Cooper.
18 *Robinson v Kilvert* (1889) 41 Ch D 88.

radio telescope in his back garden can hardly complain if his neighbours' television interferes with it. (However, even the very sensitive can complain if the defendant acted for malicious or otherwise illegitimate motives; this is one of the rare examples where English law is prepared to allow bad motives to make wrongful what would otherwise be allowed.)[19] Of course, as luxuries take the guise of necessities, sensitive uses will become normal and thus protectable; dicta in 1965,[20] for example, that television reception is an over-susceptible interest not protected by the law of nuisance are probably doubtful today.

Secondly, damage to amenity of land is not actionable if such damage is normal where that land is. Those living next to industrial estates must endure more noise than those in leafy suburbs.[1] (Oddly, this limitation does not apply where the plaintiff complains of actual damage and not of impaired amenity. So in *St Helens Smelting Co v Tipping*[2] a copper foundry was liable for damage its fumes did to shrubs in neighbouring gardens even though such damage was doubtless to be expected in the area. This exception is difficult to justify; there is no reason to distinguish land made less pleasant and things on land burnt, broken or poisoned. Continental law recognises no such distinction; English law, it is submitted, should follow suit.)

In any case, without an account of the effect of statute, stating the common law position misleads. Things drastically affecting land, such as airports, oil refineries or opencast mining, are controlled by statutes which (since statutory authority ousts common law liability) make largely irrelevant the common law of obligations. Some such statutes do what the common law cannot, justifying an activity but providing compensation for those affected by it; the benefit of this is obvious, in that it means environmental costs are ultimately paid by the enterprise engaging in the activity and (one hopes) eventually by those who benefit from it, rather than by those unlucky enough to be immediately affected by it. Unfortunately not all statutes do this; and if a statute merely authorises an activity without saying more, then the activity can simply be carried on without any liability to anyone. The House of Lords, moreover, recently made clear in *Allen v Gulf Oil Refining Ltd*[3]

---

19   *Hollywood Silver Fox Farms Ltd v Emmett* [1936] 2 KB 468, [1936] 1 All ER 825, (though see the sceptical comments on this matter in Salmond & Heuston, *Torts*, 18th edn, 53 f).

20   See *Bridlington Relay Ltd v Yorkshire Electricity Board* [1965] Ch 436, [1965] 1 All ER 264.

1   Compare Thesiger LJ's often-quoted dictum in *Sturges v Bridgman* (1879) 11 Ch D 852 at 856, that 'what would be a nuisance in Belgrave Square, would not necessarily be so in Bermondsey.'

2   (1865) 11 HL Cas 642.

3   [1981] AC 1001, [1981] 1 All ER 353. Note, however, that sometimes a statute can be construed to exclude liability for deliberate interference with property rights, but not to excuse harm caused negligently; *Geddis v Proprietors of Bann Reservoir* (1878) 3 App Cas 430.

that courts cannot plausibly construe a statute as allowing something to be done and yet as preserving any liability to damages at common law.

To return, however, to the common law. Nuisance, we have seen, is a peculiar tort in that it may make wrongful even reasonable and beneficial activity. Yet more bizarrely, a plaintiff can in at least one case use it to complain of damage he himself has brought about. One might think a person buying a house next to a very smelly pig-farm could not complain of the smell. Not so, however; it is no defence that the plaintiff came to the nuisance.[4] The reason for this extraordinary rule is, it is suggested, that nuisance, before planning controls were introduced by statute, provided a sort of private enterprise planning control. Hence noxious trades, even beneficial ones, could not be carried on in a residential area, the aim being to confine them to where they existed already rather than to prevent them being carried on at all. Hence also the newcomer to a district could get an injunction to prevent an old-established nuisance; the obligation not to commit a nuisance existed partly for the benefit of the neighbourhood as well as the for the plaintiff. (Indeed, this function of nuisance is not perhaps entirely out of date. Planning control by statute has some effect; but it provides no remedy for the householder damaged by unauthorised activities nearby. The law of nuisance does something to fill that lacuna.)

4. Who can complain of interference with property?

Were English law logical the answer to this question would be simple – the owner – and in any case it could be relegated to the law of property. As it is, however, matters are slightly more complex for both chattels and land.

(a) CHATTELS

We begin with interferences with chattels amounting to conversion, such as using, taking or destroying them. On principle the obligation not to convert a thing is owed not to its owner but to its possessor. So in the old case of *Gordon v Harper*[5] it was held that a landlord who hired out furniture to his tenant could not sue a third party who wrongfully took it. Only the tenant, who possessed the furniture, could complain. In fact, however, this did not matter in practice. An owner who was not a possessor might not be able to sue in conversion, but if he suffered actual loss from interference with his property he could recover it from the person responsible by the action for 'reversionary injury'.[6]

---

4   *Sturges v Bridgman* (1879) 11 Ch D 852.
5   (1796) 7 Term Rep 9.
6   *Tancred v Allgood* (1859) 4 H & N 438; *Lancashire Wagon Co Ltd v Fitzhugh* (1861) 6 H & N 502.

Moreover, there was one exception anyway to the rule that only a possessor could sue for conversion; an owner not in possession could sue in the normal way if he would have had the legal right, at the time his property was converted, to demand it back from the person who *was* in possession. This protected the owner whose goods were stolen and then converted in the hands of the thief, and also the bailor at will, who lent goods to another on terms that they were to be returned on demand. (Moreover, even where goods were bailed for a fixed period, as in hire purchase, courts were adroit to find some act by the bailee that extinguished his right to hold on to the goods for the agreed period and turned him into a bailee at will.)[7]

Conversely, at common law, the possessor always could sue for conversion, even if (because the goods did not belong to him) he personally suffered no loss. Superficially peculiar, in fact the rule made good sense where it was unclear who *did* have the best title to goods (many owners, indeed, would be hard put to it to prove more than possession of what they think they own[8]). Much less defensible was the right of a possessor to recover where it *was* clear that someone else had a better right (on principle even a self-confessed thief could sue[9]); and the Torts (Interference with Goods) Act 1977, s 8, now allows a defendant sued for conversion to show a named person has a better right to the goods concerned than the plaintiff.

So much for conversion. As for interferences covered by trespass to goods, this tort too is a tort against possession, and more strictly so since only a possessor can sue for it and not a person who, though not a possessor, nevertheless has an immediate right to possess. Thus if A's goods are stolen by B and interfered with while in B's hands by C, A can sue C in conversion but not trespass. (Perversely, however, a bailor at will, though not a possessor, *can* sue in trespass; apparently on the basis that he is in possession through the agency of his bailee.)

As with conversion, the possessor can sue for trespass even though not the owner; this right, however, has been curtailed in the same way as the right to sue in conversion, by s 8 of the Torts (Interference with Goods) Act 1977.

(b) LAND

With interference with land, we are dealing effectively with trespass to land. This is completely a tort against possession. The possessor can sue even if the land is clearly owned by somebody else; there is no

---

7   See, eg, *North Central Wagon and Finance Co Ltd v Graham* [1950] 2 KB 7, [1950] 1 All ER 780.

8   Cf W. Buckland & A. McNair, *Roman Law and Common Law*, 76 f.

9   For obvious reasons this probability is rather academic. A thief sued and won in the New York case of *Lieber v Mohawk Arms Inc* 314 NYS 2d 510 (1970).

limitation on this right equivalent to that in the Torts (Interference with Goods) Act 1977 relating to chattels.[10] The non-owning possessor cannot sue. However, if he can show actual loss he can apparently recover that from the person responsible by an equivalent of the tort of 'reversionary injury' relating to chattels that we have already mentioned.[11]

Similar principles apply to the tort of nuisance, that governs indirect or more insubstantial injury to land; this is again a tort against possession, with similar results.

Odd though it may seem, this solution is right. In practice trespass and nuisance protect land not as a valuable thing in abstracto (which broadly marks the extent of the owner's interest in it); but instead protect the interests of those on land, who live or work there. Hence in the commonest case where ownership and possession of land are split, the lease, it is appropriate that any action in respect of interference with the land should prima facie be brought by the lessee and not the lessor.

---

10   *Nicholls v Ely Beet Sugar Factory Ltd* [1931] 2 Ch 84 at 86, per Farwell J.
11   *Jones v Llanrwst UDC* [1911] 1 Ch 393.

Chapter 3

Interference with the person

Persons are like things in that they can be interfered with in numerous ways; and just as disparate torts have grown up to cover interference with things, so also with interference with persons. Different sorts of interference give rise to different kinds of liability; and English law has rejected the idea (present in, say, German law[1]) of a single tort in interference with personality in general.

Interference with personality takes at least four forms. One may be deliberately injured; or touched but not injured in circumstances clearly demanding a remedy (as with indecent assault); or frightened or distressed without being touched at all; or affected merely in one's freedom, as where one is confined or simply prevented from going where one wants. To cover these various interferences, there are four particular torts; assault, battery, false imprisonment and a fourth, which we will call 'unjustified injury', to fill some of the gaps left by the other three.[2]

1. Physical injury

Here, if nowhere else, English law approaches an acceptable general theory of liability. It is tortious deliberately and unjustifiably to cause physical injury to another. Injury for these purposes includes, besides injury in the normal sense, any substantial physical incursion whether or not harmful (for instance, an unauthorised operation); and further, 'nervous shock' – a convenient, rather than informative, description covering any recognised psychiatric complaint due to traumatic events which goes beyond mere grief or distress.[3]

Two torts go to make up this general liability; battery and 'unjustified injury.' The former, whose essence is the deliberate physical interference with another's person, covers cases where injury is in some

---

1 Art 823.1 of the German Civil Code makes actionable unlawful violation of the 'life, body, health, freedom, property or similar right' of another.
2 This head of liability is sometimes also called 'residuary trespass to the person.' Its name is, of course, irrelevant; what matters is whether the liability exists.
3 *Hinz v Berry* [1970] 2 QB 40 at 42, [1970] 1 All ER 1074 at 1075, per Lord Denning MR.

sense forcible (whether the force amounts to a direct blow, a trip-wire placed in front of an unsuspecting walker, or an unauthorised operation on a sleeping patient). The latter applies to other cases of deliberate injury where there is no residual element of force. Since it is not easy to injure another without at least some force it is a rare liability; but it is typefied by Wright J's decision in *Wilkinson v Downton*[4] that a hoaxer was liable for the nervous shock he caused to a woman by falsely telling her that her husband had been injured some distance away. Although authority for this separate head of liability is scanty, and its boundaries a little uncertain,[5] it must be sound because it is unthinkable that any civilised system of law would deny a remedy in such cases. Moreover, the existence of 'unjustified injury' as a separate head of liability removes a difficulty that would otherwise exist, that some kinds of liability fit obviously into no established tort. A surgeon, for instance, who misinforms his patient on the nature of a serious operation may or may not be liable in battery[6] (there being some sort of consent, his intervention is forcible only in a remote sense); but this does not matter since even if not liable for battery he is liable for 'unjustified injury'.

2. Interference without injury

Quite apart from deliberate *injury*, the tort of battery makes wrongful deliberate *touching* of another, even if no harm is caused or intended. A kiss is as actionable as a slap where the victim does not consent. The reason for this liability is not so much injury as offence. Hence the law distinguishes between inadvertent contact with others, something which (in the absence of injury) is not actionable because it is simply a hazard of social life; and deliberate interference which, because it is deliberate, offends others sufficiently to justify making it wrongful even in the absence of loss.[7]

3. Distress and fear

Apparently on the basis that distress and fear, as such, are less serious incursions than injury, the law refuses to make a person liable simply for deliberately and without excuse causing another to be distressed or

---

4   [1897] 2 QB 57.
5   Is one, for instance, necessarily justified in *truthfully* telling a woman that she has just been widowed if the result will clearly be to cause her traumatic nervous shock?
6   Though a Canadian court has said he is – *Lepp v Hopp* (1979) 98 DLR (3d) 464.
7   Oliver Wendell Holmes once remarked that even a dog knows the difference between being stumbled over and being kicked.

afraid, as against being actually injured. Instead deliberate distress or fear is actionable only in one case; where A, being in the immediate vicinity of B, attacks him or makes as if to do so (as by pointing an unloaded gun at him) then he is liable to B for the tort of assault. Actual contact is unnecessary; liability depends simply on B's apprehension of what A did.[8] (Indeed, in theory even apprehension is unnecessary; if a reasonable person would be frightened at what the defendant did, it is irrelevant that the plaintiff was in fact unusually strong-minded and did not fear a thing. But this case is abnormal).

But this liability is surprisingly narrow. True, it seems words spoken in a person's presence, if menacing enough, may be actionable ('Hands up' from a motionless robber);[9] but more remote threats, such as by telephone or letter, are not; nor are other forms of fear deliberately caused, if they fall short of nervous shock (which, as we have seen, is treated as a form of injury).

4. Freedom of movement

The law distinguishes, understandably, two rather different ways of restricting another's freedom of movement; preventing him going in a particular direction where he wants to go (but allowing him freedom to go in other directions), and completely circumscribing his movements. As the remedies provided by the law emphasise, the former is obviously less serious than the latter.

Stopping a person going in a particular direction, however deliberately, is not as such wrongful.[10] There is one narrow exception; obstructing a highway so as to stop another going along it is the tort of public nuisance, and anyone suffering special (normally financial) loss as a result, over and above that suffered by the public at large, can claim it.[11] Effectively, therefore, one's interest in going where one wants is protected only in a limited way, and even then as a commercial, rather than a personal, interest.

Confining a person, by contrast, is treated much more seriously; in effect, indeed, in the same way as injuring him. Deliberately preventing a person leaving a given area[12] – physically or by threats – without lawful excuse amounts to the tort of false imprisonment, and is

---

8   Indeed, the victim need be in no real danger at all, provided he thinks he is; pointing an unloaded gun is just as much an assault as pointing a loaded one. See *Stephens v Myers* (1830) 4 C & P 349.

9   Most instructive here is the New Zealand case of *Police v Greaves* [1964] NZLR 295.

10 *Bird v Jones* (1845) 7 QB 742.

11 *Rose v Miles* (1815) 4 M & S 101.

12 How large the area must be before confinement in it ceases to be imprisonment at all is a matter for conjecture, but not a very important one.

actionable as such, even though no further loss is caused. Means do not matter; in an interesting parallel with *Wilkinson v Downton*[13] and the tort of 'unjustified injury', it is enough for A, intending to imprison B, to start a chain of events that will have that effect (for instance, by supplying information to the police[14]). The importance placed by the law on freedom of movement is further emphasised, in that it is imprisonment itself, and not its effect on the individual plaintiff, that apparently matters; thus it seems one may recover for false imprisonment even though one does not know one is being imprisoned, for instance because one is unconscious.[15]

5. Malicious prosecution

Any legal system must protect citizens against malicious use of the criminal law against them when they are in fact innocent; English law does so through the tort of malicious prosecution. In practice, however, this is not a very important tort, and there is little point in dealing with it in any detail. The decline in private (and thus possibly very ill-founded) prosecutions, and the practice of paying costs of successful criminal defendants out of public funds,[16] have made it redundant in all but a very few cases. Moreover, even when the tort was more significant than it is now, the plaintiff was deliberately placed under a very heavy burden of proof, to prevent discouragement to those with public spirit enough to enforce the criminal law at all, and as a result comparatively few actions in practice succeeded anyway.

6. Justification for interference with the person

As with protection of property, the torts protecting the person – assault, battery, false imprisonment and unjustified injury – carry a form of strict liability. Although they cover only intentional interferences, a person committing them is liable unless what he did was in fact legally justified. It is no defence as such that he thought it was justified, however reasonably;[17] nor yet that the action he took was reasonable in the circumstances.

---

13 [1897] 2 QB 57.
14 *Hopkins v Crowe* (1836) 4 Ad & El 774.
15 *Meering v Grahame-White Aviation Co Ltd* (1919) 122 Lt 44. The authority often cited to the contrary, *Herring v Boyle* (1834) 6 C & P 496, is unconvincing and in any case obiter. By analogy, moreover, other interferences with persons asleep, such as unauthorised operations, are clearly tortious.
16 Pursuant to the Costs in Criminal Cases Act 1973, ss 1–3.
17 A good example is *Walters v W H Smith & Sons Ltd* [1914] 1 KB 595.

Equally, however, in many cases what would otherwise be breaches of the obligation not to interfere with others will (as might be expected) be justified. One may use force to defend oneself of one's property, for example. Most important by far, however, in this connection are the rights of the State; to arrest, detain, and so on. Now there are various ways to reconcile these rights with the general law of obligations and yet provide a remedy where the State exceeds its powers. One way is to exempt State action altogether from the ordinary law of obligations but then to allow a special cause of action in certain cases as a matter of administrative law for compensation. English law, however, rejects this solution. Instead, the general law of assault, battery and so on apply to public authorities and other State agencies as much as anyone else: and rights of arrest and similar rights are expressed simply as exceptions to it. A police constable, for instance, may arrest only (a) for a breach of the peace and (b) where he reasonable believes a person is committing, has committed or is about to commit, certain serious offences (known as 'arrestable offences'); in other specific cases laid down (normally) by statute.[18] If the policeman goes outside these cases, however reasonably or justifiably, he commits a tort and can be sued for it like anyone else.

At first sight the distinction we have drawn seems to make little difference. Liberty is equally well protected whether those who infringe it without justification are liable under the general law of obligations or under specific principles regarded as part of administrative law. Nevertheless, the English system we have just described has one serious drawback. Under it, an arrest (or, for that matter, any other interference with the person undertaken by public authority) is either rightful, so it cannot be complained of at all; or wrongful, when it may be prevented by injunction, reasonable force used to resist it, and so on, as well as its giving rise to a right to compensation. There is little room in the common law for a power which authority acts lawfully in exercising, but which, if it in fact turns out to have been exercised without foundation, gives the person it is directed against a right to compensation. This lacuna, it is submitted, has caused a proliferation of justifications for interference with the person, in the shape of vast numbers of miscellaneous police and other powers, which rather reduces the value of the general obligation of non-interference. Arguably, it also gives those who have been arrested or otherwise inconvenienced in error, a justifiable feeling that, by going un-compensated, they individually are bearing a burden that ought to be borne by the community at large.

---

18 See E. C. S. Wade & G. G. Phillips, *Constitutional and Administrative Law*, 9th edn, 443–448, and in particular the Criminal Law Act 1967, s 2(1), for when powers of arrest exist.

7. Insult and humiliation – a note

Although this book primarily concerns interests that *are* protected by the law of obligations, the interests a legal system chooses *not* to protect can be equally significant. One such interest in English law is, perhaps oddly, self-respect. Insult causing humiliation, even if deliberate, is not actionable as such. (It may be incidentally wrongful, of course; if false and communicated to a third person it may be defamatory, and humiliation may increase damages where other breaches of obligation are involved.)[19] But only in one or two cases, normally statutory, is a remedy provided essentially to protect *amour propre*. The best examples are anti-discrimination legislation; in particular the Sex Discrimination Act 1975[20] and the Race Relations Act 1976,[1] whereby a person dismissed from work, or refused employment, or refused other goods or services, on grounds of sex or race may claim substantial damages for the humiliation and other non-pecuniary harm caused thereby.

---

19   See Ch 17, below.
20   SS 65, 66(4).
1   SS 56, 57(4).

Chapter 4

Protection of reputation

Through the twin torts of libel and slander (which share many of the same rules and can be conveniently known collectively as 'defamation'), English law protects reputation straightforwardly, individualistically and very generously. When in doubt, the interest in reputation prevails over that in active news reporting and over the defendant's claim not to be penalised for innocent reporting; a strict attitude existing partly (one suspects) because English law, unlike many Continental systems, regards defamation largely as a tort and plays down its criminal aspect.[1] (Libel is a crime, but is very rarely prosecuted.)

1. The means of defamation – libel and slander

The difference between libel and slander goes to the means of defamation; written defamation, broadly, is libel, spoken defamation slander. (What of ambivalent forms of communication? These are treated, it seems, as libellous if permanent – tape-recordings or films –and slanderous if transient. Wireless and television broadcasts are statutorily assimilated to libel.)[2]

The only important distinction between libel and slander is in the sort of loss the defamed plaintiff can claim compensation for; in libel he can claim independently of whether he has suffered any actual money loss, whereas with slander he must prove some such loss. Even this difference is discounted since four kinds of allegations are actionable in slander even in the absence of proved damage (accusations of serious crime, contagious infection, professional incompetence, and – for women – unchastity).[3]

To distinguish defamations by the medium of expression is

---

1 A more insidious reason is that an English court cannot order the *retraction* of a defamatory statement, but only award damages for the harm it has done. Damages are a crude way to undo the harm done by a defamatory statement, but are nevertheless generously awarded because they are the only one.

2 Defamation Act 1952, s 1.

3 Moreover, it seems a plaintiff in slander who *can* prove pecuniary loss is not *limited* to it; he can claim non-pecuniary losses as well.

intellectually indefensible; whether that condemns the distinction is more doubtful. In practice it does little injustice and some good; the requirement of special damage rightly excludes many minor complaints of verbal slanging, while the exceptions to it prevent many serious complainants going uncompensated.[4]

2. The interest protected – reputation

Defamation is a tort protecting *reputation*; it deals solely with statements tending to make a person[5] less attractive to others as a person, to lower him 'in the estimation of right-thinking members of society generally'. To call a shopkeeper dishonest or incompetent is defamatory; but not to say that (without being himself at fault) he once sold bad meat, or that he has gone out of business. Such allegations may damage, and may comprise malicious falsehood,[6] but they do not defame because they reflect not on the plaintiff but on his business.

What matters is, of course, that an allegation *actually* tends to make others think less of the plaintiff; whether as rational people they *ought* to, is irrelevant. Obviously we ought not to think worse of a woman who has been raped; what matters is that some people do, and so to say so is defamatory.[7] Again – and less defensibly – this means that undeserved reputation is protected as much as deserved; a war criminal who has hitherto hidden his complicity in past atrocities can recover handsomely for a false allegation that he is guilty of other atrocities.[8] By way of exception, illegitimate reputation – that is, reputation for acting illegally or otherwise undesirably – is not protected; one cannot complain of allegations, however false, that one is a police informer, since such activity is a social duty.[9]

Falsehood is necessary in defamation; truth is an absolute defence, though the defendant bears the burden of proving it. The law has refused to protect privacy by extending defamation, or any other tort,

4   Were libel and slander assimilated, there ought to be a specific exclusion of any complaint relating to allegations that did the complainant no appreciable harm. See J. G. Fleming, *The Law of Torts*, 5th edn, 527.
5   Or, it seems, a corporation: *Bognor Regis UDC v Campion* [1972] 2 QB 169, [1972] 2 All ER 61. This is odd, because it is hard to see how corporations can have any interest in reputation except as a financial asset.
6   See Ch 8, below; cf *Ratcliffe v Evans* [1892] 2 QB 524. Distinguishing falsehood and defamation is a delicate task; see, eg *Capital & Counties Bank Ltd v Henty* (1882) 7 App Cas 741.
7   *Youssoupoff v Metro-Goldwyn-Mayer Pictures Ltd* (1934) 50 TLR 581.
8   *Plato Films Ltd v Speidel* [1961] AC 1090, [1961] 1 All ER 876. If the plaintiff's previous misconduct *is* known, however, he will have less of a reputation to lose, and damages will reflect this fact.
9   *Byrne v Deane* [1937] 1 KB 818, [1937] 2 All ER 204.

to make wrongful illegitimate, as against false, attacks on reputation. One cannot complain of the revival, however malicious or unjustified, of a discreditable incident in one's past life;[10] here, as elsewhere, the law refuses to penalise a person for doing what he has a right to do (tell the truth) merely because his motive in doing so was unjustified. Of course, for defamation purposes truth is relative; literal truth can be defamatory if untruth is inferrable from it. To say, *tout court*, that X has often been seen with a murdered girl may be true; without more, it may still imply X's implication in the murder. Again, a statement ex facie innocent may be otherwise to those with particular knowledge (the doctrine of the 'innuendo'); to say Mr X has promised to marry Miss Y may be defamatory of Mrs Y to those who know her, since it suggests she is living in sin with Mr Y.[11] Of course, the doctrine of 'innuendo', pushed too far, seriously threatens freedom to speak the truth; hence the law is careful to limit the extent to which secondary meanings can be attached to apparently innocent assertions. How it does so is too detailed for coverage here.

Further, in order to protect honest reporting, the right to complain of merely technical untruth is limited: a bank-robber, for instance, cannot complain of an allegation that he stole £10,000 on the ground that he only stole £9,000. The Defamation Act 1952, s 5, extends this principle to cases where, of several statements made, some are not true but are piffling in comparison with those that are.

3. What is actionable interference with reputation?

(a) PUBLICATION

On the ground that reputation is not *amour propre*, defamatory statements are not actionable unless communicated to a third person. However, this requirement is less limiting than it seems. Formal publication, even to a secretary writing a letter, seems to suffice; further, in cases where third persons can be expected to find out about a communication (for instance where it is displayed publicly or contained in an unsealed postcard), publication is presumed.[12] In fact, the requirement of publication is rapidly becoming merely formal; which perhaps explains why, once a falsehood has been communicated, it remains actionable even though no-one is proved to have believed it.[13]

---

10 With one exception. The Rehabilitation of Offenders Act 1974, s 8, provides a remedy for 'maliciously' (*sc* illegitimately) reporting certain long-dead convictions.
11 *Cassidy v Daily Mirror Newspapers Ltd* [1929] 2 KB 331.
12 Cf *Huth v Huth* [1915] 3 KB 32.
13 See *Hough v London Express Newspaper Ltd* [1940] 2 KB 507 at 515, [1940] 3 All ER 31 at 35, per Goddard LJ.

(This latter rule also seems justified on pragmatic grounds; proving belief of scandal can be difficult, and the assumption that scandal harms is doubtless right often enough to justify treating it as though it always did).

(b) HARM TO REPUTATION

Reputation is valuable; but it is primarily a moral, not a pecuniary, interest. Hence libel and the four varieties of slander mentioned allow an award of damages (and often a substantial one) independently of money loss suffered. (Actual loss is recoverable as well, of course.)[14] The characterisation of reputation as a moral interest also explains and justifies the rule that the right to sue for defamation does not survive the plaintiff's death; there is no justification in allowing an executor to recover for the estate damages that would have gone to console, not to reimburse, the deceased.

(c) THE ACT OF INTERFERENCE

As might be expected, a defamatory assertion may be indirect as well as direct; implied or express. To take a well-known example,[15] to picture a well-known amateur sportsman in an advertisement may suggest prostitution of amateur status; it may even be defamatory for the police ostentatiously and justifiably to watch an innocent person's house.[16]

In short, what matters is what others believe from the defendant's action, not what the defendant intended to assert. The consequences are sometimes drastic. Not only can one be liable for a statement that one reasonably believed to be true; a statement about a fictitious person sharing the plaintiff's name may attract liability if it could also refer to the plaintiff,[17] and so even can quite true assertions about a namesake of his.[18] These last two rules, while logical (defamation is a

---

14   But not damages for injury. At first sight this is odd; but it is right. Defamation is a tort of strict liability; it would be anomalous to introduce it adventitiously into the general scheme of negligence liability for personal injury.

15   *Tolley v Fry & Sons Ltd* [1931] AC 333.

16   See *Robertson v Keith* 1936 SC 29. Extending defamation too far outside what people *say* to what they *do* can be problematical; for instance, justifications for what would otherwise be defamation do not sit easily where action, rather than speech, is involved.

17   *E Hulton & Co Ltd v Jones* [1910] AC 20.

18   *Newstead v London Express Newspaper Ltd* [1940] 1 KB 377, [1939] 4 All ER 819. Equally to defame the members of a small group is to defame each of them, even though none is named. See *Knupffer v London Express Newspaper Ltd* [1943] KB 80, [1942] 2 All ER 555, and *Morgan v Odhams Press Ltd* [1971] 2 All ER 1156, [1971] 1 WLR 1239.

tort of result, not intention), are however intolerable to authors and reporters; hence the Defamation Act 1952, s 4, provides a limited defence of 'innocent publication'. A person defaming another merely because he did not know he existed or because he really meant to refer to someone else, can escape liability in damages by a suitable apology and retraction.

(d) LIABILITY IN DEFAMATION

Not only the writer of defamatory material, but the publisher, printer and even the distributor (for instance, bookshop or newsvendor) are liable;[19] the essence of the tort is publication. Logically all should be liable regardless of intent; in fact only writer, printer and publisher are. The distributor, exceptionally, is liable only for negligence; if he had no reason to know what he distributed was libellous, he escapes.[20]

4. Defences and justifications

(a) PRIVILEGE

English law may constrict zealous reporters; but efficient government and business often requires a right to pass on doubtful or even false information without being sued for it. Privilege in defamation satisfies this need.

In some circumstances 'absolute privilege' applies, meaning total immunity from the law of defamation. These include things said in court; and things said in, and papers published by, Parliament; the same goes, for obvious reasons, for accurate contemporaneous reports of legal proceedings[1] and republication of Parliamentary papers,[2] and also, apparently, for certain communications between very senior Government officials.[3]

More interesting, and much more extensive, is 'qualified privilege'. Where this applies, liability depends, exceptionally, not simply on falsity, but also on 'malice'; meaning publication either in the knowledge that what is communicated is false, or alternatively without such knowledge but for an illegitimate reason.

19 Salmond & Heuston on *The Law of Torts*, 18th edn, 146.
20 *Emmens v Pottle* (1885) 16 QBD 354; cf *Goldsmith v Sperrings Ltd* [1977] 2 All ER 566, [1977] 1 WLR 478.
1 Law of Libel Amendment Act 1888, s 3; *McCarey v Associated Newspapers Ltd* [1964] 2 All ER 335, [1964] 1 WLR 855.
2 Parliamentary Papers Act 1840, s 1.
3 Eg *Chatterton v Secretary of State for India* [1895] 2 QB 189. This interesting, as being one of the very rare cases where a public official is exempted from the ordinary law of obligations at common law merely because of his position.

The justification for strict liability in defamation is the argument that if one does not know that what one is saying is true, one should not say it. Now, qualified privilege applies broadly where this argument does not hold good and to expect silence would be quixotic: particularly, where one has a legal (or moral) duty to warn another of what one suspects but cannot prove, and where one has an interest of one's own (or sometimes of another) to protect.

Examples of defendants under a duty include an employer providing a reference for an employee; or a company secretary receiving an adverse report on a company official from the auditors, who must be able to pass it on to the shareholders without danger of being sued.[4] The duty may, of course, be limited to informing particular people; an employer suspecting an ex-employee of dishonesty may voice his suspicions without fear to other prospective employees, but to no-one else.[5]

The interest one is entitled to protect is rather more nebulous. Proprietary interest suffices; if my goods are in your warehouse, I can without danger tell you I suspect your employees of pilfering them. Similarly the interests of companies or trade unions extend to those administering them; internal communications on their affairs are thus normally privileged.[6] By an analogy with the right to self-defence, communications issued to defend oneself against other allegations carry qualified privilege.[7] Again, administrators[8] and, indeed, all of us, have some etiolated interest in good government; hence a letter to once's MP alleging maladministration is privileged.[9] And, of course, it is under the head of protecting one's interests that professional privilege for communications between client and legal adviser is justified.

Privileged reports

News is not protected from the law of defamation in general; but certain reports are protected ad hoc. These include, at common law, fair and accurate reports of judicial proceedings abroad. The Defamation

4   As in *Lawless v Anglo-Egyptian Cotton Co* (1869) LR 4 QB 262.
5   This is sometimes confusingly expressed as the rule that the recipient must have an 'interest' in receiving the communication. See generally *Adam v Ward* [1917] AC 309.
6   *Bryanston Finance Ltd v De Vries* [1975] 2 All ER 609 at 629–630, per Lawton LJ. But it is not sufficient that both parties stand to gain by the communication. News agencies sell news to newspapers for profit; but news is not per se privileged. Compare too *Macintosh v Dun* [1908] AC 390 and *London Association for Protection of Trade v Greenlands Ltd* [1916] 2 AC 15.
7   See *Turner v Metro-Goldwyn-Mayer Pictures Ltd* [1950] 1 All ER 449 at 470–471, per Lord Oaksey.
8   *Adam v Ward* [1917] AC 309.
9   *Beach v Freeson* [1972] 1 QB 14, [1971] 2 All ER 854.

Act 1952, s 7, adds a large and varied collection which attract qualified privilege. If what is reported is of public concern, reports of proceedings of international organisations and courts, Commonwealth legislatures and courts, and English public registers, among other things, attract qualified privilege; provided the publisher also prints an answer by the person defamed, the same goes for reports of the proceedings of public bodies and, significantly for free discussion, public meetings.

(b) FAIR COMMENT

Any law of defamation must deal with the problem of statements, not of fact, but of opinion: allegations by one journalist that another publishes a 'low' newspaper, or by a theatre critic that a performance is 'disgraceful'. Apart from the theoretical question how far statements of opinion can be untrue at all, there must be room for legitimate artistic and political criticism.

Where a statement is not on a matter of public concern, English law holds – oddly – that statements of opinion are like statements of fact; they may be defamatory, and if they are must be shown to be true.[10] How to do this with a statement of opinion is unclear; presumably a bald assertion that X behaved 'disgracefully' would be justified by proving some behaviour that could reasonably be called disgraceful.

Where matter is of public concern (and this includes most of government, public and artistic life and a good deal besides), and where – as in the arts – comment is the rule anyway, the law is more intelligent. Provided the defendant is not 'malicious' in the sense of spiteful, his opinion need only be honest (that is, honestly based on true facts[11]) in order not to be actionable.[12] This is the defence of 'fair comment'. If any of the above features are lacking – if the defendant is malicious[13] or what he said was really an assertion of fact and not opinion (a narrow distinction in many cases),[14] he will have to justify his opinion in the normal way. But if fair comment applies, any statement of opinion is protected, however partisan or unreasonable. The question, in short, is not whether comment is *legitimate*, but rather whether it is *honest*.[15]

---

10 See *Sutherland v Stopes* [1925] AC 47 at 62, per Viscount Finlay; *Kemsley v Foot* [1952] AC 345 at 356, per Lord Porter.
11 See the Defamation Act 1952, s 15.
12 See, eg, *Turner v Metro-Goldwyn-Mayer Pictures Ltd* [1950] 1 All ER 449.
13 *Thomas v Bradbury Agnew & Co Ltd* [1906] 2 KB 627.
14 Eg *London Artists Ltd v Littler* [1969] 2 QB 375, [1969] 2 All ER 193. Apparently imputations of dishonesty are always questions of fact; cf *Campbell v Spottiswoode* (1863) 3 B & S 769.
15 See eg *Merivale v Carson* (1887) 20 QBD 275 at 280–281. It is sometimes said that the comment must be such as a reasonable man *could* have made; but this is misleading, as prejudiced judgments can be fair comment, while reasonable men are (presumably) unprejudiced.

Chapter 5

Liability without fault

The protection of persons, property and reputation, which we have dealt with hitherto, are specialised subjects; hence the particular coverage given to each. But any legal system must have general rules to deal with other forms of loss or damage; financial losses, inadvertent damage to property and personal injury in particular. Now a person causing any loss to another[1] may face several schemes of liability. He may not be liable at all; he may be liable only if he deliberately caused the loss; he may be liable only if he, or perhaps certain other persons, were at fault; or he may be liable strictly, independently of fault. The next few chapters deal with liability for loss in general; this one deals specifically with causes of liability without fault.

English law, when it imposes[2] liability without fault, may do so for one of three reasons. First, and most obvious, is simple social policy; although A may not be *criticised* for carrying out a given activity, nevertheless he ought to bear the costs it causes, because (for instance) it is unfair to let the activity harm outsiders without harming them. Secondly, there is a 'semi-fault' argument; those pursuing very extraordinary or unreasonable activities ought not to be able to exonerate themselves from the consequences merely by proving they acted with all care. Keeping a tiger as a domestic pet is a far-fetched, but clear, example. Thirdly, there are 'doctrinal' reasons for liability without fault. Some obligations, especially contractual ones, are strict, not because anyone strongly feels that they ought to be, but simply because traditionally contracts embody promises that a person is liable for breaking whether or not he is at fault. The best example is the liability of a seller of goods to the buyer for damage done by latent defects in the goods. Of course these reasons may combine in individual cases, especially since English law never developed a general theory of

---

1 This phrase obviously assumes damage being compensated, directly or indirectly, through some person who is 'responsible' for it (rather than, for instance, by the State on 'social security' principles). Whether that is the right way of going about designing a system of compensation is too large a question to be dealt with here; we touch on it in Ch 7.

2 A word betraying (intentionally) the assumption pervading English law that strict liability is the exception rather than the rule, and that individual instances of it stand to be justified.

liability without fault anyway; most cases, however, may be brought under one or other of them.

Of course, to bear the *risk* of an activity is not necessarily to bear the *expense*. Liability without fault on keepers of dangerous animals puts the risk on the keepers, but the expense (in practice) on their insurers, and through them, eventually, on other keepers; again, a strict duty on a Government department to compensate damage caused by defective vaccine (as provided by the Vaccine Damage Payments Act 1979) puts the ultimate expense on the taxpayer.

1. Liability without fault on social grounds

The deep-seated idea of damages as compensation for a *wrong*,[3] together with judicial cautiousness, make English law chary of imposing liability without fault on merely social grounds. This is most commonly done, if at all, by statute; for instance with nuclear installations,[4] and less melodramatically, as we have seen, vaccine damage. Common law liability under this head is limited to two cases – dangerous premises and noxious activities.

(a) DANGEROUS PREMISES

The liability of an owner of premises to persons *in* them is based on negligence;[5] to those *outside* them, by contrast, it is on occasion stricter. Where premises adjoin a highway, then if because of their decrepitude (for instance, when a tile falls off the roof) a passer-by[6] or neighbour is injured or has his property damaged, the owner of the decrepit premises is liable without proof of fault. His only defence, the Court of Appeal said in 1939,[7] is that his premises were dangerous only because of the act of a trespasser, or a 'secret and unobservable operation of nature.' This seems at first sight to make the landowner's liability practically fault-based,[8] but in fact it does not. The point seems to be that the landowner is exculpated if, without negligence on his

---

3 'Our law of torts is concerned not with activities but with acts' – Scott LJ in *Read v J Lyons & Co Ltd* [1945] KB 216 at 228, [1945] 1 All ER 106 at 109.

4 Nuclear Installations Act 1965, s 12.

5 This can be regarded as peculiar. A seller of goods impliedly promises that they are not defective, and is liable to the buyer without proof of fault if they are. The law could have implied an analogous obligation with respect to landowners, but never did. This is a good example of English law drawing distinctions by accident of thought rather than design of system.

6 See *Tarry v Ashton* (1876) 1 QBD 314.

7 *Wringe v Cohen* [1940] 1 KB 229, [1939] 4 All ER 241.

8 Though admittedly the burden of proof would be reversed, so the occupier would have to prove lack of negligence.

40   5 *Liability without fault*

part, outside causes, such as subsidence, damage his property; but not if the property itself is defective. In other words he is strictly liable if his building is *bad*, but liable only for negligence if it is *damaged*. Certain features of this liability without fault are difficult to defend. It oddly applies only to buildings, not to natural growths such as trees.[9] Again, protecting highway users is understandable; but why should liability to one's neighbour depend on the proximity of a highway? Why distinguish bad and damaged premises? Nevertheless, the principle of greater liability to those outside buildings than to those in them is sound, if only because the passer-by does not choose to come into contact with the building while the visitor does. Hence, if the present law is anomalous, the anomaly is best removed by taking away indefensible limits on liability without fault, not abolishing it altogether in this area.

(b) HARMFUL ACTIVITY

In contrast to great American willingness to impose liability without fault for 'abnormally hazardous acts',[10] English judges have consistently refused to say that activity likely to hurt others, *for that reason alone,* engenders liability without fault. (The Pearson Commission, however, in 1978 recommended approaching nearer to this position.)[11] But the general does not exclude the particular, and in at least one case the tort of nuisance has created just such a liability. As already touched on in Ch 2, if I deliberately carry on activities on land that harm neighbouring land or buildings, or (in some cases) those in them, I am liable for any damage I do, however much care I took to stop it. The activity must in some sense be inherently harmful;[12] but if it is, it then does not matter how reasonable or usual it otherwise is. I am as liable when my neighbour's horse dies from eating the leaves on my yew-tree as when his house is burnt down because of my experiments with explosives.[13] Nor does it matter that the damage is 'one-off', provided it results from activity pursued by the defendant. So a manufacturer of aluminium foil found himself liable when some of it blew away and fouled a neighbouring factory's electrical system with predictable results.[14]

Because, however, nuisance is essentially a tort about interference with land, the sorts of damage recoverable under this head of liability

9   *Caminer v Northern and London Investment Trust Ltd* [1951] AC 88, [1950] 2 All ER 286.
10   See the American Law Institute's *Restatement of Torts, 2d,* para 519.
11   See Cmnd 7054 (1978), Ch 31.
12   Cricket is not – *Bolton v Stone* [1951] AC 850, [1951] 1 All ER 1078.
13   *Crowhurst v Amersham Burial Board* (1878) 4 Ex D 5.
14   *British Celanese Ltd v A H Hunt (Capacitors) Ltd* [1969] 2 All ER 1252, [1969] 1 WLR 959.

without fault are limited. Noxious activity creates liability for damage to land, and by extension to occupiers of that land; but to no-one else. So if my experiments with explosives cause a fire that demolishes my neighbour's house and injures him and his wife, I am liable to my neighbour for his injuries and the damage to his house; but I am not liable to his wife.[15]

As part of a rational scheme of liability without fault, to impose such liability in the isolated case of damage to neighbouring land makes little sense. It is not clear why such liability grew up, and disinclination to subvert existing schemes of liability elsewhere has prevented it being extended to other fields. It has remained in its present form for a long time, one suspects, largely because in so many cases of nuisance specific relief, such as an injunction, has been in issue, and here negligence in the normal sense is largely irrelevant.

(c) FIRE

The common law may once have treated fire as a species of the genus noxious activity; if I lit a fire on my land, however reasonably, or if I negligently let one start there, I was strictly liable for all the damage it did without further negligence. Statute,[16] however, now exonerates any person on whose land fires 'actually begin'; and this has been interpreted as making them not liable unless they were negligent in letting the fire escape.[17] Now, therefore, liability is effectively based on fault. But, of course, storage or use of inflammable materials may come under the 'semi-fault' liability of *Rylands v Fletcher*, which we now turn to.

2. Strict liability on 'semi-fault' grounds

(a) *RYLANDS V FLETCHER*

In 1867 Blackburn J held a millowner liable when his industrial reservoir sprang a leak and flooded adjacent mine-workings, even though the defendant had not been negligent. He said, in *Rylands v Fletcher*,

> . . . the person who for his own purposes brings on land and collects and keeps there anything likely to do mischief if it escapes must keep it in at his peril, and if he does not do so is prima facie answerable for all the damage which is the natural consequence of its escape.[18]

---

15 *Malone v Laskey* [1907] 2 KB 141.
16 The Fires Prevention (Metropolis) Act 1774, s 86.
17 *Sochacki v Sas* [1947] 1 All ER 344; *H & N Emanuel Ltd v Greater London Council* [1971] 2 All ER 835.
18 (1866) LR 1 Ex Ch 265 at 279; affd (1868) LR 3 HL 330.

The House of Lords upheld him.

Such an assertion, eclectically generalised from existing liability without fault in nuisance and for certain sorts of animals, could have generated a principle of liability appropriate to the previous section; anyone injured by activities which social policy demands ought to bear the risk of the damage they do automatically has a claim. The width of what Blackburn J said recalls a parallel provision in the French Civil Code,[19] which has been very expansively interpreted, creating liability for damage done by things 'in one's keeping'. In fact, partly from fear of excessive burdens on nascent industry, partly from judicial temperament, *Rylands v Fletcher* liability developed the other way and imported substantial elements of fault liability. The key was a suggestion of Lord Cairns in the house of Lords[20] that it only applied to 'non-natural' use of land. Originally interpreted as meaning 'artificial', to exclude strict liability for escape of weed seeds or accumulated rainwater, it later came to mean 'unreasonable' or at least perverse. A commentator later summarised this development; 'non-natural use', he said, was a matter of a 'value-judgment on the defendant's conduct, taking into account its social utility and the care with which it is carried out.'[1] So now *Rylands v Fletcher* effectively makes an occupier liable for damage done by dangerous things on his land only if he acted unreasonably or eccentrically in bringing them there; in other words, such conduct raises an irrebuttable presumption of fault. So if I keep large amounts of petrol in my garage which catches fire and burns my neighbour's house down or operate a peculiar kind of fairground amusement that injures an outsider I am liable; by contrast, piping gas through the streets[2] or operating an explosives factory,[3] while dangerous, are neither unreasonable nor eccentric and attract no liability in the absence of negligence. Moreover, liability under *Rylands v Fletcher* further approaches fault liability because it cannot arise out of activity statutorily authorised;[4] a factor that logically ought to be out of account where liability depends – nominally – on risk and not on wrongfulness.

As with the rule concerning decrepit premises, this head of liability encompasses only damage done outside the defendant's land; the dangerous thing, it is said, must 'escape' from the land. Often criticised as unduly restrictive, this limitation on liability has much to be said for

19   Art 1384.
20   (1868) LR 3 HL 330 at 338.
 1   Winfield & Jolowicz on *Tort*, 11th edn, 407.
 2   *Dunne v North Western Gas Board* [1964] 2 QB 806, [1963] 3 All ER 916.
 3   *Read v J Lyons & Co Ltd* [1947] AC 156, [1946] 2 All ER 471.
 4   *Dunne v North Western Gas Board*, above. The illogicality is observed by Windeyer J in the Australian decision in *Benning v Wong* (1969) 43 ALJR 467 at 489. (See too the old case of *Batcheler v Tunbridge Wells Gas Co* (1901) 84 LT 765 at 766.)

it. As with liability for decrepit premises, complete outsiders damaged by my activity have more claim to sympathy than those who, however innocently, voluntarily involve themselves in it.

More problematical is the received wisdom that one cannot use *Rylands v Fletcher* to recover damages without proving fault for personal injury, as against damage to land and things on it.[5] This limitation, never unequivocally accepted in England, has been rejected in Australia;[6] and indeed any such rule deliberately preferring property to people seems unacceptable in any coherent scheme of obligations. The one argument in its favour, that *Rylands v Fletcher* is akin to nuisance – which does not generally compensate personal injury, except to occupiers[7] – is not a good one. Obligations that are akin are not necessarily identical, and there is no reason why personal injury should not be one of the differences between *Rylands v Fletcher* and nuisance; particularly as one of the sources from which *Rylands v Fletcher* was synthesised, liability for animals, clearly always did cover personal injury.

(b) ANIMALS

One can always be liable in negligence for failing to control an animal; but the Animals Act 1971, replacing and updating similar ancient common law rules, provides a further, statutory, 'semi-fault' liability.

The basis of this is that a person is liable without fault for damage done by two sorts of animal in his keeping. One is naturally dangerous animals such as tigers or elephants; here the keeper is liable without more.[8] The other is animals that, although belonging to a species normally relatively harmless, the keeper knows in this particular case to be dangerous.[9] Apart from these two liabilities, which in fact depend on some fault or at least eccentricity in the defendant, there are two other minor ones justified on grounds of convenience. The owner of 'livestock', that is, effectively, most farm animals, is liable without fault when they stray and damage others' property; conversely, the owner of a dog is liable for damage done by it to someone else's livestock.[10]

As might be expected from a statutory scheme of liability, the Animals Act liability is generally rational and straightforward. In particular, there is no limit to property damage; personal injury is covered equally well. Indeed, in one case liability is perhaps wider than

---

5 See especially per Lord Macmillan in *Read v J. Lyons & Co Ltd* [1947] AC 156 at 173, [1946] 2 All ER 471 at 477.
6 *Benning v Wong* (1969) 43 ALJR 467.
7 See p 41, above.
8 Animals Act 1971, s 2(1).
9 Animals Act 1971, s 2(2).
10 Animals Act 1971, ss 3,4.

it need be; unlike the case with *Rylands v Fletcher* or decrepit buildings, it does not matter whether the damage took place on or off the defendant's property. The zoo is as liable when a tiger mauls a visitor as when it escapes and attacks an outsider, even though arguably the latter has a more plausible claim than the former.

(c) EMPLOYERS' LIABILITY

Employers sit rather uneasily in this chapter; in general their liability for injury to their employees depends on negligence (though an unusually high degree of care is expected of them). But there is an exception where the action for 'breach of statutory duty' applies. If statute requires an employer to maintain a certain kind of machinery, or to keep it fenced, he incurs civil as well as criminal liability if he does not; further, since the criminal liability is independent of fault, so is the civil liability. An employer is liable to an employee injured by illegally unfenced machinery even though he had no reason to know it was unfenced, and indeed even if though he acted in no way reprehensibly because the machinery would have been unusable had it been fenced.[11]

In practice, however, liability for breach of statutory duty is often nearer to fault than to strict liability.[12] The 'dangerous machinery', for instance, that must by s 14 of the Factories Act 1961 be fenced, is machinery that is a foreseeable source of damage, and hence foreseeability of damage is imported as a requirement for liability.[13] Much industrial legislation, moreover, does not require precautions to be taken if they are 'impracticable' (or some similar adjective):[14] here the element of fault is obvious. It should be noted, however, that recent industrial safety legislation returns somewhat to the principle of liability without fault; while providing an 'impracticability defence' in criminal law, it excludes it specifically where civil liability is involved.[15]

3. Liability without fault on doctrinal grounds

(a) REPRESENTATIONS CONTAINED IN CONTRACTS

A person should not normally be liable, in the absence of fault, merely because a statement he makes turns out to be untrue, and someone else suffers loss by relying on it. However, by way of exception, in practice

---

11   *J Summers & Sons Ltd v Frost* [1955] AC 740, [1955] 1 All ER 870.
12   One commentator pointedly calls breach of statutory duty 'statutory negligence' – Williams (1960) 23 MLR 433, 436 – for just that reason.
13   See *Hindle v Birtwistle* [1897] 1 QB 192.
14   Eg Mines and Quarries Act 1954, s 157.
15   Health and Safety at Work etc Act 1974, s 47(3).

any legal system must make it possible to guarantee the truth of an assertion, undertaking liability in damages to the representee or others if, even without fault on one's own part, the statement is untrue. Otherwise, for instance, it would be impossible for a seller of goods to guarantee them against latent defects.

In this connection, English law distinguishes between representations which are incorporated into a contract, in which case prima facie the person making them warrants their truth on a basis of liability without fault; and other representations, where liability is for negligence only. So if a seedsman assures a farmer who buys his seeds that they are of a given variety, whereas (without any negligence on his part) in fact they are not, he is liable for the farmer's loss of profit on his year's crop only if his assertion was incorporated into the contract of sale. As to whether assertions are so incorporated, there is considerable learning.[16] Express incorporation in a written contract obviously suffices; otherwise, there seems to be a weak presumption that any assertion inducing another to enter into a contract, especially by a person in a good position to know whether it is true, is incorporated. On occasion, where for some reason the assertion cannot be part of the contract it induces, courts have inferred a second contract that does certain it appendant ('collateral') to the main contract, that does not.[17]

(b) OTHER CONTRACTUAL LIABILITIES

So much for express warranties. However, it is the warranties that are *implied* into certain kinds of contract that make contractual liability such a fecund source of liability without fault. Furthermore, despite superficial similarity, express warranties represent obligations accepted, implied warranties obligations, at least to some extent, imposed; hence implied warranties are more significant in the general scheme of liability recognised by the law.

English law is generous in implying warranties comporting liability without fault. The Sale of Goods Act 1979, for instance, implies into every contract of sale warranties by the seller that the goods sold correspond with their description, are reasonably fit for any purpose the buyer has said he wants them for, and are of 'merchantable quality'. Strict liability for breach of these warranties can have spectacular results; it means, for instance, that the corner grocer selling a tin of salmon containing (unknown to him) contamination is liable,

---

16 Compare *Schawel v Reade* [1913] 2 IR 64; *Oscar Chess Ltd v Williams* [1957] 1 All ER 325, [1957] 1 WLR 370, and *Dick Bentley Productions Ltd v Harold Smith (Motors) Ltd* [1965] 2 All ER 65, [1965] 1 WLR 623.

17 See, eg *De Lassalle v Guildford* [1901] 2 KB 215; the assertion there could not be incorporated into the main contract itself because of the rule that a contract finally reduced to writing is deemed to enumerate its terms exhaustively.

without proof of fault, to the purchaser for any injury he suffers.[18]
Such liability is drastic. It has advantages. The victim is compensated for food poisoning without having to prove fault; the shopkeeper can insure against liability, and in any case pass it up the chain
towards the manufacturer or importer by suing his wholesaler in turn.[19]
More importantly, however, it emphasises once again that liability
based on implied contractual terms is a creation of the law, rather than
genuinely an accepted liability. Yet this in turn raises a further point.
Despite the opportunity that implied terms offer for creative mani-
pulation of the law of contract so as to provide strict liability where it
might be desirable, English law has refused to develop liability without
fault in contract on the basis of any rational plan.

Take, for example, the distinction currently drawn between the supply of
things, where liability for defects is independent of fault, and supply of
services, where it is not. Thus where goods are sold, or supplied in the course
of another contract (as where a garage, in servicing a car, changes the oil),
or hired out,[20] the obligation of the supplier is to see they are of merchantable quality; merely taking care to do so will not suffice. There is no reason
as such not to import a similar strict obligation to supply of services as well.
French law, for instance, early made railways liable without fault for injury
to passengers, by implying a term into the contract of carriage that the
passenger *would* reach his destination safe and sound – not simply that
reasonable care would be taken to make sure he did. English law never
took this line,[1] instead stoutly insisting that services could never comport
any obligation more stringent than one to take care. The results can be
bizarre. If a garage, in servicing a car, supplies a defective tyre, it is liable
without fault when the tyre bursts and the car owner is injured. If, by contrast, the garage supplies a good tyre but fits it badly with the same result, it
is liable on proof of fault. With transport contracts the result is even odder.
Where goods are carried by water, the accent is on the supply of the ship to
carry them; if the vessel is defective ('unseaworthy') the carrier is liable
without fault for any damage done thereby to the cargo.[2] With carriage by
land, however, the accent is on the service; hence the early decision that a
railway company was not liable without proof of fault for damage resulting
even from defective rolling stock.[3]

18   Cf *Frost v Aylesbury Dairy Co* [1905] 1 KB 608.
19   Not that the situation is ideal, even here. One of the chain of sellers may be insolvent
    or unknown. French law has an elegant solution allowing the consumer to 'short
    circuit' the line of strict liabilities between himself and the manufacturer and sue
    the latter directly.
20   For this latter case, see now the Supply of Goods and Services Act 1982, ss 4(2),
    9(2).
1   It finally decided not to in *Readhead v Midland Rly Co* (1869) LR 4 QB 379.
2   See *Lyon v Mells* (1804) 5 East 428; *Kopitoff v Wilson* (1876) 1 QBD 377. Statute
    modifies this rule in certain cases: Carriage of Goods by Sea Act 1971, s 3.
3   See *Readhead v Midland Rly Co* (1869) LR 4 QB 379.

If there is no coherent pattern behind the instances of contractual strict liability in English law, why is contract such a powerful source of strict liability?

There are two reasons for this. First, English law does not distinguish 'promises to' (for instance, supply 20 tons of coal) from 'undertakings that' (for instance, the coal is best quality anthracite). Since liability for breaking a 'promise to' is independent of fault (the seller's obligation to supply is actually to supply, not to make reasonable endeavours to do so) it has been assumed, without much thought, that the same must apply to any promise that something is the case. Secondly, there is failure to realise that a condition precedent to the one party's obligation under a contract does not necessarily amount to an obligation on the other side. In other words, a buyer must be able to reject defective goods whether or not the buyer was at fault in tendering them; this ought not of itself to mean that the seller is liable in damages for all loss suffered by the buyer as a result of the goods being defective, even though in practice it does.

Chapter 6

Liability for fault – Part I

From strict liability we turn to the much larger question of liability for fault; when must a person make good loss suffered by another on the grounds that his conduct, while not deliberately intended to cause the loss, nevertheless fell short of some standard?

Fault as a ground for liability is pervasive. It appears primarily as the tort of negligence; but by no means exclusively, since it applies also in the law of contract (for instance, governing the standard to be reached by those supplying services); in liability neither contractual nor tortious, such as that of a bailee for loss of the goods bailed to him; in the relationship of trustee and beneficiary; and elsewhere. Moreover, it reflects an instinctively plausible principle; that as between a person who is at fault and one who is not, prima facie the one who is at fault should pay for any losses resulting.

It is misleading, however, to generalise. Liability for fault arises in at least four different contexts, all of which raise rather different issues; in particular, it is not always equally acceptable either to insist that any fault leads to liability, or to deny compensation of a loss merely because no-one has been at fault.

First, fault liability supplements other sources, such as personal insurance and social security, of compensation for personal injury (an area so important that it is not clear that compensation ought to be dependent on anyone else's fault). Secondly, comparatively unimportantly, it compensates incidental damage to property (where a car demolishes a garden wall). Third, it redistributes losses arising from certain kinds of business disaster (as where an oil refinery is shut down because the pipeline leading to it is cut). Fourthly, fault liability governs certain business relations, as where a surveyor is negligent in advising on the value of a house, or a trustee in looking after the trust property.

We begin, then, by asking when a person is liable for loss caused by his own fault. First, it is clear that the mere fact that A has been at fault and B has suffered loss as a result ought not of itself to be sufficient to make A liable to B. An owner of property, for instance, who negligently lets thieves steal it, is under no liability to the innocent third party who loses money in buying that to which he gets no title.[1] Besides fault and

---

1   Cf. *Moorgate Mercantile Ltd v Twitchings* [1977] AC 890, [1976] 2 All ER 641.

loss, a third thing is needed, known as a duty to take care. (So, at least, runs the theory of English law. In fact, the cases where fault does give rise to liability for loss resulting, are – as will appear – so generalised that the need for the duty of care is better expressed negatively; there must, as well as fault and loss, be no good reason to *deny* liability. Provided this is kept in mind, the concept of the duty of care is harmless.)[2]

The obligation to take care may arise either specifically or generally. Its specific sources are relationships between two parties such as a contract, or the giving of advice in a business context, or the relation of trustee and beneficiary, or bailor and bailee; we deal with those later. Generally, however, there is a principle as follows: a duty to take care prima facie arises in tort if A and B are in such a relation of proximity that, if A is at fault, B is likely to suffer loss. It is this general duty, for instance, which provides compensation for road accident victims, and others suffering loss at the hands of those with whom they have no connection. (However, the general duty of care, while it does deal with such cases, is not the only one to do so. A person may be obliged to take care concurrently under the general duty of care and also under some specific relationship; a doctor, for instance, who is paid by his patient owes a duty to him both under the general law and because of his contract with the patient).

1. The extent of the general duty of care

(a) IN GENERAL

The general duty of care in tort was first recognised in respect of personal injury and property damage. By 1932, in the course of holding that a manufacturer could be liable in negligence for injury suffered by a user of his product, Lord Atkin could say that

> the rule that you are to love your neighbour becomes in law, you must not injure your neighbour

and to define a neighbour as anyone

> so closely and directly affected by my act that I ought reasonably to have them in mind as being . . . affected.[3]

The generality of that statement was further emphasised in 1970 when the House of Lords, discountenancing mere novelty as a reason against liability, stressed that any act causing foreseeable damage to another

---

2 See generally on this, B.S. Markesinis, *The not too dissimilar tort and delict* (1977) 93 LQR 78.

3 *Donoghue v Stevenson* [1932] AC 562 at 580.

(or his property) should prima facie be compensable in negligence unless there was good reason to the contrary.[4] Non-liability, in other words, is now the anomaly; and, if foreseeability of damage is present, it must be justified.

Such pronouncements were limited to personal injury and property damage, and did not extend to other forms of loss, for at least two reasons. One was historical; the roots of the tort of negligence lay in trespass, a tort always primarily connected with physical interference. The other, probably more important, was pragmatic. For accident compensation purposes, which it seems Lord Atkin primarily had in mind in 1932, a general/liability for personal injury and property damage is enough; there-is no need to extend liability to other sorts of damage.

However, accident compensation, while an important aspect of fault liability, is not the only one; and in other situations, limitation to physical damage simply breeds anomaly. Take, for instance, liability for commercial disasters; if an explosion cripples a factory, the owner's right – or lack of right – to recover should not depend on whether the explosion damaged the fabric of the factory itself or merely broke a pipe belonging to someone else that led to the factory. The loss is the same whether or not due to damage to the owner's property.[5] Similarly in business relations; if the buyer of a house that turns out to have been badly built should be able to sue the builder for negligence it should not matter whether the house damages him, itself or merely transpires to be less valuable.

As a result the general principle was later extended to cover all sorts of loss. Lord Wilberforce in *Anns v Merton London Borough Council*,[6] a case concerning a badly-built house, clearly thought that any damage or loss, provided it was foreseeable and resulted from another's fault, should prima facie be compensable, whether it was physical or merely financial. This authority has been subsequently reinforced, including once by the House of Lords in 1982 in *Junior Books Ltd v Veitchi Co Ltd*.[7] So now, at least in theory, a similar principle applies to give a plaintiff compensation whether he has been injured in a car-crash, poisoned by defective ginger beer, damnified by buying a defective house, or even deprived of a legacy he thought he would get because a will was carelessly misdrafted;[8] if his loss results from another's fault, he recovers. Having started by saying, 'No recovery unless a duty of care is shown to exist,' the law has ended by approaching the diametrically

4   *Dorset Yacht Co Ltd v Home Office* [1970] AC 1004, [1970] 2 All ER 294.
5   See the reasoning in the instructive Australian decision in *Caltex Oil (Australia) Pty Ltd v The Dredge 'Willemstad'* (1977) 136 CLR 529.
6   [1978] AC 728, [1977] 2 All ER 492.
7   [1982] 3 All ER 201, [1982] 3 WLR 477.
8   As in *Ross v Caunters* [1980] Ch 297, [1979] 3 All ER 580.

opposite view that (at least prima facie) fault, coupled with loss to another, comports of itself an obligation to compensate that loss.[9] (A collateral result has been the slightly untidy one that many business relations, such as solicitor and client, now engender two concurrent, parallel, duties of care; one in contract, one in the general law of tort.[10] Apart from a few technical points, however, such as the effect of limitation statutes, this is practically not very significant.)

(b) THE GENERAL DUTY OF CARE: LIMITS ON RECOVERY

Even though there are now no theoretical limits on the sort of loss that can be recovered in negligence, this does not mean that all sorts of loss can be recovered to the same extent. Liability in negligence, we said, exists only if there is no good reason for it not to; and a good reason to deny or limit one kind of recovery may not be good reason to deny others.

We begin with personal injury. Here there are practically no limitations on recovery: a result of bias in favour of accident compensation in principle, appreciation that many defendants to such actions are insured and thus do not pay damages out of their own pocket (motorists, for instance, or employers), and realisation that damages are unlikely to be astronomical in any case (though this is less true now). Indeed, a recent attempt to limit recovery for even the most abstract and evanescent personal injury, nervous shock, was roundly rebuffed by the House of Lords.[11]

Property damage is effectively treated as generously as personal injury;[12] understandably where it is similar or incidental to personal injury (damage to clothes and car, for instance, in a road accident), less so in other cases. Where, for instance, a large explosion causes widespread damage to property, arguably traders and householders should regard this, like periodic power-cuts, as simply a normal risk of business and life and protect themselves against it – if at all – by insurance rather than seek to pass the loss on to anyone else. Otherwise, it could be argued, there is the danger of one incident giving rise to excessive numbers of claims. In fact practical considerations largely oust these fears. Catastrophic property damage from one event is rare; and in any case certain potential causes of catastrophe (for instance, nuclear explosions[13]) are removed from the law of obligations altogether and statutory compensation, not based on fault, substituted.

---

9 Cf the terms of Art 1382 of the French Civil Code.

10 As in *Midland Bank Trust Co Ltd v Hett, Stubbs & Kemp (a firm)* [1979] Ch 384, [1978] 3 All ER 571.

11 *McLoughlin v O'Brien* [1982] 2 All ER 298.

12 With a very few exceptions. S 1(8) of the Occupiers' Liability Act 1984 provides a rare example of discrimination between personal injury and property damage.

13 Nuclear Installations Act 1965, ss 7–11, 12(1) (b).

Much less straightforward is the treatment of financial loss, especially since liability for it developed only recently in tort and principles have not had time to become established. In some cases recovery obviously ought to be allowed; where, for instance, goods are damaged but the loss is suffered by someone other than the owner (such as a buyer who has paid for the goods and accepted the risk[14]) that person ought to be able to sue. But various features militate against generosity. One is very extensive liability; the thoughtless cutting of one cable could dislocate untold numbers of businesses. To make the person who did it personally responsible would clearly be quixotic; and even insurance cover against such open-ended liability might be difficult to get. More to the point, compensation for this sort of business loss is not so imperative as for personal injury. Office dislocation by power cut is arguably a risk that ought not to be shifted at all. As a result, it seems that the person negligently cutting a cable and causing such dislocation, however foreseeable such dislocation may be, would not be liable.[15]

Similarly with many other business losses. Many such losses, if not covered by some specific relation between the parties (such as a contract) should be regarded as normal business risks. This, it is submitted, justifies the rule that (for instance) a person losing money through buying goods that turn out to have been stolen cannot recover that loss from the original owner of the goods who carelessly allowed them to have been stolen in the first place. Such losses are normal risks accepted by those in the market. Indeed, this is one criticism of the decision in *Junior Books Ltd v Veitchi Ltd*,[16] that a subcontractor on a building site can, if he does his work badly, be sued by the site owner as well as the main contractor; it is arguable that the main contractor, by putting the work into the hands of a main contractor, should be taken to trust him, and him alone, to make sure the work was done properly.[17]

(c) THE PROBLEM OF LIABILITY FOR OMISSION

One limitation cuts right across the general duty to take care; there is prima facie no liability for mere omission. A strong swimmer failing, however culpably, to rescue a drowning man is not liable to him; nor a

---

14 See *Schiffhart und Kohlen GmbH v Chelsea Maritime Ltd* [1982] QB 481, [1982] 1 All ER 218.
15 See *Spartan Steel and Alloys Ltd v Martin* [1973] QB 27 at 37, [1972] 3 All ER 557 at 563–564, per Lord Denning MR. Interestingly enough, similar results have been reached by courts not recognising any difference between physical and financial loss – Markesinis (1977) 93 LQR 78 at 119.
16 [1982] 3 All ER 201, [1982] 3 WLR 477.
17 Further problems arise if the subcontractor has limited his liability to the main contractor by contract; how, if at all, can such a limitation affect the site owner's rights against him?

publican for failing to look after customers' cars in the car park.[18] Much criticised, in fact this rule is highly defensible. The individualistic argument from freedom is obvious. Moreover those who fail to take steps to benefit others will often be bystanders neither employed to rescue nor insured against liability, and hence not worth suing. Lastly the rule is so riddled with exceptions that it applies effectively only in the rare situation where contract between plaintiff and defendant is completely casual. Relationships of bailment, contract, trustee and beneficiary and others all comport a duty to act; and sometimes, even where one of these specific relations is missing, a duty to refrain from culpable omission will be inferred.

Thus first, an omission may be coupled with a positive act. Culpable omission in a driver to brake before running down a pedestrian attracts liability because it is counted not as an omission, but as driving badly.

Secondly, there may be liability for culpably failing to live up to an undertaking that someone else has relied on; a window-cleaner who fails, as promised, to shut the door behind him will be liable when the house is burgled as a result.[19]

Thirdly, one who has created or augmented a risk, culpably or not, may be obliged to mitigate it. A person unavoidably spilling oil on a factory floor must clean it up, or at least take steps to warn those liable to slip on it.[20] Similarly, it seems, a person inviting his friends for an outing on his private yacht cannot do nothing if one of them falls overboard and pray in aid the rule of non-liability for omissions.[1]

Fourthly, there is public law. Once accepted that government exists to help its citizens positively rather than keep out of their way as far as possible, the State (in the shape of public authorities) is less easily exonerated from liability for failure to act than a private person. I am not liable for failing to warn motorists of a traffic hazard ahead; a traffic policeman might well be.[2] Closer to home are the statutory powers of local authorities to inspect buildings being erected; if an authority improperly omits to inspect a given building and a third party suffers loss as a result of its having been put up defective, the authority may be liable.[3] Hence the authority's discretion whether to act or not, unlike a private person's is not absolute.

(When is an authority's failure to act improper? Whenever, it seems,

---

18 *Ashby v Tolhurst* [1937] 2 KB 242, [1937] 2 All ER 837. Cf *P Perl (Exporters) Ltd v Camden LBC* [1983] 3 All ER 161, [1983] 3 WLR 769.

19 *Stansbie v Troman* [1948] 2 KB 48, [1948] 1 All ER 599.

20 See the Canadian case of *Oke v Carra* (1963) 38 DLR (2d) 188 (revsd on other grounds, (1963) 41 DLR (2d) 53): cf *Johnson v Rea Ltd* [1962] 1 QB 373, [1961] 3 All ER 816.

 1 See the decision of the Canadian Supreme Court in *Horsley v Maclaren*, 'The Ogopogo' [1971] 3 Lloyds LR 410.

 2 *O'Rourke v Schacht* [1976] SCR 53.

 3 *Anns v Merton LBC* [1978] AC 728, [1977] 2 All ER 492.

the decision not to inspect was, according to the criteria of administrative law, taken either for an improper motive, or an irrelevant criterion. Why liability in negligence should depend on the motivation behind an act (or failure to act) is unexplained; hence this form of liability is puzzling and intellectually unsatisfactory. In any case it is rarely directly applied. Rather, its existence is asserted as a matter of theory the argument based on causation, that a local authority that (say) does inspect, but does it badly, should escape liability because it could not have been liable had it not inspected at all).

2. Specific duties of care

(a) DUTIES ARISING FROM OCCUPATION OF LAND

The law singles out the occupier of land for special treatment in respect of damage done by the state of the land, or what goes on on it, for two reasons. First, land is – besides motor-cars – the sort of property most non-owners come into contact with most often; secondly, there is a diffuse, but strong, feeling that the benefits of being in control of land – especially for profit – ought to comport a special duty to control what goes on on it.

The rights of those damnified by the state of land and buildings vary according to which of three classes they fall into. They may be on the land lawfully or with the owner's permission; his visitors. They may be on the land as trespassers. Lastly, they may not be on the land at all, but passers-by injured by falling slates, or neighbours whose houses are undermined by spreading tree roots.

(i) Obligations to visitors

At common law liability to visitors was on a stark and simple scheme. Just as a person who has bought a thing has a strong case for complaint if it is defective, the person who has been given it a much weaker one, and a person who has stolen it hardly any, the contractual visitor was well-protected, the visitor by bare permission of the owner less well so, and the trespasser not at all.[4] Such distinctions, being unfashionable, have now largely vanished. To those on his land by his permission or by right (thus covering a policeman exercising a right of entry), whatever the reason, the occupier owes under the Occupiers' Liability Act 1957 the 'common duty of care'.[5] This is a modification of the general duty of care in tort. Thus the rule of non-liability for omissions does not apply; one may not be obliged generally to warn another not

---

4   See the argument in *Indermaur v Dames* (1866) LR 1 CP 274 at 286; and also *R Addie & Sons Ltd v Dumbreck* [1929] AC 358.
5   Occupiers' Liability Act 1957, s 2(4).

to walk over a cliff, but the case is different if the cliff is on one's land and that other is one's visitor. Moreover, two statutory extensions of the law of contract provide extra protection for visitors. If an occupier contracts with A to allow B onto his premises and agrees to accept a higher duty vis-à-vis B than he would otherwise be under, that undertaking is enforceable against the occupier by s 3(1) of the 1957 Act. Further, by the Defective Premises Act 1972, s 4, if a landlord of leased premises is obliged, as against the tenant, to repair them, then a third party injured as a result of the non-repair can sue the landlord.

(ii) Obligations to trespassers
At common law, as we have mentioned, trespassers got short shrift; an occupier was obliged not deliberately to harm them, but that was the limit of his duty. The Occupiers' Liability Act 1957 left the position unchanged; but in 1971 the House of Lords, influenced doubtless by the fact that most injured trespassers are children who do not know what they are doing, decided that trespassers were owed a limited duty of care, not as high as that owed to lawful visitors, epitomised in the phrase 'common humanity'.[6] This development itself, however, was overtaken by the Occupiers' Liability Act 1984, which now by s 1(4) obliges the occupier to take 'such care as is reasonable in all the circumstances' to prevent personal injury to trespassers. How, if at all, this new duty differs from that owed to lawful visitors is not clear. One clue is that, by s 1(5) of the 1984 Act, reasonable warnings or discouraging notices may discharge the duty to a trespasser, whereas as against a lawful visitor this is not enough.[7] Again, in assessing the limited duty owed to trespassers at common law after 1971, the occupier's own resources were in account; a poor occupier was obliged to do less. Arguably a similar approach might be appropriate under the 1984 Act.

What of really blatant cases of trespass, such as the armed robber tripping over a loose stair-rod? Presumably it would be unreasonable for him to expect any duty of care at all; in any case, public policy, increasingly available as a defence in tort,[8] would, it is thought, be likely to bar any action.

(iii) The duty to those outside premises
Those not on land who are nevertheless affected by what goes on there – the passer-by injured by a falling tile, the neighbour whose foundations are undermined by tree-roots – could well be left to prove

6 *Herrington v British Railways Board* [1972] AC 877, [1972] 1 All ER 749.
7 See Occupiers' Liability Act 1957, s 2(4) (a).
8 Cf *Ashton v Turner* [1981] QB 137, [1980] 3 All ER 870.

fault like victims of other accidents. In fact they are often rather better protected; but, as might be expected from the pragmatically chaotic approach of English law, their protection varies according to a number of factors: whether they are on the highway or an adjoining land, and if the latter, whether they are occupiers of that land or not.

OUTSIDERS ON THE HIGHWAY. Where the state of premises or land endangers highway users, as where a tile falls from a roof, there is an intriguing mixture of fault and no-fault liability. We saw in Ch 5 that, if a defective building causes injury to a passer-by, its occupier is liable in nuisance without proof of fault. But this strict liability is limited to buildings; with other things, such as trees, the occupier remains liable in nuisance, but here his liability does depend on fault. The only difference between this liability and ordinary liability for negligence in general is that, like most liabilities attaching to occupation of land, it extends to cover omissions as well as acts.[9]

ADJOINING PREMISES. We saw in Ch 2 that, where one occupier damages his neighbour's property by doing something on his own land, he is liable to compensate his neighbour if the activity foreseeably harms the latter beyond what he can reasonably be expected to tolerate. This is not really liability for fault, though, since one may be liable for carrying on activities even though those activities are not unreasonable. Where, however, an occupier merely *omits* to prevent something already on his land from damaging his neighbour, as where he allows part of his garden on a hillside to subside and bury his neighbour's,[10] then effectively liability depends on fault. The occupier is liable if, and only if, his omission is unreasonable in the circumstances. Thus in *Goldman v Hargrave*[11] a farmer was held liable when a fire spread from a tree on his land and engulfed his neighbour's property; but only because he had been at fault in not putting it out on his own land. This liability now applies to any danger on one's land; a previous bucolic belief that if something came naturally on one's land (as with thistles) one was entitled to do nothing about it, has now been exploded.[12] (Oddly, however, in one respect the duty of care owed in this connection is lighter than that in negligence generally; as with liability to trespassers at common law, the defendant's own resources, or lack of them, is relevant in deciding what he must do to fulfil his duty.)

As regards those on adjoining premises suffering injury who are not

---

9   As, for instance, in *Slater v Worthington's Cash Stores (1930) Ltd* [1941] 1 KB 488, [1941] 3 ALL ER 28.
10   *Leakey v National Trust for Places of Historic Interest or Natural Beauty* [1980] QB 485, [1980] 1 All ER 17.
11   [1967] 1 AC 645, [1966] 2 All ER 989.
12   Compare *Leakey v National Trust*, just mentioned, with *Giles v Walker* (1890) 24 QBD 656, now discredited. Cf Weeds Act 1959, ss 1, 2.

occupiers but merely visitors to it or otherwise there by right, the rules of the tort of nuisance do not apply, and they can recover only by proving negligence in the normal way.[13]

THE OCCUPIER: A NOTE. One reason to apply special rules to liability arising out of the occupation of land is that, unlike other property, more than one person is often interested in land; notably with landlord and tenant. Now, primarily liability to third persons outside property attaches to the 'occupier' or person in actual possession – thus, if there is a tenancy, the tenant. Nevertheless, for practical and social reasons, sometimes the landlord is made liable too.

First, a landlord who lets premises he knows to be decrepit remains liable for damage resulting from that deprepitude even after the letting (so a landlord who lets a house with loose tiles on the roof to his knowledge is liable if one of them later falls on a passer-by). This is so even if it is the tenant who by the lease is obliged to repair the premises. That is an odd rule, given that a letting of land is like a sort of partial sale, and no-one suggests a *vendor* of premises should be liable after the sale for the effects of obvious defects in them. Moreover, liability for damage to third persons arising from the state of land is generally insured against, and it is largely business tenancies that oblige the tenant to repair; so there is not even the residual justification of saving a plaintiff from the impecunious residential defendant.

Secondly, by a statutory exception to the rule of privity of contract, a landlord obliged vis-à-vis his tenant to repair the leased premises, who negligently fails to do so is liable, by s 4 of the Defective Premises Act 1972, to anyone 'who might reasonably be expected to be affected' by a defect in the premises – a phrase that clearly includes a passer-by.

Thirdly (though this is a little out of place here) where the tenant is strictly liable to a passer-by in nuisance, the same liability applies to the landlord if he has the duty or right as against the tenant to repair the premises – even if the landlord did not know of the defect.[14] This rule is justified, if at all, pragmatically; lessors of residential property (who are normally by the lease obliged to repair it) will often be in a position to arrange insurance against liability themselves, whereas their tenants are unlikely to do so.[15]

(b) LIABILITY FOR NEGLIGENT MISSTATEMENT

In practice, any legal system must provide some remedies in respect of those who suffer loss by relying on statements that, because of the

---

13 *Malone v Laskey* [1907] 2 KB 141.
14 *Mint v Good* [1951] 1 KB 517, [1950] 2 All ER 1159. (Contra, *Wilchik v Marks* [1934] 2 KB 56 at 67, per Goddard J).
15 It should not be forgotten that residential lettings are very largely by public authorities to the less well-off.

negligence of those who make them, turn out to be untrue; not so much because the plaintiff necessarily deserves a remedy, as because efficient business depends on reliable information. One must have some assurance that the surveyor's report on a house and the auditor's report on a company are trustworthy.

Liability in this field grew up unplanned and haphazardly, and still comes from at least four sources. First is *contract;* in many sorts of contract, such as that of a solicitor or stockbroker with his client, concerned with the giving of advice, a duty to take care in giving that evidence is easily and obviously implied. Secondly, there are *fiduciary relationships,* where equity, rather than common law, imposes various duties, including on occasion one to give careful advice. (This class overlaps with the previous one; thus a solicitor's relation with his client is both contractual and fiduciary, and if the advice is careless the client may claim against the solicitor on either basis.[16] But it is also wider; it includes, for instance, the relation of banker and customer in so far as the banker gives advice gratis and therefore non-contractually,[17] and also that of trustee and beneficiary.) Thirdly, there are cases where a statement by A induces B to contract with him. At first sight this does not look like fault liability at all, since as we have seen in Ch 5 a representation incorporated into a contract makes the representor strictly liable if it is false,[18] and the drastic remedy of cancellation of a contract ('rescission') is available even for an innocent, non-negligent misrepresentation. Nevertheless, elements of fault liability exist even here. Statements are more readily incorporated into contracts, for instance, so as to engender 'strict' liability, if made by those who may be expected to know if they are true.[19] Much more importantly, the Misrepresentation Act 1967 now provides a general remedy in damages in respect of negligent statements made by a party to a contract inducing another to contract with him (with, moreover, the burden on the defendant to disprove negligence).

In all these cases, however, there still lacked any general duty covering advice given in a business context but not in the course of any relationship that could be called contractual or fiduciary. (The doctrine of consideration in contract, of course, precludes the natural solution of allowing contractual liability to fill the gap). As a result the House of Lords decided in 1963 in *Hedley Byrne & Co v Heller &*

---

16 *Nocton v Lord Ashburton* [1914] AC 932. The client can for that matter equally well sue in tort: *Midland Bank Trust Co Ltd v Hett, Stubbs & Kemp (a firm)* [1979] Ch 384, [1978] 3 All ER 571. Thus this particular obligation to take care seems to be one that subsists in contract, tort and equity.

17 See *Woods v Martins Bank Ltd* [1959] 1 QB 55, [1958] 3 All ER 166.

18 See pp 44–45, above.

19 *Oscar Chess Ltd v Williams* [1957] 1 All ER 325, [1957] 1 WLR 370, is a clear example of this process at work.

Partners,[20] that a bank owed a duty of care, and owed it in tort, when it gratuitously gave a credit reference to a person other than its customer. That is, it decided that a duty to take care in making statements could arise as a matter of general principle even where none of the relations that would previously have given rise to it existed. That general duty not to make negligent statements, and to compensate those who rely on them, has since been confirmed and extended to various business contexts; assertions made in negotiations leading to a lease,[1] statements made by accountants to those about to invest in a company about its financial state, and so on. In short the present rule quickly was settled, that any statement seriously made, in a business context, or such that it is clearly likely to be relied on, prima facie attracts a duty of care in the person making it.

Hedley Byrne v Heller having generalised liability for negligent misstatement, one is tempted to add it to *Donoghue v Stevenson* and *Anns v Merton LBC* for further generalisation; any fault, of any sort, in word or deed, causing loss of any kind, should prima facie be actionable. But except as an exercise in academic abstraction, this temptation should be resisted. Liability for negligent misstatement raises enough different issues to discourage one from adding it to the general law of negligence; and *Hedley Byrne v Heller,* it is submitted, is better regarded as a useful exercise in gap-filling than as anything wider. The differences between liability for misstatement and other liability are twofold.

First, liability for negligent misstatement is, unlike most other 'tort' liability, *accepted* and not *imposed*; Lord Devlin in *Hedley Byrne* itself made liability depend on the defendant's 'assumption of responsibility'.[2] It therefore is closer to the contractual and equitable remedies already mentioned for negligent misstatement, than to the general law of tort;[3] it is best regarded as a sort of semi-contractual liability avoiding such troublesome requirements for contractual liability as consideration and privity.

Secondly, it is a limited liability, largely because (in contrast with the rest of the law of tort, where plaintiffs come into contact with defendants willy-nilly) negligent misstatement does no harm until someone voluntarily relies on it. Hence there is no liability for mere casual statements; the old opinion still holds, that one cannot complain if casual advice given by a lawyer on a train-journey turns out erroneous.[4] The House of Lords in *Hedley Byrne* expressed this

20 [1964] AC 465, [1963] 2 All ER 575.
1 As in *Esso Petroleum Ltd v Mardon* [1976] QB 801, [1976] 2 All ER 5, CA.
2 [1964] AC 465 at 529, [1963] 2 All ER 575 at 610-611.
3 Hewson J's notorious observation that *Hedley Byrne* liability is 'nearer contract than tort' (*The World Harmony* [1967] P 341 at 362) [1965] 2 All ER 139 at 155 is nevertheless perceptive.)
4 *Fish v Kelly* (1864) 17 CBNS 194 at 207, per Byles J. The parallel is, once again, with contractual liability, where obligation cannot arise unless there is 'intent to create legal relations.'

positively; plaintiff and defendant must be in a 'special relationship' with each other; but the message is the same. Of course, there is no such rule in the general law of tort; the casual bad driver is just as liable (if not more so) as the serious one.

Of course, *Hedley Byrne v Heller* has one thing in common with tort liability in general, especially for economic loss; both involve potentially very large numbers of claimants, and hence the fear of unworkably extensive liability. Even here caution is necessary; liability for negligent misstatement being fundamentally accepted and not imposed, the intent of the defendant to accept liability must ultimately govern. A person who clearly states that he accepts liability for a statement, and that he does so as against anyone at all relying on it, should be held to what he said.

(c) LIABILITY OF CONTRACTING PARTIES

Contract traditionally concerns the enforcement of promises (on which see Ch 11, below).[5] Nevertheless, it is equally, if not more, important as the source of an obligation to take care. Where a contract involves a person rendering another a service, such as carrying his goods, advising him on the stock market or mending his shoes, the most important term of the contract is likely to be the 'implied' one that reasonable care will be taken.[6] It would of course be possible to undertake that shoes, once repaired, will be perfect; that goods carried will arrive come what may; or that a stock market tip is in fact a profitable one; but in fact contracting parties rarely do so. The duty to take care is the rule, the guarantee the exception. (Sometimes, indeed, promissory obligation as such becomes effectively dependent on fault; a landlord may undertake to repair premises leased, but is not liable in damages for the effects of defects he had no reason to know about.)[7]

Contractual duties of care resemble often those in tort; many professional persons, indeed, now owe concurrent duties of care in contract and tort, the plaintiff being able to rely on whichever is more advantageous.[8] Nevertheless the scope of the two duties of care is not necessarily the same. First, contractual duties to take care are, like all contractual duties, owed only to the other contracting party. If a building society commissions a survey of a house, the surveyor who

5   See eg Anson's *Law of Contract*, 25th edn, 1 f. Cf P.S. Atiyah, *An Introduction to the Law of Contract*, 3rd edn, 1 f.

6   See now s 13 of the Supply of Goods and Services Act 1982, which codifies the common law.

7   *O'Brien v Robinson* [1973] AC 912, [1973] 1 All ER 583; Defective Premises Act 1972, s 4.

8   For example, on limitation grounds; this was why the plaintiff sued in tort, rather than contract, in *Midland Bank Trust Co Ltd v Hett, Stubbs & Kemp (a firm)* [1979] Ch 384, [1978] 3 All ER 571.

performs it negligently is liable in contract only to the society; to anyone else relying on his survey – for instance, a purchaser – he is liable, if at all, in tort.[9] Secondly, contract involves payment, and at least in practice this often pitches the duty of care rather higher. In particular, contractual duties generally embrace omissions as well as acts. A paid carrier will be liable in contract if he negligently fails to deliver goods on time, but an unpaid carrier will not; again, a retained investment adviser who negligently fails to tell his client of a good investment opportunity will be lible to him in damages, despite the lack of any general duty to advise another for his own benefit. Thirdly, the level of care demanded by a contract depends less on the disembodied standard of the 'reasonable man' and more on the concrete circumstances of the relationship. The more skill (or esoteric knowledge) a contractor professes, and the more he is paid, the better he must perform so as not to be negligent. Structural engineers, for example, professing expertise in particular sorts of work are held to a higher duty of skill in such work than normal structural engineers.[10] Fourthly, the extent of liability, and the sorts of damage, subsumable under a contractual duty to take care may differ from that elsewhere. In particular, fear of indeterminate liability, which potently restrains extensive *tort* liability for financial loss, does not apply to contractual obligations, which are ex hypothesi owed to particular persons only. A demolition contractor who thoughtlessly severs a cable may not be liable to all those whose electricity is cut off as a result;[11] there is no reason why he should not be liable in contract for such losses to the person employing him, however, if he happens to be among them.

(d) BAILOR AND BAILEE

A bailee is liable for the loss of the bailor's goods, not strictly (unless he agrees to be) but on the basis of negligence. Nevertheless, his liability is peculiar, sharing some features with contractual, some with tortious, obligation, some with neither. (Indeed, it has been said that, because of this, bailment fits more easily into the sphere of property than that of obligations.)

A person may thus be a bailee, and liable as one, even though there is no contract – or even any agreement – between himself and his bailor; a gratuitous bailee, and a sub-bailee (that is, a bailee of a bailee) may owe an owner of goods the same duty as a bailee himself.[12]

9 As in eg, *Yianni v Edwin Evans & Sons (a firm)* [1982] QB 438, [1981] 3 All ER 592.
10 *Greaves & Co (Contractors) Ltd v Baynham Meikle & Partners* [1974] 3 All ER 666 (affd [1975] 3 All ER 99).
11 See *Spartan Steel and Alloys Ltd v Martin* [1973] QB 27, [1972] 3 All ER 557.
12 For a neat example, see *Gilchrist Watt & Sanderson Pty Ltd v York Products Pty Ltd* [1970] 3 All ER 825, [1970] 1 WLR 1262.

However, it goes without saying that if there is a contract between bailor and bailee, then the bailee's obligations are governed by that contract and not otherwise. A bailee who exempts himself from liability by contract cannot be sued on the general law of bailor and bailee so as to by-pass the exemption.

Further, though all bailees, whether there is a contract between them and the bailor or not, must take care of the goods bailed to them, the bailee's duty, it seems, varies according as whether the bailment is gratuitous or for reward. In the latter case it is higher; the man who borrows his neighbour's lawnmower has to take less care of it than the warehouseman paid to house and guard a valuable cargo of whisky.[13] (Strictly speaking, this duty seems to apply to all who are bailees of others' goods in the course of a business; but since this generally involves their being paid by someone, even if not the bailor, the difference is minor.)

Thirdly, at least where bailment is for reward, the bailee's duty approximates to that in contract rather than that in tort. He is, for instance, liable for the fault of independent contractors as well as employees[14] although there is no such liability in the general law of tort (on which see Ch 12). His duty, moreover, embraces omissions. In general I am not obliged to guard my neighbour's bicycle against theft; but if I am a bailee of it, then I must at least take reasonable steps, such as locking it and keeping an eye on it, to protect it. Of course, in marginal cases this raises nice questions as to whether there is a bailment at all; a question answered in practice, not according to the formal criterion of whether the alleged bailee has possession; but rather whether in the circumstances he ought to have to take positive steps to guard the thing concerned. Thus an innkeeper is not a bailee of cars left in his car park, and so owes no duty to take steps to exclude thieves; on the other hand, a fairly expensive hotel charging a fee for the use of an underground car park is a bailee and does owe such a duty.[15]

Lastly, in all cases of bailment, and in contrast to the rule in contract and tort, the bailor has the advantage that although the bailee is liable only for negligence, the burden of proof is on him to disprove it. Unexplained losses are thus borne by the bailee and not the bailor.[16]

---

13   See, eg, *Ross v Hill* (1846) 2 CB 877, where all three judges make the point. True, it is sometimes said (eg in *Buchanan & Co Ltd v Hay's Transport Services Ltd* [1972] 2 Lloyds Rep 535 at 539) that all bailees, paid or not, must simply behave as reasonable men; but presumably a reasonable man takes more care of property he is paid to look after, so it comes to the same thing.

14   *British Road Services Ltd v Arthur V Crutchley & Co Ltd* [1968] 1 All ER 811.

15   Compare *Ashby v Tolhurst* [1937] 2 All ER 837, with *Adams v Trust Houses Ltd* [1960] 1 Lloyds Rep 380.

16   *Houghland v R R Low (Luxury Coaches) Ltd* [1962] 1 QB 694, [1962] 2 All ER 159.

(e) TRUSTEE AND BENEFICIARIES

Viewed dispassionately and free from the traditional English separation of law and equity, trust is very like contract. A trustee is typically a person accepting the obligation to look after someone else's property (such as his investments) and distribute income and capital to those entitled to it, having a right to be paid his expenses in doing so and, provided the instrument appointing him allows it (which it invariably does) to be paid for his services. Thus in all but name he is a person contracting, for a fee, to look after someone else's property. (Of course this is not true of all trustees; nevertheless it is true of a significant majority of them.)

Not surprisingly, therefore, a trustee owes a duty to take care while acting as a paid – or unpaid – investment manager. In particular he must exercise reasonable care in deciding what to invest in; and in supervising the investment once made. To take just one example, trustees with holdings in, and representation on the board of, a private company were held liable to their beneficiaries when they failed to prevent the company sinking money in an obviously unsound speculation.[17]

Since, moreover, it is a trustee's duty to look after the trust property, it goes without saying that, like a contractor and bailee, he is liable for omissions as well as acts. His liability when those appointed by him to look after the trust property, such as solicitors or stockbrokers, lose or steal the trust property is more difficult. Certainly if the trustee himself is not at fault he is not strictly liable for what his appointees do; for instance, if the trust stockbroker steals the trust funds.[18] What, however, if the trustee is personally at fault; for instance, by not supervising the agents appointed by him closely enough, or leaving money in the hands of someone obviously incompetent or dishonest? The better view is that then he is liable for the loss suffered by the beneficiary.[19] The difficulty is how to reconcile this position with two sections of the Trustee Act 1925, ss 23 and 30. Section 23, having allowed the trustee to appoint agents to do various things for the trusts, then says he 'shall not be responsible for the default of any such agent if employed in good faith.' Section 30, apparently even more straight-forwardly, excludes a trustee's liability where a 'banker, broker or other person with whom trust property is deposited' fails in his obligation, unless the trustee showed 'wilful default.' However, both sections can

---

17   *Bartlett v Barclays Bank Trust Co Ltd* [1980] Ch 515, [1980] 1 All ER 139. For other cases of failure to supervise see *Learoyd v Whiteley* (1887) 12 App Cas 727; *Fry v Tapson* (1884) 28 Ch D 268.
18   *Speight v Gaunt* (1883) 9 App Cas 1.
19   Eg *Learoyd v Whiteley* (1887) 12 App Cas 727; *Re Lucking's Will Trusts, Renwick v Lucking* [1967] 3 All ER 726, [1968] 1 WLR 866.

be interpreted otherwise than as exonerating a trustee from responsibility for his own failure to take care.

Section 23 can be interpreted as merely emphasising that the trustee is under no liability in the absence of personal fault, on the mere ground that the agent has defaulted; and 'wilful default' in s 30 reflects the use of that form of words in equity draftsmanship as extending to negligent as well as deliberately dishonest conduct. Given how anomalous it would be were trustees alone among managers of other people's property to be exempted from liability for personal negligence, it is submitted this interpretation ought to be adopted.[20]

All trustees, paid or unpaid, must take care of the trust property; paid trustees, like paid bailees, must take more care.[1] This rule is fairly easily justified; unpaid trustees are likely to be private persons unversed in the skills of managing property, whereas trust corporations generally profess considerable skills, and settlors may be taken to know this.

The liability of a contractor or bailee affects only the parties to the relationship; third parties cannot be liable for breach of bailment. By contrast, a trustee's obligation may affect third parties. That is because of the doctrine that where a fraudulent breach of trust is committed, not only the trustee is liable, but also anyone who 'knowingly' assists in it. Once thought to catch only those who *knew* what they were participating in was a breach of trust – who ought for obvious reasons to be liable in the same way as anyone else participating in another's wrong – the doctrine now apparently embraces even those who merely *ought* to know. Thus a bank that inadvertently, but negligently, helps company directors to defraud their company (directors, in their relations vis-à-vis their company being for these purposes treated as trustees) is liable to the company thus defrauded.[2] This obligation to take care not to be made the unwitting instrument of another's fraud has been heavily criticised,[3] but never actually overruled; further, it is submitted that, in line with the general extension of negligence liability elsewhere,[4] there is much to be said for putting even third parties under

20   See Jones [1959] 22 MLR 381, criticising *Re Vickery, Vickery v Stephens* [1931] 1 Ch 572.
 1   *Bartlett v Barclays Bank Trust Co Ltd* [1980] Ch 515 at 534, [1980] 1 All ER 139 at 152, per Brightman J.
 2   *Selangor United Rubber Estates Ltd v Cradock (No 3)* [1968] 2 All ER 1073, [1968] 1 WLR 1555. In this case the bank was also held liable to the plaintiff company for breach of an implied term in its contract that it would take care in handling the account. If, as seems not inconceivable, it would also have been liable in tort under the wide liability suggested by *Junior Books Ltd v Veitchi Co Ltd* [1983] 1 AC 520, [1982] 3 All ER 201, this would be another case of concurrent liability in contract, tort and trust. The proponents of a united law of obligations would have a field day.
 3   Eg *Carl Zeiss Stiftung v Herbert Smith & Co (No 2)* [1969] 2 Ch 276 at 301, [1969] 2 All ER 367 at 381–382, per Edmund Davies LJ: *Belmont Finance Corpn Ltd v Williams Furniture Ltd* [1979] Ch 250, [1979] 1 All ER 118; Snell, *Equity*, 28th edn, 195.
 4   Megarry J has pointedly remarked that there is no reason why the reasonable man should not 'labour in equity as in law': *Coco v A N Clark Ltd* [1969] RPC 41 at 48.

at least some minimal duty to take care not to become involved in others' dishonesty. The degree of fault required can always be pitted high enough to prevent any resultant burden becoming excessive.

Company officers: a note
In some cases those in charge of companies are in equity treated as owing the same obligations as trustees. This does not mean, however, that they are in all respects treated as trustees. In particular, the duty of care attaching to a company director, as such, is in equity vastly lower than that attaching to a trustee. For instance, a trustee who, indifferent to the affairs of the trust, failed to notice or supress speculation by employees of the trust, would have no hope of escaping liability to the beneficiaries for the loss resulting. But a company director who did the same would apparently not be liable, at least in the absence of actual knowledge of what was going on.[5] In fact, however, this difference is not as significant as it sounds. The very light burden just described effectively applies only to 'honorary' or decorative directors not employed under a contract of service; if there is such a contract, as there is in the vast majority of cases, the duty of care it supports will be much higher.

---

5 *Re Cardiff Savings Bank* [1892] 2 Ch 100; cf *Re City Equitable Fire Insurance Co* [1925] Ch 407.

Chapter 7

Liability for fault – Part II

The previous chapter dealt with the question of when A comes under a duty to take care not to harm B. This chapter continues by asking two further questions. First, assuming that A is bound to take care not to harm B, what amounts to 'fault' so as to be a breach of that obligation? Secondly, what are the limits of recovery, given that A was under a duty of care, broke it and someone, somewhere, suffered loss as a result?

Lastly, there is a brief attempt to stand back and see the position of fault liability in connection with the rest of the law, and ask what, if any, its place is in any rational law of obligations.

1. The nature of fault

'Fault' and 'negligence' are confusing concepts. Since, as we shall see, one can sue for negligence under the general law only if one is a foreseeable plaintiff suffering foreseeable damage (foreseeable, that is, to a reasonable man in the defendant's position), it is tempting to regard negligence, or fault, as consisting in the causing of foreseeable loss. It is also wrong. Foreseeability is not a *criterion* of liability based on fault; it is a *limitation*. In the case of liability under the general law, it limits both the plaintiffs who can sue and what they can sue for; in the case of liability arising from contract and other specific relations, there is no need to limit the possible plaintiffs who might be able to sue, but foreseeability is still used to circumscribe the damage that can be sued for.

In fact, the nature of fault depends, not on what happened to the plaintiff and whether it was foreseeable, but on what the defendant did and whether there was anything wrong with it. This criterion in turn breaks down into two further questions. First, there is that of justification; was the defendant wrong in doing *what* he did? Secondly, there is the standard of care; can the defendant, even though there is nothing wrong with his action as such, be criticised for *how* he did it?

(a) JUSTIFIABILITY

Any system of law must face the fact that many activities, perfectly justifiable in themselves (such as driving a car), nevertheless cause substantial risk to others. Yet it would make nonsense of fault liability to say that, for that reason (say), driving a car was ipso facto negligent, and therefore the driver was automatically liable for any damage resulting. As a result the law divides activities into two categories: justifiable activities, which the reasonable man would be prepared to carry on despite the risk, and others, which have no social or other justification at all.

With justifiable activities, these may be carried on without fear of liability, provided they are carried on with the smallest reasonable risk. It is not negligent for an employer to employ someone on dangerous work, even though there is a substantial chance of injury resulting;[1] again, cricket may obviously injure someone when a ball is hit hard, yet playing cricket on a properly conducted ground is not negligent.[2]

The rule about justifiable activities also provides, in cases where liability is based on fault, an effective defence of necessity. A fire service may engage in dangerous practices in an emergency that would otherwise be considered negligent;[3] further, despite doubts,[4] it seems that certain means of driving normally negligent will not be if the driver is in charge of an emergency vehicle, such as a police car or fire engine. (In fact, though logically unassailable on the premise of fault liability, this latter rule is less justifiable than it looks. The bystander injured by a speeding fire engine has plausible grounds for complaint if denied compensation simply because of the urgent need of a third person he has no connection with. There is a strong case for removing the defence of necessity, at least from public emergency services. On a sort of analogical unjustified enrichment argument, as the public benefits from such services, it should pay the costs they entail; and abolishing the defence of necessity would have just this effect.)

Some activities, we mentioned, are regarded as completely unjustified. With these, the law is not particularly concerned with how they are carried out; if they carry the slightest risk of harm, they automatically attract liability. A shipowner illegally discharging oil into the sea is liable if it catches fire and damages shore installations; the fact that the damage was freakish or not very likely is irrelevant.[5]

(b) THE STANDARD OF THE REASONABLE MAN

Justifiable activities attract liability only if done in an unacceptable way; that is, if the person doing them failed to reach the standard of the

1 *Withers v Perry Chain Co Ltd* [1961] 3 All ER 676, [1961] 1 WLR 1314.
2 *Bolton v Stone* [1951] AC 850, [1951] 1 All ER 1078.
3 *Watt v Hertfordshire CC* [1954] 2 All ER 368, [1954] 1 WLR 835.
4 See *Gaynor v Allen* [1959] 2 QB 403, [1959] 2 All ER 644. The thinking behind these doubts is understandable; negligence in traffic cases has in practice ceased to mean wrongdoing, and if so justifiability should equally be irrelevant. Nevertheless it is still heterodox.
5 *Overseas Tankship (UK) Ltd v Miller Steamship Co Pty, The Wagon Mound* (No 2) [1967] 1 AC 617, [1966] 2 All ER 709.

reasonable man. It is, of course, fundamental to this standard that it is objective, ignoring personal shortcomings; the learner driver must show the same skill as the reasonably experienced one.[6] Despite the lack of moral failing, as between the defendant and the innocent plaintiff the latter is preferred.

Objectivity, however, is mitigated. The standard the defendant must reach is that of the reasonable person in his position. A child is judged by the standard of the reasonable child; a home handyman by that of the reasonable amateur, not the experienced contractor.[7] The distinction between these cases and that of the learner driver seems to be that between competence and status; competence is not in account, but status is. This distinction, though, while in no way formally illogical, does seem at the very least arbitrary. Moreover, at times the distinction between competence and status may be difficult to draw; does the failure of a small country firm of solicitors to measure up to the standard of a large city practice go to competence or merely to status?

Despite his down-to-earth name, the concept of the reasonable man is highly factitious; as a result, how high his standard is pitched depends on a number of factors. If a duty of care emanates from some specific relationship, such as contract or trust, the standard is (as we mentioned in Ch 6) less disembodied and depends much more on the concrete circumstances of the case; the more the defendant is paid, or the more skill he professes, the higher his duty. With duties to take care arising under the general law, standards are less variable, but the law takes the opportunity, in certain cases, to raise them for social and other reasons. Long-standing compulsory third-party insurance, for instance, has in practice put drivers under a duty of care always high and sometimes impossibly so. Again, for obvious reasons, the duties of employers towards their employees and doctors towards their patients are almost equally onerous.

(c) THE PROOF OF FAULT: A NOTE

Except in relations such as bailment, a plaintiff alleging fault bears the burden of proof. Unfortunately this rule means no-one is liable for unexplained accidents; and, in the nature of things, many accidents tend to be unexplained. The problem, which is faced by all legal systems, can be alleviated by various devices; for instance, a presumption of fault where damage is done by something (such as a car) in the control of the defendant; or even conclusive presumption of fault in certain cases. But English law largely rejected these solutions,

6   *Nettleship v Weston* [1971] 2 QB 691, [1971] 3 All ER 581.
7   See *McHale v Watson* (1964) 111 CLR 384, and *Wells v Cooper* [1959] 2 QB 265, [1958] 2 All ER 527.

developing instead the doctrine of *res ipsa loquitur*. The point of this doctrine is that, if an accident happens which is otherwise unexplained but which in the normal course of things would not have happened unless the defendant had been negligent, the court is entitled – in the absence of further evidence – to infer negligence on the defendant's part. (Examples are a road accident due to a defect in part of a car that can be inspected, or a brick mysteriously falling from scaffolding on a building site.)[8] Once such an unexplained, but apparently negligent, accident is proved, the defendant is liable unless he in turn can show, not that he might not have been negligent, but affirmatively that he was not.[9] The power this doctrine gives to a court to manipulate a particular case in favour of a deserving plaintiff, is obvious.

2. Limitations on liability for fault

(a) WHO CAN SUE FOR NEGLIGENCE

With duties of care arising out of specific relations like bailment, contract and trust, it goes without saying that there is no problem in this connection; a bailee owes his duty to his bailor, a contractor to the other contracting party, and so on. However, there is a need for some limit on those who can sue under the general law of tort; and this limit is that one is liable for failing to take care only to those reasonably foreseeable as likely to suffer loss if one does not. A motorist may carelessly swerve, and the resulting accident may start a fire that spreads to a cottage half a mile away; but the owner of the cottage cannot recover from the motorist.[10] Now reasonable foreseeability, of course, is a matter of hindsight, and the obvious aim of the rule we have just described is to limit the number of claims arising out of an incident to a reasonable number. It has therefore been suggested, not implausibly, that where there is a danger that claims might proliferate more than usual, the requirement that the plaintiff be foreseeable will be more strictly construed. For example, while a motorist who fails to take proper care will be liable to anyone injured provided merely that he ought to have foreseen that there might be someone in that position likely to suffer, it has been suggested that a contractor who negligently cuts an oil pipeline will be liable for the resultant business dislocation to the plaintiff only if that particular plaintiff ought to have been

---

8   See, for instance, the decision in *Henderson v Henry E Jenkins & Sons* [1970] AC 282, [1969] 3 All ER 756: and *Byrne v Boadle* (1863) 2 H & C 722.
9   *Colvilles Ltd v Devine* [1969] 2 All ER 53, [1969] 1 WLR 475.
10 This is implicit from *Bourhill v Young* [1943] AC 92, [1942] 2 All ER 396. The principle developed late: cf the old case of *Smith v London and South Western Rly Co* (1870) LR 6 CP 14.

foreseeable to him.[11] Financial loss being potentially more prolific, the class of foreseeable plaintiffs who can sue for it is likely to be more circumscribed.

(b) LIMITS ON THE LOSS FOR WHICH THE DEFENDANT IS LIABLE

Perhaps because duties to take care vary so much, English law has no general theory of what damage a defendant admittedly at fault ought to be liable for. Indeed, in one case, negligent breach of trust, the law bravely refuses to set any limit at all, making the trustee liable for *all* the consequences of his fault, however remote.[12] But that is exceptional, and trustees' liability is, one suspects, rarely ruinously excessive in practice. Elsewhere there are limits, even though precisely where they are set depends on what sort of claim is involved. Where a duty of care arises from a contract, the actual damage the defendant is liable for depends, at least formally, on the rules established in *Hadley v Baxendale*[13] in 1854. According to these rules, a contract breaker is liable for the loss if one of two criteria is met. Either the loss must have been made clear to the delinquent party as likely to happen before the contract was made; alternatively, the loss may have resulted 'in the normal course of events'. The former criterion is straightforward; according to the latter, it seems that the loss must be more than a little foreseeable, and not simply the result of very unusual or freakish events.[14] It is the loss, incidentally, that must be appropriately foreseeable, not the amount of it; if, while carrying out work at a farm, a contractor negligently poisoned the farmer's cattle so they were likely to become ill, he would remain liable if, by unlucky and unlikely chance, complications developed and they died.[15]

Where the basis of the plaintiff's claim is the general law of tort, a similar result is reached (though perhaps slightly more generous to the plaintiff[16]), but by a completely different route. Prima facie a defendant is liable for all the loss or damage to a foreseeable plaintiff resulting from his fault. Unlike the case with contractual claims, intervening

11   Compare *Farrugia v Great Western Rly Co* [1947] 2 All ER 565 with the majority judgments in *Caltex Oil Australia Pty Ltd v The Dredge 'Willemstad'* (1977) 136 CLR 529.

12   See *Caffrey v Darby* (1801) 6 Ves 488. There is little justification for treating trusts so idiosyncratically. The argument that liability in equity is for 'restitutio in integrum', rather than damages, though often advanced, does not answer the question why different rules ought to apply.

13   (1854) 9 Exch 341.

14   As in *Hadley v Baxendale*, itself, above; cf *Victoria Laundry (Windsor) Ltd v Newman Industries Ltd* [1949] 2 KB 528, [1949] 1 All ER 997.

15   Cf *H Parsons (Livestock) Ltd v Uttley Ingham & Co Ltd* [1978] QB 791, [1978] 1 All ER 525.

16   In fact any difference between tort and contract liability is unlikely today to be very significant, because now most contractual duties to take care also subsist in tort.

freakish circumstances are irrelevant. *Hughes v Lord Advocate*[17] neatly illustrates the point. Contractors leaving a dangerous naked light in unattended road works were held liable when a small boy picked it up and was injured in the resulting (unforeseeable) explosion. However, whereas this may seem to extend liability considerably, two further rules limit the losses a defendant is liable for. First, as we point out in Ch 15, some events intervening between the defendant's fault and the plaintiff's damage are said to justify the conclusion that the former was not a cause of the latter at all. Secondly, there is no liability for damage of a completely different sort from that which was foreseeable as a result of the defendant's act. In extreme cases this is obvious: a motorist causing an accident through his own fault can hardly be held liable to the bystander who as a result is not injured, but instead has his attention distracted and misses a bus to a lucrative appointment. The question is how far this principle extends; the question whether damage is of a completely different kind from what was foreseeable is a rather subjective one. In *Overseas Tankship (UK) Ltd v Morts Dock & Engineering Co Ltd, The Wagon Mound*[18] in 1961, the Privy Council applied the principle generously; as a result, a shipowner carelessly discharging oil in navigable waters escaped liability when some of it caught fire and destroyed neighbouring property; while damage by pollution was foreseeable, reasoned the court, damage by fire was not, and moreover this was a completely different kind of damage. But this decision is in practice less significant than it looks. To begin with, one of the Privy Council's reasons for reaching it, that it was somehow immoral to make a defendant liable for damage he could not foresee, is unconvincing; negligence in the law, as we have seen, has little to do with the personal morality of the defendant. More to the point, what is a different sort of damage is a question of fact in each case, and subsequent courts have in general been unwilling, even in the face of quite stark differences between what was foreseeable and what happened, to allow defendants to escape on that ground.[19] (It remains open whether, in those areas such as liability for financial loss where there is a need for means to limit liability, courts will use this means more willingly to do so. If, for instance, a bank negligently advises X that Y Ltd, a customer of the bank, is in good standing, it will be liable if X loses through giving credit to Y; but will it be liable if X instead buys shares in Y that turn out to be worthless?)

17 [1963] AC 837, [1963] 1 All ER 705.
18 [1961] AC 388, [1961] 1 All ER 404, ostensibly overruling *Re Polemis and Furniss Withy & Co* [1921] 3 KB 560.
19 Most extreme in this connection is *Warren v Scruttons Ltd* [1962] 1 Lloyds Rep 497. But the trend is not universal – see, eg, *Doughty v Turner Manufacturing Co Ltd* [1964] 1 QB 518, [1964] 1 All ER 98.

(c) THE EXTENT OF LOSS FOR WHICH THE DEFENDANT IS LIABLE

In contract, as we mentioned, if a negligent contract-breaker is liable for a loss at all, he is liable for its full extent, even if through freakish chance the loss is greater than foreseeable. A similar principle applies elsewhere; in the general law of tort, it is sometimes known as the 'eggshell skull' principle, whereby if X is liable for any harm to Y he remains liable even if the hurt is unexpectedly catastrophic. If I negligently cut your finger, but complications ensue and blindness results, I am liable for the latter;[20] similarly, if I mistake a mildly inflammable liquid for a harmless one, I remain liable if, by unlucky chance, it causes not a minor fire but a tremendous explosion.[1] Admittedly, this rule sits a little ill with the exclusion by the law of liability for loss substantially different from the loss that is foreseeable. In fact, however, it is largely justified by convenience. It is difficult enough to work out whether harm of this, rather than that, kind is foreseeable, and whether one is substantially different from the other anyway. But compared with this, the difficulty of finding out (for instance) just how violent an explosion a reasonable man would foresee as a result of certain conduct, is quite horrific.

3. Accident compensation, fault liability and the law of obligations[2]

The last three chapters have largely, though by no means exclusively, concerned accident compensation; in particular, the right to damages for personal injuries. The picture that has emerged is that, at present, the right to compensation for injury depends on proof of fault in varying degrees, with more or less haphazard exceptions of strict liability. Such a picture is incomplete, however. Quite apart from the law of obligations, state benefits provide minimum protection against destitution for everyone (accident victims included); and, further, provides rather greater payments for some particular classes, such as mobility allowances and disability pensions for the disabled, industrial injury benefit for those injured at work, and so on. Indeed, social security, in one form or another, represents over half of all accident compensation payments in England.[3] This raises acutely the question whether the present scheme of

---

20 See *Warren v Scruttons Ltd* [1962] 1 Lloyds Rep 497.
1   *Vacwell Engineering Co Ltd v BDH Chemicals Ltd* [1971] 1 QB 88, [1969] 3 All ER 1681.
2   This section is too brief, of course, to do anything like justice to the issues. For more extended treatment of them, P. S. Atiyah, *Accidents, Compensation and the Law*, 3rd edn, and G. Calabresi, *The Costs of Accidents*, are highly recommended.
3   See the Pearson Commission, Cmnd 7054 (1978), Vol II, Table 158.

liability, and in particular the law of obligations in its present state (dependent as it is on ideas of fault), should be retained. Indeed, is there any basis for ever making liability depend on fault, given that fault in law does not normally represent personal failing at all? Certainly, it seems that any attempt to justify fault liability on the ground that it makes those pay who have shown some moral failing is doomed. Fault in law does not depend on blameworthiness, since one can be negligent merely because one fails to reach a standard one could not have reached anyway. In any case, many defendants held liable for negligence are not individuals but corporations, and thus incapable of moral blameworthiness anyway.[4] Many defendants, moreover, are liable not because they were negligent, but instead because someone else whom they employed was. Yet again, substantial damages for personal injury and other accidental damage are generally not paid by those at fault but by their insurers. Except in isolated cases, (for instance, medical or legal practice, where findings of negligence may damage professional reputation), liability for fault is unlikely to deter; again, because in practice the person at fault does not pay.[5]

Apart from this, a system of liability for fault does not seem to be economically efficient in that it promotes the most efficient use of resources; at least with personal injuries, the Pearson Commission reported in 1978 that the present system cost over four times as much to administer, proportionately, as the social security system.[6]

Nevertheless, despite the arguments just advanced, there is in certain kinds of case a plausible argument in favour of fault liability. Essentially, the justification of fault liability lies not in what the defendant did, but in the question what the plaintiff can complain of. Its basis is an individualistic moral assumption, that prima facie losses due merely to the proper carrying on of others' business are an integral part of life that one cannot complain of; an assumption that, outside the field of personal injury, is surprisingly often unexceptionable. If my car is damaged few would argue that any injustice was done by making me bear the loss myself unless I can prove fault in someone else. Similarly uncontroversially, the recipient of advice that turns out to have been misguided should have no complaint unless he shows the advice was negligent; nor should the beneficiary be able to complain against the

---

4 Of course this does not mean those in charge of directing the policies of corporations may not be morally at fault; of course they may. But then it is not they who pay the damages, so the point in the text stands.
5 It is true, however, that very risky businesses may find the expense of insuring against liability so high that they must become less risky or cease their activity – a phenomenon known as 'general deterrence.' See G. Calabresi, *The Costs of Accidents*, Ch 5.
6 See the Pearson Commission, Cmnd 7054 (1978), Vol II, Table 158. The figures are 46% and 10% respectively.

trustee if the value of the trust fund goes down without mismanagement on his part. If any generalisation can be made, it is that most cases of damage to property and financial loss are cases where the person suffering it can reasonably be expected to bear it himself in the absence of negligence on the part of someone else.[7]

But, as might be expected, there are losses which it is unjust to expect a person to bear as part of the ordinary costs of life. One is losses, or at least some losses, falling within public law and caused by State action. As we suggest later, the power of the State to cause disastrous losses by wrong decisions is so great that, at least in some cases, an authority taking a decision that is later quashed on administrative grounds ought to be strictly liable for any loss caused by the decision that, ex hypothesi, should not have been made. But much more important than losses caused by State action is personal injury. Society (or the State) may owe no duty to preserve wealth, but it does owe at least a minimal moral duty to mitigate the effects of ill-health and injury, whatever their causes. It is for this reason that making compensation essentially dependent on proving fault is unacceptable; in other words, the assumption that personal injury, like damage to one's property, is a risk one can be expected to shoulder oneself or make one's own arrangements to deal with, is unfounded.

Now, if it is accepted that society owes its members, if not protection of their wealth, at least protection of their health, not only liability based on fault but also strict liability are difficult to defend. After all, even strict liability leaves unjustifiably uncompensated those whose injuries are caused by *no-one*, whether at fault or not. Ideally, some kind of compensation scheme based on 'social security' principles, providing compensation according to the injury suffered, ought to replace any existing scheme based on the law of obligations.

At this point, of course, it could be argued that limited alleviation of hardship is already available under the present social security arrangements; that this fulfils the state's moral obligations (which few would argue would extend to full compensation for injury suffered); and that therefore it was justifiable to leave the situation as it is at present, with compensation over and above the State minimum, and up to the full amount of the loss, available on the basis of fault. Unfortunately this argument seems to break down on the facts: social security provision is neither very equitably distributed nor (it is suggested) really adequate to fulfil the State's moral obligations.[8] If, as

---

7   The protective State, however, intervenes even here on occasion. Banks and even holiday travel operators are legally compelled to contribute to funds to compensate members of the public who would otherwise lose from their insolvency; see the Air Travel Reserve Fund Act 1975 and Part II of the Banking Act 1979.

8   P. S. Atiyah observes, for instance, in *Accidents, Compensation and the Law*, Chs 14–16, the disparities in social security provision and in particular the generous treatment of industrial injuries.

seems to follow, the only way to alleviate the situation is to divert resources from the present system based on the law of obligations to some new social security provision, then it would seem that this ought to be done.

That, however, is a radical solution; though adopted in New Zealand with some success, the Pearson Commission in 1978[9] refused to recommend its adoption in England. An intermediate suggestion, bottomed on a sort of moral equivalent of the idea of unjustified enrichment rather than on arguments about moral claims, is to extend strict liability very widely. The aim of this is that, as far as possible, those indulging in any activity should be made to bear its costs in terms of the damage it causes to others' interests. For instance, strict liability for road or industrial accidents would in practice, through liability insurance, make the motoring or industrial community bear the whole of its risks; it would therefore prevent it being unjustifiably enriched by being allowed to carry on its activity effectively at the expense of those innocently injured as a result of it. Now, if the present scheme for personal injury compensation were to be replaced as unsatisfactory, this scheme would on practical grounds be an attractive alternative. Not only would it mark less of a break from the present system, which in any case does provide for strict liability on occasion; it has the additional advantage that it could be brought in piecemeal in various areas in the law as thought fit – or politically expedient.

---

9 For the not very satisfactory reason that, even had it wanted to, its terms of reference would not have let it.

Chapter 8

Liability for financial loss deliberately caused

1. In general

How far must one refrain from deliberately causing another person financial loss? Despite superficial similarities, the issues raised here are rather different from those raised in Chapter 2 on 'Protection of Property.' The reason is the nature of economic free enterprise. As against deliberate damage to things, which is hardly ever justified, and nearly always attracts liability, two vital factors must narrow any general principle of liability for deliberately caused financial loss.

One is that property implies freedom; the right to do as one wishes with one's own must to some extent justify one in causing loss to others. There would, for instance, be something odd in a legal system that said that a householder who chopped down a particularly handsome tree in his garden had to compensate his neighbours for the depreciation in their houses due to the view from them being taken away (even if the householder knew this was certain to happen). This reasoning underlies the theoretically significant decision in *Bradford Corpn v Pickles*[1] that a landowner incurred no liability by drawing off percolating water under his land, however much loss he caused his neighbour by doing so. His right of property justified what he did, *tout court*.

The second – and vastly more important – factor is the right to compete. A shopkeeper cannot be liable for driving his neighbour out of business by successfully competing with him. Of course, this is only a beginning. *Some* competition is always justifiable; what matters is how far the law takes the right to compete. English law in fact takes it far, indeed extending the right to compete using lawful methods not only to business competition as such but even to acts done in the course of industrial conflict. In all these cases it stands back and allows commercial forces to take effect.

Now, there are two ways to fit a right to use one's property, or to compete, into a general scheme of liability for deliberately caused economic harm. One is the method of French law; this makes it prima facie wrongful to damnify another deliberately, but exculpates a

---

1   [1895] AC 587.

defendant who is exercising a right, such as the right to compete. This approach deals characteristically with two problems; unfair competition and the malicious or unjustified use of property. The right is to compete *fairly*; to use one's property *reasonably*; and in the absence of fairness or reasonableness the immunity disappears and the original liability revives. However, English law rejects this solution. Excepting liability for conspiracy, which is anomalous and not very important, it assimilates the right to compete with the right to compete *lawfully*, not *fairly*, and similarly with property rights. As a corollary, its theory is that what is actionable is not damage done to one's neighbour as such, but loss deliberately caused to another unlawfully – that is, by committing a breach of contract, tort or other wrongful act, or getting someone else to do so. Hence, characteristically, competition unfair but lawful, and property used lawfully but without good reason, remain largely untouched by the law of obligations. (Statute, however, has now forbidden the worst excesses of unfair competition and severely restricted once absolute rights of property, so the theoretical issue of the basis of liability matters less today than it might).

Why have English lawyers thus, rather crudely, made everything depend on rightfulness and wrongfulness? Two reasons stand out. One is judicial diffidence. English judges mistrust their own ability to mark off convincingly what is fair and unfair competition, good and bad business practice. The distinction between what the law allows and what it does not is simpler and safer.[2] The other reason is political sagacity. Unwillingness (at least in the last fifty years) to take overt sides in the fight between labour and capital – the subject of much of this law – has predictably discouraged judges from deciding what is fair and unfair in this connection; easier, again, to distinguish simply the lawful and unlawful, leaving Parliament to make adjustments.[3]

Hence we have the principle that it is wrongful to damnify another deliberately through wrongful means. But this principle is too general, and in practice resolves itself into a number of different torts, reflecting different situations such liability covers. Thus deceit largely concerns unfair trading; passing off, unfair competition; causing loss by unlawful means, labour relations, and so on. Hence we deal with each separately.

2   As Fry LJ put it in 1889: 'To draw a line between fair and unfair competition, between what is reasonable and unreasonable, passes the power of the courts.' (*Mogul SS Co v McGregor Gow & Co* (1889) 23 QBD 598 at 625–626). Nearly a hundred years on these words are still applicable in general, although EEC law now requires judges, however unwillingly, to make just this sort of decision.
3   Lord Devlin admitted as much in *Rookes v Barnard* [1964] AC 1129 at 1218–1220, [1964] 1 All ER 367 at 405–407. In that case Parliament took the hint; the result was the Trade Disputes Act 1965, now the Trade Union and Labour Relations Act 1974, s 13(1) (b).

2. Particular forms of liability

(a) DECEIT

Deliberate untruth is an obviously illegitimate means of causing loss to another. If A makes a statement to B which he knows[4] is false (or at least knows might be) and B suffers loss by acting on it, A is liable for that loss. Similarly where A's statement to B is relied on by C; as where the seller of a business fraudulently misstates its value not to the buyer but to his accountant. Historically, deceit has concerned mainly unfair trading (typically where a seller of goods deliberately misdescribes them to the buyer); but it is not, of course, limited to those cases. The hoaxer who misdirects a tourist, or (as in *Wilkinson v Downton*[5]) sends another on a false errand of mercy, is equally liable for the wasted expense he causes.

In fact, with the growth in liability for negligent misstatement, deceit in business relations is not now very significant. Where A induces B by misstatement to contract with him, the Misrepresentation Act 1967, s 2(1), gives B a far more efficacious remedy than deceit to recover damages, since A will be liable unless he can prove he was not only honest but careful in saying what he did. And even where the Misrepresentation Act does not apply, liability for negligent misstatement now in practice covers most representations made in the course of a business. Obviously these forms of liability, requiring less to be proved, are likely to supplant deceit.[6]

Reflecting dislike of those who deliberately deceive others, the plaintiff to sue for deceit need merely have relied on the defendant's statement; whether his reliance is reasonable is irrelevant.[7] Strictly speaking a statement must be one of present fact, not future fact or opinion. But this limitation is deceptive; to say one will do something is construed as implying one intends to do it at present, and to express an opinion implies also that one has reasonable grounds for holding that opinion. A seller of a business must not say that in his opinion it is financially 'healthy' if to his knowledge there are facts that would make a reasonable man think it was not 'healthy'. Another rule more important in theory than in practice is that a positive statement is necessary; it is not tortious knowingly to allow another to act on a mistake of his own making. Much of the sting is taken out of this rule owing to the principle that a misleading half-truth is deemed a lie, and

---

4 And not merely ought to know – *Derry v Peek* (1889) 14 App Cas 337.
5 [1897] 2 QB 57.
6 There are exceptions. Liability in deceit applies where advice is given merely casually, and probably even where there is a disclaimer of liability. In neither case is there liability in negligence.
7 *Redgrave v Hurd* (1881) 20 Ch D 1.

that any positive deceptive act (such as deliberately positioning merchandise to hide defects) takes the case out of the category of mere acquiescence.

Talk of justification sounds odd when it comes to deceit; when could telling lies ever be justified? Yet one case shows neatly how even here right and wrong must bow to business practice. Where two parties are negotiating over price, a statement by one of them that he does not intend to deal on certain terms ('I will not sell for less than £1,000') is not actionable even if known to be false.[8] Otherwise negotiation would be, to say the least, impaired.

(b) MALICIOUS FALSEHOOD

Like deceit, malicious falsehood involves telling lies in order to cause loss to another; unlike deceit, the statement here is made not *to* the plaintiff, but *about* him – or his business, or his property – with intent to cause him loss.[9] This tort involves primarily, though not exclusively, unfair competition; typically saying untruthfully that a person is bankrupt, or has gone out of business, or that the house he is trying to sell is haunted, or is not his to sell.

The resemblance to defamation is striking, but superficial. Defamation protects primarily personal, non-pecuniary interests, but makes a defendant liable for interfering with them even if he acted innocently and reasonably; further, it is limited to statements damaging to reputation. Malicious falsehood, by contrast, covers all statements damaging the plaintiff financially, not merely those damaging his reputation: on the other hand, financial loss must normally be shown and a defendant is not liable unless he knew what he said was false (or at least might be).

Malicious falsehood, therefore, requires an untruth about the plaintiff intended to cause him loss. It is said, however, that the untruth must also be 'malicious'. This is puzzling at first sight; surely lies deliberately told about another should make one liable for loss caused without more. The explanation is, it is submitted, that malicious falsehood includes also statements made in the knowledge that they might be false, and these, unlike deliberate lies, may often be justified. For instance, if B is trying to sell a house which A bona fide claims to be his, A must be entitled to assert his own claim, even though he knows it may be ill-founded and that asserting it will probably lose B the sale to C. This result is neatly reached by saying A's statement is made without 'malice'.

At common law, pecuniary loss was essential to malicious falsehood.

8 *Vernon v Keys* (1810) 12 East 632.
9 See eg *Ratcliffe v Evans* [1892] 2 QB 524.

Harmful allegations that nevertheless caused no loss in hard cash were not actionable. This was right. Malicious falsehood is a business tort; business exists to make money, and a person has little to complain of merely because his business, rather than he himself, has been traduced if he has not suffered any loss thereby. But the Defamation Act 1952, s 3, effectively reversed this rule for statements likely to harm business; damages are now available even in the absence of proved penuniary loss, on the specious ground that since proving pecuniary loss can be difficult the need to do so should be abolished.[10] The Court of Appeal eloquently commented on this odd law reform by pointedly giving very little to a plaintiff who used the section to claim substantial redress for business losses he could not show he had suffered.[11]

(c) PASSING OFF

The essence of passing off is that the public is deceived, and the plaintiff thus damaged, by the defendant stating falsely that his product[12] is the same as the plaintiff's. This tort is fundamentally one of unfair competition, in this case the gaining of a market for goods that ought to go to somebody else.

If deceit is present, liability is general; the defendant, for instance, need not have misrepresented his product as being actually the plaintiff's provided he attributed to it some quality possessed by the latter. An inferior vintner can be prevented by a maker of champagne from selling what he makes as champagne even under his own name.[13] Some form of deception, however, remains essential; mere 'unfair competition' without deception of somebody is not wrongful. So, for instance, one may quite legitimately direct one's own advertising to capture with little effort a market for a given product painstakingly – and expensively – built up by someone else.[14] One may even, indeed, use someone else's name or picture without his consent, provided one avoids statements or suggestions that he somehow endorses, or approves of, what one is trying to sell.

As a tort aimed at one sort of unfair competition, passing off is limited to *business* contexts. Indeed, in England it is even further limited, to where both plaintiff and defendant are engaged in the same

10   See the report of the Porter Committee on Defamation, Cmd 7536 (1948), paras 50–54.
11   *Fielding v Variety Inc* [1967] 2 QB 841, [1967] 2 All ER 497.
12   Or services. This matters because the statutory protection of the Trade Marks Act 1938 extends to products but not services.
13   *Bollinger v Costa Brava Wine Co* [1960] Ch 262, [1959] 3 All ER 800; *Erven Warninck BV v Townend & Sons Ltd* [1979] AC 731, [1979] 2 All ER 929.
14   *Cadbury Schweppes Pty Ltd v Pub Squash Co Pty Ltd* [1981] 1 All ER 213, [1981] 1 WLR 193.

sort of business. So a famous footballer may stop his name being used to sell footballs by suggesting he approves of them, but not, say, cosmetics.[15]

Strictly speaking, even though passing off is a business tort, liability for it does not depend on financial loss. Perhaps because in the formative years of the tort, lawyers introduced the red herring of a trader having a 'property' in his name to justify protecting it at all, there is (as with trespass to property) a right to nominal damages for any act of passing off. But this illogical rule is not very significant. Substantial, as against nominal, damages cannot be claimed in the absence of pecuniary loss (or perhaps other reckonable damage, such as damage to business reputation). In any case, in most passing off cases injunctions are a more important remedy than damages anyway, so the question when damages are available is not as important as it seems.

(d) BREACH OF CONFIDENCE

If a person receives information on terms that he is not to reveal it to third parties, any legal system must, at least on occasion, enforce such a duty of confidence. English law is no exception. Often such an obligation is incidental to ordinary promissory liability; an employee, for instance, impliedly promises in his contract of employment not to reveal his employer's trade secrets.[16] However, equity enforces obligations of confidence much more widely than this. Broadly it obliges a person to keep information confidential if: (i) he received it expressly or impliedly on terms that it was not to be disclosed further; or (ii) he received it from another, knowing that other himself to be under such an obligation; or (iii) he obtained it himself, say surreptitiously, knowing that the person in control of it wished it kept confidential. Hence a prospective licensee receiving details of a secret process in the course of negotiations must keep them secret even though no contract, and thus no contractual obligation, ever arises;[17] and so must anyone else to whom the prospective licensee discloses the information, provided he knows of its secrecy.[18] Similarly it would seem a person who purloins information from the boardroom safe can be in no better position than if he had been told it in confidence.[19] Breach of

---

15 See *Wombles Ltd v Wombles Skips Ltd* [1977] RPC 99. Other Commonwealth jurisdictions ignore this limitation – see eg *Henderson v Radio Corpn Pty Ltd* [1969] RPC 218.

16 *Robb v Green* [1895] 2 QB 315.

17 *Saltman Engineering Ltd v Campbell Engineering Co Ltd* [1963] 3 All ER 413n, 65 RPC 203.

18 Eg *Fraser v Thames Television Ltd* [1983] 2 All ER 101, [1983] 2 WLR 917.

19 *Lord Ashburton v Pape* [1913] 2 Ch 469, but cf *Malone v Metropolitan Police Comr (No 2)* [1979] 2 All ER 620.

confidence, moreover, while primarily protecting commercial interests, also protects personal ones; the doctor is equally obliged to keep his patient's secrets and the husband his wife's.[20]

There are two main exceptions to the duty of confidence. One, as might be expected with restrictions on information, is public policy. This is a limited exception mainly concerned with obvious cases such as information disclosing the commission of a crime, or other information whose withholding is obviously contrary to the public interest. The other exception is existing publicity of the information concerned. If information is well-known to those likely to be interested in it anyway, and possibly if the person seeking to protect it has himself previously revealed it in a public source, the right to protect it is lost.

(e) THE ECONOMIC TORTS

Except for breach of confidence, the liabilities we have dealt with, deceit, malicious falsehood and passing off, have in common one thing: the use of unlawful means (deception) to cause loss to another. This apart, however, they are rather disparate; they cover different problems and obey different detailed rules. By contrast, the 'economic torts' we deal with next – creating liability for participation in another's wrongdoing, causing loss by unlawful means and intimidation – are much more closely related. They combine to produce a general liability something like this. If A, intending to cause loss to B, (i) commits a wrong, including a tort, breach of contract, breach of trust or other actionable wrong, vis-à-vis B or a third person C; or (ii) threatens such an act against B or C with the same intent; or (iii) participates knowingly in such an act committed by C against B, then A is liable to B. This is in fact the working out of the principle mentioned at the beginning of this chapter, that one must not use unlawful means to damnify one's neighbour; equally, it complements rule that pressure or competition using lawful means is generally acceptable.

A preliminary warning, however. The economic torts appear largely, though not exclusively, in connection with two subjects; commercial competition and labour relations. In both cases, statute has largely overlaid the common law. With competition it has reduced freedom to act, outlawing some competitive methods even if they do not use means otherwise illegal (for instance, collective action to enforce minimum prices). With labour relations the opposite has happened. Effective industrial action means interfering with economic expectations, including contractual rights (calling a strike often means inducing employees to break contracts of employment, for example); to protect the freedom to take such action, certain forms of industrial action are made lawful even though they otherwise would not be. We deal in summary with such statutory changes later on.

(i) Participation in another's wrongdoing

If A knowingly assists in, or encourages, a breach of contract, breach of trust or other wrongful act against B committed by a third person, C, A is liable for the loss he causes to B. A trader must not suborn a competitor's employee to break his obligation of confidentiality by passing on trade secrets; nor persuade him to work for him in the face of a term in his contract giving his exclusive services to his present employer.[1] Similarly a trade union official can be prevented from telling employees not to account to employers for cash received on their account; the obligation to account exists in both contract and equity, and it is wrongful to tell another to break it.[2]

This form of liability is odd. In contrast to the case of the joint wrongdoer, it makes a person liable for participating in a wrong he cannot himself commit (only contracting parties can break contracts; only trustees commit breaches of trust); and its only rational defence is a very broad, abstract idea of illegitimacy. Breaking trusts, contracts and other obligations is wrong, and so persuading others to break them is an illegitimate way to compete with, or pressurise, others. This broad justification also explains why similar liabilities apply to inducing breach of contracts and participating in breaches of other obligations, even though these are normally regarded as belonging to completely different parts of the law.[3] The point is that trusts have much in common with contracts; indeed, many obligations can be based alternatively on breach of trust or breach of contract.

Liability depends on 'participation' in a breach of obligation. Now the obvious case of this is persuasion; but it is not the only one. Any participation suffices, even though the initiative came from the obligation breaker himfelf. If A agrees with B not to sell a thing to C, C commits a wrong in buying it even though the idea came from A and not himself;[4] again, one who assists a company director in breaking his fiduciary duty to his company is liable to the company wherever the initiative came from.

---

1   *Lumley v Gye* (1853) 2 E & B 216.
2   *Prudential Assurance Co Ltd v Lorenz* (1971) 11 KIR 78. (Compare the liability that has always existed for assisting in more conventional breaches of trust, as in *Barnes v Addy* (1874) 9 Ch App 244).
3   Eg the obligation of an employer not to reveal his employer's trade secrets is normally regarded as based on contract, while the obligation to account is regarded as primarily equitable; see above.
4   *Earl Sefton v Tophams Ltd* [1964] 3 All ER 876, [1964] 1 WLR 1408 (revsd on other grounds, [1967] 1 AC 50, [1966] 1 All ER 1039).

Some sort of active participation in a breach of obligation is, however, necessary. Merely bringing it about is not enough; otherwise many acts of justified competition would be harmful. So A may legitimately buy up all supplies of a given commodity even though he knows that as a result B will be in breach of a contract he has with C to supply the same commodity. He may have caused B's breach; he has not participated in it.

Further, participation must be knowing participation. One cannot be liable for persuading A to do an act that amounts to a breach of his contract with B unless one knows of that contract.[5] Similarly too, it is suggested, with participation in a breach of trust; the better authority is that one cannot be liable for this unless one actually knows of the relationship of trustee and beneficiary.[6]

Although one must know one is participating in a breach of obligation, one can be liable even though one does not intend such a breach to take place. The competitor who hires his rival's employee despite the latter's contractual obligation to his previous employer is still liable even though doubtless his aim was to advance his own business interests and not to cause loss to his rival.

Naturally, what the defendant participated in must actually have been a breach of obligation. One cannot be liable for inducing breach of a defective contract;[7] similarly, if a contract is effective one cannot be liable for persuading someone to do an act that is not a breach of it.[8] There is, however, one exception to this latter principle. If the only reason why an act which A persuades B to do is not a breach of B's obligation to C, is that the contract between B and C specifically exonerates B if his 'breach' is due to A's influence, then A cannot take advantage of that exoneration and is liable to C notwithstanding. A trade unionist who persuades a fuel merchant not to deliver fuel as promised to an employer is liable to the employer even though the contract between the employer contains a clause exonerating the fuel merchant if his failure to deliver is due to a trade union action.[9] Just as a contracting party cannot rely on a frustrating event to excuse him if it

5   Of course one need not know all the terms of that contract; it is enough if one knows it exists, and what sort of contract it is – *Emerald Construction Ltd v Lowthian* [1966] 1 All ER 1013, [1966] 1 WLR 691.
6   *Re Gross, ex p Adair* (1871) 24 LT 198 (affd sub nom *Re Gross ex p Kingston* (1871) 6 Ch App 632). Once a person knows of the trust relationship, however, it apparently suffices if he has constructive knowledge of the fact that he is helping to break it; *Selangor United Rubber Estates Ltd v Cradock* (No 3) [1968] 2 All ER 1073, [1968] 1 WLR 1555.
7   Eg a minor may be encouraged to break a contract not binding on him – *De Francesco v Barnum* (1890) 45 Ch D 430.
8   Eg one may call on employees to strike, provided they give due notice – *Morgan v Fry* [1968] 2 QB 710, [1967] 3 All ER 452.
9   *Torquay Hotel Co Ltd v Cousins* [1969] 2 Ch 106, [1969] 1 All ER 522.

was due to his own fault, an instigator of a breach of contract cannot take advantage of a provision designed to protect the parties from the effects of his own intervention.

(ii) Intimidation

Intimidation is a threat to commit a breach of obligation that causes another to act to his own or a third person's detriment. Some cases are straightforward. A person forced to give up a lucrative business because of threats of violence must be able to recoup his loss. Similarly, though not so obviously, with threats to break a contract. A purchaser of a house, forced by a last-minute threat by the vendor not to complete to pay an extra £5,000, can recover it.[10] In both cases, the alternative idea, that the loss was the plaintiff's own fault because he gave in to the threat rather than seeking legal remedies (such as an injunction), is unattractive. It would make wrongdoing pay with a vengeance and contradict the general rule elsewhere that liability for a loss carries with it liability for the reasonable effect of avoiding it.[11]

Parallelling liability for participation in another's wrongdoing, on principle a threat to commit any wrong – breach of contract, tort, breach of trust, and so on[12] – except a mere crime, should suffice. This comports a very wide liability; in fact, however, another factor greatly narrows it. A person who gives in to a threat as part of a bona fide compromise, or pays a claim he knows unjustified in order to cement future business relations, cannot complain; nor the victim of a threat genuinely content to waive his rights and pay up.

More difficult is the case where three persons are involved – where A threatens a wrong against B unless B acts to the detriment of C. Older cases established liability in respect of damage done to a plaintiff's business by blatant threats to his customers;[13] more recently the tort has been applied to labour relations. In *Rookes v Barnard*[14] trade unionists threatened an employer with a strike (amounting to a breach of contract) unless the latter dismissed another non-union employee;

---

10 Because the extra £5,000 is not only lost by B but gained by A, many authorities here – eg *North Ocean Shipping Co Ltd v Hyundai Construction Co Ltd, The Atlantic Baron* [1979] QB 705, [1978] 3 All ER 1173, – based the right to recover on unjustified enrichment (see Ch 10, below). But the result would hardly be different if A never benefited – for instance, if A insisted it should be given to some charity. ✗

11 A rule applying both in tort – *Jones v Boyce* (1816) 1 Stark 493 – and elsewhere, for instance in insurance; see eg *Symington & Co v Union Insurance Co of Canton Ltd* (1928) 97 LJKB 646, 139 LT 386.

12 Even, perhaps, misuse of public authority – *Central Canada Potash Co Ltd v Government of Saskatchewan* (1978) 88 DLR (3d) 609. See further pp 93–4, below.

13 In *Garret v Taylor* (1620) Cro Jac 567 the defendant was held liable for driving away the plaintiff's customers by threatening to 'mayhem and vex them with suits.'

14 [1964] AC 1129, [1964] 1 All ER 367.

the employer unwillingly did so. The non-union employee recovered from the trade unionists for the loss of his job, on the ground that it had been caused by the threat of an unlawful act. This result is at first sight difficult to justify. If the plaintiff was lawfully dismissed by his employers, why should he have a claim against anyone; equally, why should a breach of contract between the trade unionists and the employer give any rights to the plaintiff? But as soon as the case is seen as one involving the use of illegitimate means to achieve a certain financial end, then immediately it becomes rather more explicable.

(iii) Causing loss by unlawful means

If *threatening* unlawful action against B with intent to harm C is wrongful, obviously *committing* it should equally be. Threatening to assault a rival's customers unless they go away is intimidation; assaulting them with the same effect is causing loss by unlawful means. The liability extends beyond unfair competition represented by that example; in particular, to labour relations. In *Stratford v Lindley*[15] trade unionists were in dispute with X, who hired river barges to Y, among others. They were held liable to X when they caused Y's employees, in breach of contract with Y, to refuse to cooperate in returning the vessels to X.

Hence a general principle something like this. If A commits a wrongful act (tort, breach of contract or trust, or otherwise) against B, prima facie only B can complain, even though C may suffer loss as well; nevertheless, if A's act was aimed specifically to hurt C, this combines with its wrongfulness to justify making A liable to C as well. It follows, of course, that, to be liable to him, A must actually have aimed at hurting C; knowledge that what he did was likely to do so is not enough. Any seller of goods knows that, if he wrongfully fails to supply the buyer, third persons, such as sub-buyers, will suffer loss; nevertheless he is not liable for that loss because he did not intend to cause it. Again, a thief of company property is normally liable only to the company itself and not to the individual shareholders, even though they will clearly be damnified.[16] (The same rule, incidentally, applies on principle to intimidation; a person threatening a wrongful act against A is not, without more, liable to any third person suffering loss as a result. But this is not very important; in most *Rookes v Barnard*[17] situations the defendant will have aimed specifically at the third party suffering the loss.)

What, for these purposes, counts as 'unlawful means'? Torts and breaches of contract clearly do, and in the absence of authority it is

---

15 [1965] AC 269, [1964] 3 All ER 102.
16 See the classic case of *Foss v Harbottle* (1843) 2 Hare 461.
17 [1964] AC 1129, [1964] 1 All ER 367.

suggested breach of trust should as well. So a trustee of a discretionary trust who corruptly decides to give a sum of money to X rather than Y should be liable for the loss suffered by Y.[18] On the other hand, where loss is caused by acts wrongful in some etiolated sense, but (unlike torts and breaches of contract or trust) not giving rise to a claim for damages or compensation, a different rule applies; prima facie they are not 'unlawful means'. A is not, for instance, liable in damages to B merely because he causes him loss by committing a crime.[19] Any other rule, indeed, at least where statutory crimes are concerned,[20] would undermine the rule that a criminal statute never creates civil liability unless some intention to that effect can be inferred. (Not that this is a convincing justification. A better one is that criminal and civil liability protect different interests, and unfortunate results may flow from regularly allowing one to give rise to the other.) Similarly, acts on principle tortious but rendered not actionable by statute are excluded from 'unlawful means'; a provision vital in trade dispute cases to prevent statutory protection of industrial action being rendered nugatory.[1]

Exceptionally, however, some activities are regarded as 'unlawful means' despite not being actionable. One is deception causing no loss to the person deceived. If A deceives B into acting contrary to C's interests, for instance obtaining by deception goods which B has contracted with C not to supply him with, he acts wrongfully.[2] Another case, apparently, is unlawful administrative action; threatening to deprive X on legally inadmissible grounds of (say) a licence may not be actionable by X, but may, if it was aimed at hurting Y, be actionable by him. Thirdly, contrasting oddly with the law's normal refusal to create statutory causes of action by implication, acts contrary to miscellaneous statutes, such as the Restrictive Trade Practices Act 1976, have been held 'unlawful means'.[3] But such cases, it is submitted, are anomalies not to be extended.

Liability for causing loss by unlawful means is further limited because the unlawful means used must not be merely peripheral to the defendant's primary motive of harming the plaintiff. For example, in *Stratford v Lindley*[4] the defendants were liable for preventing the return of the plaintiffs' barges because they encouraged the crews to break

18 Assuming, that is, that a discretionary trust gives no-one an enforceable right to any property.
19 *Chapman v Honig* [1963] 2 QB 502, [1963] 2 All ER 513.
20 Which effectively means most criminal offences today.
1 *Hadmor Productions Ltd v Hamilton* [1983] AC 191, [1982] 1 All ER 1042.
2 *National Phonograph Ltd v Edison-Bell Ltd* [1908] 1 Ch 335.
3 *Daily Mirror Newspapers Ltd v Gardner* [1968] 2 QB 762, [1968] 2 All ER 163; *Brekkes v Cattell* [1972] Ch 105, [1971] 1 All ER 1031.
4 [1965] AC 269, [1964] 3 All ER 102.

their employment contracts by refusing to man them. What, however, if the defendants had not committed that wrong but merely the tort of nuisance by leaving the barges where they were and blocking other frontagers' access to the river? It is submitted they would not have been liable; they would have damnified the plaintiffs by doing an act that happened to be illegal, but the illegality would have been collateral and incidental.

CAUSING LOSS BY UNLAWFUL MEANS: THREE PARTIES OR TWO? Hitherto we have dealt with A infringing B's rights to the detriment of C. But what if A aimed to hurt, not C, but B himself? This is normally a silly question; if A commits a tort or breach of contract against B he is liable without the need to invoke the economic torts at all. But in a few anomalous cases, acts not actionable as such apparently count as 'unlawful means', so that if done with intent to cause loss to another they make the actor liable. In *Acrow (Automation) Ltd v Rex Chainbelt, Inc*[5] the Court of Appeal said acts in breach of a subsisting injunction fell into this category; as a result, if X deliberately broke an injunction with intent to harm Y, he was liable. Now, there is nothing wrong as such with a class of acts actionable only sub modo; that is, only where committed with intent to injure another. Yet the idea is anomalous in English law and, it is submitted, will not be extended.

(f) CONSPIRACY

Conspiracy is committed where two or more in combination injure another. Traditionally it encapsulates two sorts of liability; where damage is done by unlawful means, and where it is not. Where unlawful means are used, the separate tort of conspiracy adds little to the rest of the law of obligations; since it is wrongful for one person to injure another by unlawful means, it is equally so for two to do so. The nominally separate head of liability has survived largely because conspiracy as a tort developed before any general tort of causing loss by unlawful means.

More interesting is the liability where no unlawful means are used. Two people can be liable for combining to injure a third even if they use means otherwise lawful; combination makes wrongful what would otherwise be legitimate.[6] Industrial conflict, as might be expected, spawned this rule. In *Quinn v Leatham*[7] in 1900, trade unionists put pressure on an employer, and caused him loss, by causing his workforce to resign en masse. Though there is no law against inducing

---

5   [1971] 3 All ER 1175, [1971] 1 WLR 1676.
6   Epigrammatically, conspiracy can be described as the 'abuse' of the right to combine.
7   [1901] AC 495.

employees to resign (provided they do not break their contracts of employment) the House of Lords held the defendants liable. The reasoning was unfortunately obscure, particularly since three years earlier the House had trenchantly refused to hold liable trade union organisers who limited themselves to lawful means; nevertheless, certain suggestions in *Quinn's* case, coupled with subsequent interpretations put on it,[8] make it clear that the vital element was the element of combination.

At this point one might think a little hollow the rule that, absent illegality, one cannot be liable for malicious or unreasonable acts. Are not such acts normally done by more than one, and will not the more generous liability in conspiracy therefore normally apply? In a few cases this is true (for instance where two combine, for reasons of pure malice, to drive another out of business by ruinous competition); in general, however, conspiracy has been castigated as in 'anomalous' head of liability and so limited that it has little effect on the law of obligations. This is not surprising. It is rationally indefensible to distinguish acts done alone from acts done in concert (the only plausible argument in defence of it, that groups can coerce more effectively than individuals, was unconvincing when advanced – half-heartedly – in *Quinn v Leathem*[9] itself, and is more so now that such effective pressure can be exerted by companies and organisations that, for all their power, are still one person in law[10]). Add judicial diffidence in distinguishing good and bad business and fair industrial practice, and the prevailing mistrust of conspiracy is predictable.

Conspiracy is confined largely by manipulating the requirement of intention. As with causing loss by unlawful means, the defendant must have aimed at hurting the plaintiff; however, conspiracy has a further rule to itself, that it is a defence that the defendant, though he did aim at hurting the plaintiff, did so with the ulterior motive of serving some interest of his own. So one cannot be liable in conspiracy for anything done in order to advance one's business interests – or, for that matter, to advance the interests of a trade union[11] Indeed, ironically, even the decision in *Quinn v Leathem* would probably go differently today.

(g) JUSTIFICATION

(i) At common law
The law, as we have seen, starts by saying that one is liable if one uses unlawful means to cause loss to another. However, in certain cases even

---

8 Notably by Lord Dunedin in *Sorrell v Smith* [1925] AC 700 at 723.
9 By Lords Brampton and Lindley – [1901] AC 495 at 531 and 537–538.
10 See Lord Diplock's remarks in *Lonrho Ltd v Shell Petroleum Ltd* [1982] AC 173 at 189, [1981] 2 All ER 456, at 464.
11 See *Lonrho Ltd v Shell Petroleum Ltd*, above; *Crofter Hand Woven Harris Tweed Ltd v Veitch* [1942] AC 435.

though unlawful means are used, nevertheless the law regards the defendant's conduct as justified, so negativing the liability that would otherwise arise. In general such justification arises in two broad cases. First, there is action taken for compelling reasons of public policy or the protection of others. A doctor can advise a sick man to cease work without being sued by his employer for inducing a breach of contract; a race relations campaigner can encourage the employees of a dance hall owner not to work for him as long as he operates a colour bar.[12]

Secondly, a defendant may be under a contractual or other obligation to a third person; and this obligation, provided he undertook it in good faith and without knowing of the plaintiff's rights, he may take steps to enforce even though he may incidentally thereby infringe the plaintiff's rights. A trade union official employed to look to the interests of his union can do so, provided he acts in good faith, even though in doing so he incidentally interferes with third persons' contractual rights. Again, an employer is not liable merely because, acting in the course of his employment, he happens to cause his employer to commit a breach of contract or other obligation vis-à-vis a third person.[13]

Third, contractual (and other) rights obtained in good faith can be enforced. If A contracts independently to sell the same goods to both B and C, either B or C can try to persuade A to keep his contract with him, even though this involves procuring him to break his contract with the other.

Such cases, however, are exceptional. It is not enough that what the defendant did was reasonable, nor that it was in his interests.[14] Any protection of this kind has to be granted by statute.

It is sometimes thought that justification for conspiracy goes rather further; that in some circumstances conspiracy may be justified whereas no other economic tort would be. In fact this is not so. It is true that one cannot be liable in conspiracy for acts done with the intent to advance one's own self-interest; but that is a matter not so much of justification, but of a limit placed on liability by the definition of the tort itself. In general, it is better to regard conspiracy as subject to the same rules of justification as any other economic tort.

(ii) By statute – labour relations
The right to take industrial action would be hollow if statute did not protect trade unions and their members from liability in some cases for

---

12   *Scala Ballrooms (Wolverhampton) Ltd v Ratcliffe* [1958] 3 All ER 220, [1958] 1 WLR 1057.
13   *Said v Butt* [1920] 3 KB 497.
14   *South Wales Miners' Federation v Glamorgan Coal Co* [1905] AC 239. (This does not apply to conspiracy, however, since for that tort absence of self-interest is a pre-requisite to liability itself).

deliberately causing loss to others. The protection given is roughly as follows. In respect of certain kinds of trade dispute (what kind tends to vary with the complexion of the government in power) action taken in the course of that dispute is protected in two ways. First, a person cannot be liable in conspiracy if he would not have been liable had he acted alone.[15] The 'anomaly' in conspiracy, that it can make one liable for conduct otherwise entirely lawful, is therefore excluded from labour relations.[16] Secondly, acts are legitimised if all that is wrong about them is that they involve interference with contractual rights[17] – thus leaving liability intact in respect of violence, or interference with property rights. This is done by enacting that one cannot be liable for inducing a breach of contract, or (thus excluding *Rookes v Barnard*[18] liability) for threatening that a contract will be broken. Further, as we have said, such inducement cannot count as 'unlawful means' for the purpose of the tort of causing loss by unlawful means.

In short, the aim of the statutory limitations on liability is to licence parties to an industrial dispute to interfere with *financial* interests with impunity. No protection being given to interference with persons or property, liability remains if physical means, such as assault or sabotage, are resorted to.

(h) UNFAIR COMPETITION – A NOTE

The common law may have eschewed any obligation to compete reasonably or fairly. Legislation – in particular the Restrictive Trade Practices Act 1976 – and EEC law, among other sources,[19] however, introduce extensive administrative controls on unfair competition, which incidentally create obligations owed to its victims. In fact, it is now deceptive to say, *tout court*, that English law generally refuses to prevent unfair competition.

By the Restrictive Trade Practices Act 1976, agreements between different suppliers of goods (and, in some cases, services), if they regulate prices, conditions, output and the like, must be registered;[20] once registered, the Director-General of Fair Trading can apply to the

---

15 Trade Union and Labour Relations Act 1974, s 13(4).
16 Which it will often be at common law anyway, since by *Crofter Hand Woven Harris Tweed Ltd v Veitch*, above, self-interest, including trade union self-interest, negatives liability in conspiracy.
17 But not for participating in the breach of any other obligation. Hence the importance of obligations such as that of an agent to account for money received, which can be expressed otherwise than as based on contract: *Prudential Assurance Co Ltd v Lorenz* (1971) 11 KIR 78.
18 [1964] AC 1129, [1964] 1 All ER 367.
19 Including, eg, the Competition Act 1980, which is beyond the scope of this book.
20 S 1. Services are covered only if the Director-General of Fair Trading so orders – s 11.

Restrictive Practices Court to have them prevented if, according to a particular set of criteria, they are against the public interests.[1] If such agreements are operated without being registered, s 35(2) of the Act allows any third person damnified to recover damages from those responsible.

Much more important is EEC law, though any extensive coverage of that in this book is obviously impossible.[2] Suffice it to say, damages and other remedies are available to those damaged by breaches of the 'unfair competition' articles of the Treaty of Rome, Arts 85 and 86.[3] These are very widely drawn. Art 85 prohibits any 'agreement' or 'concerted practice' aimed at, or resulting in, 'distortion of competition' within the EEC; this includes, in particular, agreements fixing prices, sharing markets or limiting production. The agreement may look innocuous, like an exclusive distribution agreement that is aimed neither at restricting competition nor at harming any competitor; nevertheless, if it has that effect, it falls foul of Art 85.[4] (The contrast with the requirements of intention in the English torts of causing loss by unlawful means and conspiracy, could not be greater.) Nevertheless, even here a few exceptions are allowed; for instance, agreements existing for good commercial reasons and with negligible anti-competitive effect; or agreements aimed at preserving quality, for instance involving refusal to supply high-quality equipment to any but very competent, and very expensive, dealers.[5]

Art 86, aiming at cases where there is little competition to stifle or distort, prohibits 'abuse of a dominant position' within the EEC; in particular, unfair or discriminatory pricing, limiting production, and so on. Again, this is widely construed. A 'dominant position' means simply one of substantial economic strength in a given market; 'abuse' may even extend to simply selling at a larger profit than the European Court thinks reasonable.[6] Indeed, the prohibition on abuse of a dominant position negates even the fundamental right of English law, the right not to contract. Thus a major oil company which, in the midst of a shortage, refused to accept further orders from a previous customer, escaped falling foul of Art 86 only because the European Court considered its refusal reasonable in the circumstances.[7]

1   S 2.
2   For useful accounts of the law in this field, see D. Wyatt & A. Dashwood, *The Substantive Law of the EEC*, Part VI, and A. Parry & S. Hardy, *EEC Law*, 2nd ed, Ch 20.
3   *Garden Cottage Foods Ltd v Milk Marketing Board* [1983] 3 WLR 143 at 149–150, per Lord Diplock.
4   See, eg, 56 and 58/64: *Consten and Grundigs-Verkaufs v EC Commission* [1966] ECR 299.
5   See 56/65: *Société Technique Minière v Maschinenbau Ulm GmbH* [1966] ECR 235; *Re S A B A GmbH* [1976] 1 CMLR D61.
6   27/76: *United Brands Co v EC Commission* [1978] ECR 207, is most instructive.
7   77/77: *Benzine en Petroleum Handelomaelschappij BV v EC Commission* [1978] ECR 1513.

(i) Liability of public authorities for deliberate misuse of power
Public authorities, in their nature, sometimes take decisions they
should not take; further, since today – as one commentator puts it –
'increasingly, *government* is the major source of wealth',[8] these decisions
may well cause considerable loss. Normally both the wrongness of the
decision and the loss it causes will be inadvertent (in which case there
is liability for fault, albeit in a modified form). A remedy must also be
provided, however, where loss is *deliberately* caused by a wrong decision
or misuse of official power. English law deals with the problem through
the general law of obligations; the liability of public authorities in
damages for wrong decisions is a modified form of the wrongs of
intimidation and causing loss by unlawful means. If the loss was
intentionally caused, the unlawful means are provided by the
unjustified decision itself. As a result it can be said that there is a
generalised tort of deliberately causing loss by means of a decision that
should not have been taken;[9] as where police maliciously take action
causing the plaintiff's bar to be shut down,[10] or a monopoly marketing
organisation deliberately drives X out of business by unjustifiably
threatening to refuse to deal with those who deal with him.[11] It does not
seem to matter that the person affected by the decision could have
taken steps to have it annulled, or even ignored it; provided he suffered
loss, he can recover it.

The characterisation of this liability as for 'decisions that should not
have been taken', and not 'unlawful administrative action', is
deliberate, for two reasons. First, an administrative measure can be
annulled if taken for the wrong reason or by the wrong procedure,
whether or not in abstracto it was justified. An applicant refused a
licence (for example) without adequate hearing has the right to have
his case heard again properly even though the result may be the same.
But damages should be available only if the decision would not have
been reached had proper procedures been followed.[12] Secondly, many
administrative decisions, though annullable in law, are 'voidable': they
bind those subject to them unless and until annulled. In a sense,
therefore, they are not 'unlawful'; nevertheless that should not preclude
compensation if those decisions in fact ought not to have been taken.

Two features limit liability under this head. To begin with, the rule
of causing loss by unlawful means applies; there can be no liability
except for a decision particularly aimed at the plaintiff. This will be
fairly easy to show where the decision specifically concerns him; where,

8   See N. E. Simmonds [1982] *Legal Studies* 257, 267.
9   See *David v Abdul Cader* [1963] 3 All ER 579, [1963] 1 WLR 834.
10 *Farington v Thomson and Bridgland* [1959] VR 286.
11 *Gershman v Manitoba Vegetable Producers Marketing Board* (1976) 69 DLR (3d) 114.
12 See the very perceptive analysis of the problem in C. Harlow, *Compensation and Government Torts*, Part 3.

for instance, he is refused planning permission to extend his premises.
But this is not always so; deliberate aim may be difficult to show where
his house (or factory) is merely one of many being compulsorily
purchased as part of a clearance scheme.[13] The second feature is a requirement of 'malice'; even if a decision is
wrong, and directed at the plaintiff specifically, he cannot sue unless it
was 'malicious'. What does this mean? It is submitted that the question
is best viewed in reverse, as one of justification. A decision is not
malicious, and therefore is justified, if taken in the honest belief that the
authority that took it was legally entitled to take it, even if in fact it was
not. This is important, since in many cases a decision can, in
administrative law, be challenged as ultra vires even though taken in
good faith for good social objectives.[14] The object of the requirement of
malice is simply to protect authorities taking decisions in the (legally
misguided) light of what they see as justifiable social objectives.

13   Hence in *Dunlop v Woollahra Municipal Council* [1982] AC 158, [1981] 1 All ER 1202,
the Privy Council were at pains to deny that the mere wrongness of a decision,
coupled with damage foreseeably caused by it, sufficed to create liability.
14   As in, eg, *Hall v Shoreham-by-Sea UDC* [1964] 1 All ER 1, [1964] 1 WLR 240.

Chapter 9

Criminal law as a source of legal obligation

We shall see in Ch 13 that the fact that one party is in breach of the criminal law may prevent an obligation arising. So also, as one might expect, a breach of the criminal law may *cause* an obligation to arise. This may happen in two ways. First it may happen *indirectly*. The fact that someone has been guilty of a crime may make him liable for breach of contract, or for some tort, or to return enrichment as unjustified. Second, in certain cases, criminal conduct may *directly* create civil liability; the criminality of the act makes it sufficiently wrongful to put the person committing it under a duty to compensate those suffering loss thereby.

1. The indirect effect of the criminal law

Even though the mere fact that a crime has been committed may not automatically mean that anyone damnified can complain, it may trigger other forms of obligation.

For instance, commission of a crime may make conduct negligent that would not otherwise be; after all, as we pointed out in Ch 7, negligence involves conduct being in some sense unjustified and criminal conduct is likely to fall in this category. Hence in an early case[1] a railway company was held negligent in failing to provide a communication cord; what swayed the court was not so much the danger inherent in their conduct as the fact that legislation required such cords to be fitted.

Again, with contractual liability, it is an implied term in most contracts that they are to be performed lawfully; as a result a person committing a criminal offence in the course of performance may find himself liable in damages for any loss suffered thereby.[2] Hence, on the basis that selling a car known to be unroadworthy is illegal, a New Zealand court has held the seller liable in damages for breach of an implied term in the contract of sale, even though breach of the statute concerned did not as such give rise to civil liability.[3]

1 *Blamires v London and Yorkshire Rly Co* (1873) LR 8 Ex 283, 42 LJ Ex 182.
2 See the rather odd case of *Strongman (1945) Ltd v Sincock* [1955] 2 QB 525, [1955] 3 All ER 90.
3 *Dromorne Linen Co Ltd v Ward* [1963] NZLR 614.

Similar reasoning can apply, though slightly less obviously, to liability to return unjustified enrichment; for the fact that enrichment is gained criminally is potent ground for holding it unjustified. A blackmailer, for instance, obtains money by threatening (as often as not) to do that which he as a perfect right to do; yet, it would seem, at least partly on the ground that he commits a criminal offence in making the threat, his victim can recover from him anything he has paid.[4] Yet again, statute may make it a criminal offence for a landlord to demand a premium from his tenant; the Privy Council has held that, as a result, any such premium once paid can be recovered back.[5]

2. The direct effect of the criminal law

Some systems of law, notably French law, regard it as axiomatic that, if a person commits a crime and loss results to others, that of itself prima facie makes the person committing the crime liable; tort, in other words, is wrong plus harm, and breach of the criminal law is sufficient wrong. English law rejects this position emphatically. The mere fact that one has committed a crime does not of itself, even presumptively, make one liable in damages to anyone.[6] Nor even (it is now established, after a certain hesitation) can criminal conduct as such be prevented by injunction, except by the Attorney-General.[7] So much is straight-forward; sometimes, however, criminal conduct does create civil liability to damages and an injunction. The question is when.

We start with crimes at common law. Except where conduct is clearly made criminal with no view to protecting others' interests (as with offences against the State or the administration of justice[8]), it seems that where a common law crime is committed, prima facie anyone can sue the person committing it provided he suffers 'special damage' over and above that suffered by the public at large. This is clear with the crime of public nuisance, a crime covering all sorts of anti-social activity from obstructing the highway or access to it, to brothel-keeping; the highway user injured by colliding with an obstruction, or the householder damnified by the proximity of a brothel, can sue. What authority there is suggests that the same

4   See *Thorne v Motor Trade Association Ltd* [1937] AC 797 at 806–807, [1937] 3 All ER 157 at 160, per Lord Atkin; cf *Williams v Bayley* (1866) LR 1 HL 200, 35 LJ Ch 717.
5   *Kiriri Cotton Ltd v Dewani* [1960] AC 192, [1960] 1 All ER 177.
6   *Lonrho Ltd v Shell Petroleum Ltd (No 2)* [1982] AC 173, [1981] 2 All ER 456.
7   *Gouriet v Union of Post Office Workers* [1978] AC 435, [1977] 3 All ER 70; *RCA Corpn v Pollard* [1983] Ch 135, [1982] 3 All ER 771. Cf the earlier attitude in cases such as *Springhead Spinning Co v Riley* (1868) LR 6 Eq 551, 37 LJ Ch 889.
8   Eg most forms of contempt of court – *Chapman v Honig* [1963] 2 QB 502, [1963] 2 All ER 513.

principle extends to other crimes at common law.[9] In practice, however, whether it does is not very important. There are rather few common law crimes existing to protect others' interests that are not torts in their own right anyway. With statutory crimes, by contrast, the rule is much more restrictive. After briefly flirting with the idea that such crimes were to be treated like common law crimes as presumptively engendering civil liability,[10] English law abandoned it in favour of its present formally straightforward, if practically enigmatic, view: breach of a criminal statute gives rise to civil liability if, and only if, the statute can be interpreted as providing expressly or impliedly for such liability.

Increasingly often this point is dealt with expressly in legislation; where it is there is little problem. Thus (to take just one example) the Consumer Safety Act 1978, having prohibited the marketing of certain dangerous products, specifically by s 6 gives anyone injured by such marketing a right to sue. By contrast, the Guard Dogs Act 1975, forbidding the use of free running dogs to guard commercial premises, in s 5(2) (a) precludes any civil remedy arising. Moreover, there are certain fairly clear implications in some cases; for instance, even if a statute does give rise to civil liability it can engender no liability except for the sort of damage that it was aimed at preventing.[11]

Such clear cases aside, however, where there is no clear indication, the list of statutory prohibitions that have, and have not, been construed as giving rise to civil liability can only be described as bewildering. Those interpreted as engendering liability include most industrial safety legislation;[12] some road traffic laws (for instance, the duty to stop at a pedestrian crossing, or not to let uninsured persons drive one's car[13]); and miscellaneous other safety legislation concerning, among other things, bridges, level crossings and the sign-posting of fire hydrants.[14] In contrast, the prohibitions not giving rise to civil liability include the majority of road traffic legislation (such as that requiring vehicles to be roadworthy[15]); pure food and trade descriptions rules;[16] criminal prohibitions on intellectual property infringement;[17] laws against

9 See, eg, the rather odd case of *Roberts v J & F Stone Lighting and Radio Ltd* (1945) 172 LT 240.
10 *Couch v Steel* (1854) 3 E & B 402, 2 CLR 940.
11 *Gorris v Scott* (1874) LR 9 Ex 125, 43 LJ Ex 92.
12 *Groves v Lord Wimborne* [1898] 2 QB 402, 67 LJ QB 862.
13 *London Passenger Transport Board v Upson* [1949] AC 155, [1949] 1 All ER 60; *Monk v Warbey* [1935] 1 KB 75, 104 LJKB 153.
14 See *Knapp v Railway Executive* [1949] 2 All ER 508; *Dawson v Bingley UDC* [1911] 2 KB 149, 80 LJKB 842.
15 *Phillips v Britannia Hygienic Laundry Co Ltd* [1923] 2 KB 832, 93 LJKB 5.
16 *Square v Model Farm Dairies (Bournemouth) Ltd* [1939] 2 KB 365, [1939] 1 All ER 259; *London Armoury Co Ltd v Ever-Ready Co (GB) Ltd* [1941] 1 KB 742, [1941] 1 All ER 364.
17 *RCA Corpn v Pollard* [1983] Ch 135, [1982] 3 All ER 771.

unlawful harassment of tenants;[18] and statutes aimed to protect bookmakers from unfair competition by the Tote.[19]

Now, even though there are said to be rules of thumb in interpretation, such as that statutory crimes aimed at protecting everybody do not, whereas those aimed at protecting a defined class do, create civil liability,[20] it is disingenuous to regard the distinctions just drawn as depending in any real sense on statutory interpretation. As in many other situations, meaning here is the eye of the beholder (so much so that one commentator has abandoned any attempt to explain the cases and in desperation postulated a presumption in favour of liability in industrial safety cases and against it elsewhere[1]).

In fact, it is suggested, one thread does permeate the decisions on whether crime gives rise to tort; consciously or otherwise, it seems to underlie ostensible interpretation. This is that a criminal prohibition will not create civil liability if *either* such liability would effectively duplicate one already existing, *or* (more importantly) it would subvert an established pattern of liability, as for instance would happen were fault liability to be replaced in a particular field by strict liability.

An example of duplication precluding civil liability is the decision in *McCall v Abelesz*,[2] where the Court of Appeal refused to allow a civil action for unlawful harassment of tenants contrary to s 30 of the Rent Act 1965; the ground was effectively that liability for trespass or breach of the contract of lease ought not to be needlessly duplicated.

The argument that a particular statute should not give rise to civil liability because it would subvert existing patterns of liability is more subtle; but it is normally concerned with the fact that any civil liability based on them will be independent of fault. For example, criminal liability under food and drugs legislation is in general strict; yet in one case[3] the Court of Appeal refused to hold the seller of adulterated milk liable on the basis of it without fault to a consumer, since that would reverse the well-established rule that in general the civil liability of a producer of goods to the ultimate consumer was based on negligence. Again, in 1923, Bankes LJ stressed the 'far reaching consequences' of replacing fault with strict liability over a large part of road traffic law as a reason not to hold a driver strictly liable for damage done when an illegally defective axle broke.[4] It might be thought that decisions

---

18   *McCall v Abelesz* [1976] QB 585, [1976] 1 All ER 727.
19   *Cutler v Wandsworth Stadium Ltd* [1949] AC 398, [1949] 1 All ER 544.
20   This one was put forward by Bankes LJ in *Phillips v Britannia Hygienic Laundry Co Ltd* [1923] 2 KB 832 at 838.
1   G. L. Williams (1960) 23 MLR 233, 248.
2   [1976] QB 585, [1976] 1 All ER 727.
3   *Square v Model Farm Dairies Ltd* [1939] 2 KB 365, [1939] 1 All ER 259.
4   *Phillips v Britannia Hygienic Laundry Co Ltd* [1923] 2 KB 832 at 837. Cf McCardie J's decision in the court below ([1923] 1 KB 539), where other arguments for strict liability were canvassed and rejected.

allowing industrial safety legislation (which also often carries strict liability) to give rise to civil liability and thus replace the employer's traditional fault liability, belied this argument; but there is a suggestive answer. *Groves v Lord Wimborne*,[5] the case first establishing that an action lay for damages for breach of such legislation, was decided in June 1898, within three days of the coming into force of the Workmen's Compensation Act 1897, which statute itself for the first time introduced a measure of strict liability into the same field. As a result, *Groves v Lord Wimborne* was not as revolutionary a development as it seems at first sight.

We have hitherto drawn a clear distinction between criminal prohibitions that *directly* and *indirectly* create civil liability; and we have stressed that, where they do so *directly*, the effect is the creation of a new liability and not (say) a novel form of the tort of negligence. This is true in theory;[6] in practice the novelty of the liability is a little forced, and the liability often has much in common with negligence. Thus the defences of contributory negligence, act of the plaintiff and consent of the plaintiff (*volenti non fit injuria*[7]) apply in nearly the same way. Moreover, even the strict liability created when criminal statutes give rise to civil liability is less strict than it might seem. For instance, the 'dangerous machinery' that must by the Factories Act 1961 be fenced is really machinery that is a foreseeable cause of injury, thus importing a large element of fault liability.[8] Indeed, in practice, in the industrial field at least, liability for breach of statutory duty created by criminal statutes often means merely fault liability under another name; except that 'fault' is much more precisely defined that under the more nebulous law of negligence. As a result, the advantage given to the injured plaintiff is often more one of proof than of anything else.[9]

3. General reflections

As we mentioned, other systems of law, basing liability in tort on the simple and general idea of a wrongful act causing loss,[10] are more generous in allowing crime to give rise to civil liability; if crime is

---

5 [1898] 2 QB 402.

6 The theory was articulated clearly by Lord Diplock in *Gouriet v Union of Post Office Workers* [1978] AC 435, [1977] 3 All ER 70.

7 For the impact of *volenti non fit injuria*, cf *Baddeley v Lord Granville* (1887) 19 QBD 423, 56 LJQB 501, and *ICI Ltd v Shatwell* [1965] AC 656, [1964] 2 All ER 999.

8 See, eg, *Walker v Bletchley-Flettons Ltd* [1937] 1 All ER 170.

9 A point forcefully made by G. L. Williams in (1960) 23 MLR 233, already mentioned in note 12 p 44, above, and by Lord Atkin in *Lochgelly Iron and Coal Co Ltd v M'Mullun* [1934] AC 1 at 9.

10 Nicely encapsulated in the view of French law that tortious liability depends on *faute*, which is interpreted as meaning some *acte illicite*.

wrongful, and if it causes loss to another, prima facie there ought to be liability. This means of approaching the problem looks attractive; whether English law would benefit from embracing it, however, is more doubtful.

First, different levels of liability are often appropriate in crime and tort; the factors that militate in favour of strict criminal liability do not necessarily support strict civil liability as well. Of course, it would be possible for the law to evolve a doctrine that, although criminal prohibitions generally gave rise to civil liability, that liability was not necessarily on the same basis; for instance, that civil liability always depended on fault even though criminal liability did.[11] But unless this were done, there would continue to be a danger that either criminal liability would become too strict,[12] or civil liability too lax.

Secondly, in any case rather different factors justify imposing civil and criminal liability at all; blameworthiness and deterrence in the former case, efficient or fair compensation in the latter. To say, even presumptively, that criminal liability led to civil liability might therefore distort the purposes for which both exist. In short, conduct that may provide good reason to fine a person a small amount will not necessarily justify making him or his insurer liable – perhaps very extensively – for any damage that might happen to result.[13]

---

11   In *Potts (or Riddell) v Reid* [1943] AC 1, [1942] 2 All ER 161, such a principle was applied. It applies statutorily in at least one case – see Health and Safety at Work etc. Act 1974, s 47.

12   In order to provide a no-fault civil remedy, the House of Lords in *John Summers & Sons Ltd v Frost* [1955] AC 740, [1955] 1 All ER 870, were prepared to construe a criminal statute as completely prohibiting the effective use of a common sort of machinery in use in factories all over the country.

13   See *Atkinson v Newcastle and Gateshead Waterworks Co* (1877) 2 Ex D 441 at 446, per Lord Cairns.

Chapter 10

Unjustified enrichment

The legal claims that we have dealt with thus far have been claims to have loss made good. A claim based on unjustified enrichment, or restitution,[1] is rather different. Essentially it alleges, not that the plaintiff has less than he should have and that the defendant should make up the difference, but instead that the defendant has more than he should have,[2] and that to correct the imbalance the excess should be transferred to the plaintiff.

Of course, this does not mean that unjustified enrichment claims and those based on loss are mutually exclusive; on the contrary, the same situation may give rise to both. If A steals £100 from B, A's claim to recover the £100 may be based either on the fact that he has lost it, or on the fact that B has unjustifiably gained it. However, such complete overlap is limited to cases where plaintiff's loss exactly equals defendant's gain. In many cases a claim based on unjustified enrichment will be rather more lucrative for the plaintiff; the essence, for instance, of a principal's right to sue his agent for any bribe received by the latter is that it exists even though the principal has suffered no loss at all. Hence the importance of unjustified enrichment as a separate head of claim.

It is sometimes said that English law – unlike many Continental codes, which provide explicitly for the neutralisation of unjustified enrichment – recognises no general doctrine in this field. This is not true. Admittedly English law will not neutralise A's enrichment gained at B's expense merely because the enrichment is 'unjust', in the sense of 'unfair'; B's claim must come within one of the established categories of recovery. But then exactly the same is true of Continental doctrines; they also require that enrichment, to be recoverable, must also be not only 'unjust' but in some sense contrary to law.[3] And indubitably English law does recognise a class of claims bottomed on unjustified enrichment in this sense.[4] The only

---

1 The terms are interchangeable.
2 The word 'more' used here is designedly abstract; the excess in A's hands may be money, or things, or the benefit of services rendered, or expense not incurred, or the release of some obligation he would otherwise be under.
3 Thus German law requires enrichment *ohne rechtlichen Grund* (Civil Code, para 812); Swiss law, enrichment *in unrechtfertiger Weise* (Code of Obligations, para 62).
4 See, eg, *Fibrosa Spolka Akcyjna v Fairbairn Lawson Combe Barbour Ltd* [1943] AC 32 at 61, [1942] 2 All ER 122 at 135–136, per Lord Wright.

question, to which we now turn, is what heads of recovery are included in that class.

Claims to recover unjustified enrichment break down effectively into four categories. In each of them the defendant has somehow benefited (in money, goods, services or otherwise) at the plaintiff's expense; but the benefit may have been variously gained. It may have been (1) gained by the defendant's own wrong; (2) gained for the defendant by a third party's wrong; (3) conferred by the plaintiff on the defendant for a purpose that was not fulfilled; or (4) conferred by the plaintiff (or at his expense, which is effectively the same thing); but for some reason, such as lack of proper consent to render the benefit gratuitously, such that it is unfair for the plaintiff not to be paid for it.[5]

1. Benefits gained by the defendant's wrong

This head of liability is best illustrated by example. It includes, for instance, the doctrine of 'waiver of tort' at common law, whereby a tortfeasor is liable to return to his victim the gain he made from committing the tort, rather than simply the loss suffered by the latter; the equitable liability to an 'account of profits' faced by (say) a trade mark infringer, in order to make him return to the holder any profits he has made by the infringement; or an employer's claim to have his employee pay over payments he has received in exchange for wrongfully revealing the employer's trade secrets. Expressed more formally and generally, the requirements for this head of liability are: (a) a gain by the defendant; (b) at the plaintiff's expense; (c) resulting from some wrong committed by the defendant.

(a) THE GAIN

This is very widely construed; the gains that one may be obliged to return on the ground that they result from one's wrong go well beyond simple accretions of money or property. Thus if I unlawfully use your car for a week, I gain only negatively (by not having to pay for the hire of a similar vehicle); yet I must still pay you a reasonable hire charge.[6] Again, if lawfully evicted from your land, I must pay you rent for the time I should not have been there; I should not have use without

---

5   Some say there is a fifth category, transfers of money or property pursuant to void contracts. But only where a contract is void for some defect in consent (eg mistake or duress), or where the claimant does not receive something in exchange for what he has provided, is recovery allowed; so this category is really part of categories (3) and (4) above.

6   Cf *Strand Electric and Engineering Co Ltd v Brisford Entertainments Ltd* [1952] 2 QB 246, [1952] 1 All ER 796.

payment.[7] True, old authority suggests – apparently contrary to what we have just said – that a person merely trespassing on land without occupying it (for instance, by using it as an unauthorised short cut) is not liable to pay at all for the use made;[8] but this is anomalous, inconsistent with the authority on personal property, and it is suggested should be regarded as unsound.

(b) GAIN 'AT THE PLAINTIFF'S EXPENSE'

This is a much more enigmatic requirement. If A, by committing a wrong against B, makes a profit that B could not have made himself, one might think the profit was not gained at B's expense; but not so. If I unlawfully borrow your car for a week, I must pay a reasonable hire charge even though the car would otherwise have stagnated in your garage;[9] similarly a trustee who uses information gained in his capacity as such for his own purposes must return the profit thereby gained, even though the trust, say for lack of free capital or expertise, could not have made that profit itself.[10] Admittedly such a rule may be criticised on the ground that it tends to stifle enterprise or renders unjustifiable enrichment that ought to be reckoned as justified; it cannot be faulted on the ground that the profit concerned was not made at the plaintiff's expense.

If this is so, however, does it not mean that *any* gain by A resulting from a wrong against B must automatically be gained at B's expense, so that the latter requirement adds nothing? It is submitted that the answer is no, and that the real significance of the requirement for the gain to have been made at the plaintiff's expense is that only certain sorts of wrong engender an obligation to repay benefits arising. Notably, the doctrine is limited to wrongs to pecuniary, rather than moral, interests. If a profit is made as a result of infringing a merely moral interest of another, such as reputation, it is not made at that other's expense because reputation is not an interest that exists to be turned into money anyway. Hence the victim of libel or assault cannot claim the publisher's profits or the assailant's bribe;[11] yet a plaintiff whose property is interfered with can claim the interferer's profit, since

7   The right to so-called 'mesne profits.'
8   *Phillips v Homfray* (1883) 24 Ch D 439, 52 LJ Ch 833, criticised convincingly in R. Goff & G. Jones, *The Law of Restitution*, 2nd edn, 474 f.
9   Cf *Strand Electric and Engineering Co Ltd v Brisford Entertainments Ltd*, note 6 above.
10 *Regal (Hastings) Ltd v Gulliver* [1942] 1 All ER 378; *Boardman v Phipps* [1967] 2 AC 46, [1966] 3 All ER 721.
11 See *Hambly v Trott* (1776) 1 Cowp 371 at 376. On the question of libel, it is true that if the publisher knew the libel was untrue, exemplary damages might be available to punish him and prevent him making a profit overall. But this point, it is submitted, goes to remedy rather than right; punitive remedies are not the same as unjustified enrichment remedies.

property, unlike reputation or bodily integrity, is an interest that does exist to be turned into money.[12]

(c) THE WRONG

The question what wrongs should carry with them an obligation to hand over profits made thus effectively answers itself; it is those wrongs protecting commercial interests. In particular, this means torts[13] such as conversion or trespass to goods, and (it is submitted) economic torts such as inducing breach of contract; infringement of intellectual property rights, for instance, trade marks or patents; and breach of confidence and breach of trust and other fiduciary relations. The question of breach of contract is more difficult. Assume I pay you £30,000 to build me a house, specifying Material X to be used; but you do the job just as well by using cheaper Material Y and save £2,000. Can I, though suffering no loss, recover £2,000 from you as the profits of breach of contract? It seems not,[14] though breach of contract is obviously a wrong to commercial interests. This result, at first sight is nevertheless perhaps justifiable on the ground that the anomalous right to recoup unjustified enrichment can be waived and that in general a contract between A and B should be read as impliedly limiting B's rights on breach to recovering his own loss and no more.

It is sometimes suggested that gains from wrongful acts should not be recoverable unless the wrong was deliberate; but this does not represent the present law. A converter of another's goods, or a copyright infringer, to take just two cases, must account for profits even if innocent. Nor, it is submitted, ought innocent wrongdoers to be spared restitutionary liability on principle. The nature of unjustified enrichment is that the defendant has more than he ought to have; and the question whether a defendant gained the excess deliberately or inadvertently would seem irrelevant to the decision whether he should have to pay it back. True, there are occasions when a wrongdoer is stripped of his profits because he had acted deliberately, and would not be so stripped had he not; in particular, exemplary damages for libel or

---

12   Cf G. E. Palmer, *Restitution*, Vol I, 130.
13   The action to recover profits emanating from tortious action is specifically known as 'waiver of tort.'
14   See the Scottish decision in *Teacher v Calder* [1899] AC 451, 1 F(HL) 39. However, especially in contract cases, 'loss' and 'gain' are rather relative terms, and occasionally the best measure of what a plaintiff has lost through a breach of contract is what the defendant has gained. See, eg, *Wrotham Park Estate Co v Parkside Homes Ltd* [1974] 2 All ER 321, [1974] 1 WLR 798.

other deliberate torts are limited to deliberate wrongdoing, and have the effect of stripping a wrongdoer of his profit.[15] But this is better seen as an anomalous use of the law of tort for punitive purposes, rather than as an adventitious manifestation of unjustified enrichment principles.

2. Gains resulting from a third party's wrong

So far we have assumed that the defendant has gained from his *own* wrong; but what if the gain is from someone else's wrong? X, for instance, may steal A's thing and give it to B; or may deceive A into paying B £100. Much discussed in Continental theory, this problem is in England often not recognised as one of unjustifiable enrichment at all, being dealt with instead incidentally through other forms of legal liability.

Thus if X steals A's thing and gives it to B, A can recover the thing (or its value) not because B is unjustifiably enriched (although he is) but because the thing belongs to him. Similarly if X defrauds A of his thing and transfers it to B; A's remedy here is not to claim anything from B on the basis of unjustified enrichment, but to annul the transaction transferring it to X and then recover the thing as his property.

Slightly more difficult is the case where X steals A's thing, sells it, pays the proceeds into his bank account, and then draws a cheque in favour of B. B remains clearly unjustifiably enriched; but here A is not legal owner of the cheque, so a claim based on property will not succeed. Nevertheless, here and in a few other cases, where B receives the proceeds of A's property, he can be sued by A to make him restore his enrichment. The law of property does not directly allow recovery; nevertheless the law considers that the proceeds of the thing represent, as it were, in a etiolated way the thing itself, and for that reason puts whoever receives those proceeds under a duty to return the enrichment thereby gained.

However, some cases where B benefits at A's expense through a third person's wrong, are, even in England, treated as unjustified enrichment cases. One, for example, arises in the distribution of estates, where personal representatives pay B money that should have gone either to A or to pay the debts of the estate. A can claim what was transferred to B as belonging to him in equity; alternatively, however, both he and the creditors of the estate, as the case may be, also have a simple pecuniary claim against B for what was wrongly given to him (though, rather oddly, less anything they can recover from the personal representative himself).[16]

15 *Cassell & Co Ltd v Broome* [1972] AC 1027, [1972] 1 All ER 801.
16 *Ministry of Health v Simpson* [1951] AC 251, [1950] 2 All ER 1137.

3. Benefits conferred for a purpose that is unfulfilled

(a) MONEY PAID FOR SOMETHING THAT DOES NOT MATERIALISE

If A pays B a sum of money in exchange for goods or services that he does not get, he can recover his payment; were B allowed to keep it, he would obviously be unjustifiably enriched. This claim of A's sometimes overlaps with one for breach of contract, but not always. There may not have been a contract between A and B at all; A may have made a bad bargain so damages for breach of contract would be less than what he paid; or A may himself have been in breach of contract by refusing to accept the goods or services.[17] None of these factors affects A's right to recover the full amount he has paid for that which he does not get. Nor even does it matter that, although A did not get what he had paid for, he got some other collateral benefit. So a buyer of a stolen car who gets no title to it can recover the full price from the seller when forced to give it up to the owner even though he has had the use of the car meanwhile. He contracted for ownership, which he has not got; the fact that he incidentally received use is irrelevant.[18]

But this right of recovery is for money paid for a consideration which 'totally fails'; it applies in general only where A gets nothing of what he ought to have got. If B performs partly but not wholly, A has no right under the law of unjustified enrichment to recover a sum representing what he did not get. So if A pays B £500 to paint his house and B only paints half of it, A is limited to his claim (if any) for breach of contract against B.[19] This rule is odd, and sometimes unfair; its only (somewhat unconvincing) justification is that a right of partial recovery might be difficult to quantify. The unfairness is recognised in one respect, since in the vital area of sale of goods the rule does not apply. The seller who, having been paid, delivers short must return the proportion of the price representing what he has not delivered.[20]

(b) MONEY NOT USED FOR THE PURPOSE FOR WHICH IT IS PAID

If A pays B £100 to be used for a particular purpose (for instance, paying a debt of B to C) the situation is similar to where A pays the £100 for goods or

---

17   *Dies v British and International Mining and Finance Corpn Ltd* [1939] 1 KB 724, 108, LJKB 398. In these circumstances A is of course liable to a counter-claim for breach of contract.

18   *Rowland v Divall* [1923] 2 KB 500, 92 LJKB 1041. Quaere whether the seller could have counterclaimed, alleging he provided the car under the mistaken impression that the buyer was validly obliged to pay for it?

19   See eg, *Whincup v Hughes* (1871) LR 6 CP 78, 40 LJCP 104. The Law Commission (Report No 121, Part III) recommends retaining this rule, on the robust ground that the innocent party, since he can recover his loss (if any) as damages for breach of contract, cannot really complain of the other party being paid the whole price for doing half the job. The reasoning is not convincing.

20   *Behrend v Produce Brokers Ltd* [1920] 3 KB 530, 90 LJKB 143.

services to be provided by B: if B completely fails to use the money for the stated purpose A can recover £100 from him.[1] Here, however, A also has an extra remedy, ostensibly proprietary but in fact concerned with unjustified enrichment. Until the money is used for the purpose concerned, A remains owner of it in equity (though not of course in law) by virtue of a resulting trust.[2] Two results follow. First, if B becomes insolvent, then provided he still has the money A recovers it as a preferred creditor – a result of impeccable law if doubtful justice. Secondly, and rather more justifiably, it would seem that if only part of the money is spent on the stipulated purpose, the part that is not so spent can be recovered from B; that is, there is presumably no need to prove a *total* failure of consideration.

(c) OTHER BENEFITS RENDERED IN EXCHANGE FOR SOMETHING THAT DOES NOT MATERIALISE

Normally goods are supplied, and services rendered, for payment: a liquidated sum that can be recovered in the usual way without recourse to conceptions of unjustified enrichment. But what if A does something for B in exchange for something other than cash; for instance, if a builder does preliminary work for a client, both parties assuming a contract to be in the offing, but the contract is never signed? Here the builder has a restitutionary claim to cover the value of the work done.[3] This leaves the case where A transfers property or renders services and receives only *part* of the consideration in return; for instance, if the builder in our example above did the preliminary work on *two* sites, but got the contract in respect of only one of them. Here, it is suggested, he ought to be able to recover for a proportionate part of the services rendered.[4] There is no reason to introduce into this part of the law the technicality applying where money is paid, that there must be total failure of consideration; indeed, if necessary to do justice there should be inferred a promise by the client to pay a reasonable price for the goods or services supplied, in the event of the planned exchange or part of it not materialising.

4. Benefits that for other reasons cannot be retained

This is the residual category of unjustified enrichment claims, and as might be expected the largest. At bottom it concerns exceptions to, and

---

1 Aliter, presumably, if B applies part, but not all, of the £100 to the stated purpose.
2 *Barclays Bank Ltd v Quistclose Investments Ltd* [1970] AC 567, [1968] 3 All ER 651; *Re Kayford Ltd* [1975] 1 All ER 604, [1975] 1 WLR 279.
3 *William Lacey (Hounslow) Ltd v Davis* [1957] 2 All ER 712, [1957] 1 WLR 932; *Brewer St Investments Ltd v Barclays Woollen Co Ltd* [1953] 2 All ER 1330, [1954] 1 QB 428.
4 And analogously for property transferred.

glosses on, a simple rule: if A confers a benefit on B, voluntarily and without any agreement on B's part to pay for it, then no claim in unjustified enrichment lies against B. If I give you £100 or paint your house for you as a gift, or hoping to curry favour with you, I cannot later recover anything from you, however much I repent of my generosity. The various sorts of claims that can arise by way of exception to the rule just mentioned, we now go through in turn.

(a) BENEFITS NOT RENDERED GRATUITOUSLY

It almost goes without saying that benefits rendered, whether in the form of things transferred, debts paid, services performed, or otherwise, in circumstances obviously not gratuitious, and freely accepted by the recipient, raise an obligation on the latter to pay a reasonable price. So if A sends goods to B on approval and B accepts them; or if A, a decorator, at B's request paints B's house without a price being mentioned; B must pay a reasonable sum.[5] Here contract and unjustified enrichment meet; it does not matter whether we say that a person accepting goods or services impliedly promises to pay a reasonable sum for them (contract) or that he would be unjustifiably enriched if he did not.[6]

The need for acceptance
When should the rendering of services, or the provision of goods, raise an obligation to pay a reasonable sum? One line of reasoning is as follows. Unjustified enrichment is about benefit to the defendant. A defendant may benefit from what the plaintiff did either objectively, as where the plaintiff does something for him that he would have paid someone else to do anyway, or subjectively, as when he requested or freely accepted what the plaintiff did (a person who asks for something, as it were, is precluded from denying that it benefits him). As a result, *either* benefit *or* request should raise the obligation to pay. If A painted B's house at B's request B should have to pay A; similarly if A by mistake[7] painted B's house while B was away, provided B's house was in need of painting anyway (but not if it were not[8]).

However, with exceptions (a person improving another's chattel thinking it is his own is relieved from the obligation to return it unless paid for the work he has done[9]) English law has never adopted this

---

5   *Way v Latilla* [1937] 3 All ER 759; *British Steel Corpn v Cleveland Bridge and Engineering Co Ltd* [1984] 1 All ER 504; cf Supply of Goods and Services Act 1982, s 15.
6   Except that the promise does not exist, whereas the enrichment does. Cf P. S. Atiyah, *Promises, Contracts and the Law of Obligations* (1978) 94 LQR 193, 204.
7   Not as implausible a mistake as it seems; A might paint B's house thinking it was C's, which he *had* agreed to paint.
8   The principle described here has been felicitously christened that of 'incontrovertible benefit' – R. Goff & G. Jones, *The Law of Restitution*, 2nd edn, 16–17.
9   Torts (Interference with Goods) Act 1977, s 6.

attitude.[10] Instead, benefits in terms of things supplied or services rendered need be paid for if, and only if, requested or accepted.[11] It is not enough that the recipient would – or even rationally should – have accepted them; nor, a fortiori, that the benefits were rendered with the best of motives. If I spend £50 to save your house from thousands of pounds' worth of storm damage while you are away, I still have no claim; again, a garage repairing my car on the orders of a thief, however innocently, cannot sue me for the cost of the repairs however much they benefit me.

The apparent harshness and injustice of this rule is tempered, not only by the exceptions to it, but also because in practice acceptance of benefits is inferrable from rather exiguous material. For instance, in many kinds of contracts prospective acceptance of other, extra-contractual services can be surprisingly easily inferred, especially if those services are rendered in an emergency. Thus a carrier may, by an 'implied term' in the contract of carriage, store goods – and charge for doing so – if no-one collects them when they arrive;[12] again, by the principle of 'agency of necessity', an agent entrusted with goods to sell can in emergency charge his principal with the reasonable cost of measures to preserve them.[13] Indeed, even contract as such is not necessary, since other relationships such as bailment suffice; thus a bailee may be able to charge his bailor for necessary measures of preservation even in the absence of any actual contract between them.[14]

Further, there are in any case several exceptions to the rule that only benefits accepted need be paid for.

First, A may have been forced by law to render the benefit; here, as we shall see, the plaintiff's compulsion outweighs the defendant's lack of acceptance.

Secondly, there is public policy. The right to refuse, however unreasonably, a benefit offered depends on the right to do as one wants with one's own; and, predictably, that right is in certain cases curtailed. One such case, which we have no space to cover in detail, is maritime salvage. A salvor of a ship at sea (whose fate, and that of its crew, clearly ought not to hang on its owner's whim) can claim for salvage services rendered whether or not the owner accepted the

---

10 This is the result of any but the narrowest reading of *Falcke v Scottish Imperial Insurance Co* (1886) 34 Ch D 234, 56 LJ Ch 707, and *Sorrell v Paget* [1950] 1 KB 252, [1949] 2 All ER 609.

11 In one case, indeed, English law denies that a benefit is conferred at all unless it is accepted. If A purports to pay off B's debt to C, the debt is effectually extinguished only if B accepts A's munificence by ratifying his act. Only when he has done so may he become liable to A for the amount of the debt.

12 Cf *Tetley & Co v British Trade Corpn* (1922) 10 Lloyds Rep 678.

13 Eg *Prager v Blatspiel, Stamp & Heacock Ltd* [1924] 1 KB 566, 93 LJKB 410.

14 See *China Pacific SA v Food Corpn of India, The Winson* [1982] AC 939 at 960–961, [1981] 3 All ER 688 at 694–695, per Lord Diplock.

services, and indeed even if he (unreasonably) refused them.[15] Similarly, the better view is that a man's life is not wholly at his own disposal so as to allow him perversely to refuse to pay for emergency medical attention[16] (though in England, with universal free medical care, the question is a little academic). Yet again, if A is under a legal duty to maintain B, as with parents and children, anyone else with reasonable cause carrying out A's duty for him can, it seems, claim recoupment from A, whether or not A asked him to do what he did.[17]

Thirdly, in certain (unspecified) special cases, it seems that a benefit even if unaccepted may raise an obligation to pay for it. In *Owen v Tate*,[18] for instance, the plaintiff by spontaneously paying off a bank overdraft automatically cleared a mortgage on the defendant's property, which was security for it. Although the plaintiff failed in this case to recover from the defendant on the ground that the benefit had not been accepted, the Court of Appeal left it open whether a person with some (unspecified) very good reason for intervening might have succeeded.

The value to be put on this dictum is unclear. In any case, discharge of obligations is perhaps a special case because here a third person intervening can always make himself a creditor of the defendant anyway by taking an assignment of the obligation concerned;[19] hence to allow him to obtain the right to sue the person subject to the obligation merely by paying it off is merely allowing him to do more simply what he could do in any case.

(b) BENEFITS RENDERED SUBJECT TO DEFECTIVE CONSENT

As we said before, if A willingly does B a favour, or gives him £100, or sells his car to him at an undervalue pursuant to a valid contract, he cannot complain. Consent bars recrimination; it justifies B's enrichment. But the argument from consent is obviously weakened if A's action was due to a mistake, or to very serious pressure (including, but obviously going beyond, crude physical threats), or to a good reason that no longer applies (for instance, a contractual obligation that has been annulled by frustration). This section deals with cases of defective consent; for convenience's sake, it is divided into benefits rendered under defective contracts, and other benefits.

(i) Benefits rendered pursuant to defective contracts
In general the same factors, such as mistake, nullify contractual

---

15 *The Kangaroo* [1918] P 327, 88 LJP 5.
16 A Canadian court has said as much – *Matheson v Smiley* [1932] 2 DLR 787.
17 ıSee *Jenkins v Tucker* (1788) 1 Hy B1 90.
18 [1976] QB 402, [1975] 2 All ER 129.
19 See Ch 16, below. An assignment is valid, indeed, even if the assignee acted quite unreasonably in taking it – *Fitzroy v Cave* [1905] 2 KB 364, 74 LJKB 829.

obligation as nullify other legal acts such as transfers of property. However, because contracts aim partly at finality and at precluding subsequent dispute, it is more difficult to annul a contract and recover benefits transferred pursuant to it than it is simply to recover in unjustified enrichment where no contract is involved. An example makes this abstraction clearer. If A pays B £100 by mistake, thinking he owes him it, he can recover it. But if A, thinking B can sue him for £100, contracts to pay B £90 in exchange for a release of B's rights and pays that sum, he cannot later upset that contract and recover the £90 on the basis that the £100 was not owing at all.[20] This is a sound distinction, not only because the very function of contract is to evidence willingness to risk certain errors (eg as to value, or background circumstances), but also because those taking benefits under contracts have generally paid for those benefits or given value for them, and therefore ought to be better protected in their tenure of them.

As might be imagined, not all defective contracts are treated in the same way when it comes to unjustified enrichment. Despite what we said above, some factors annul the obligation inherent in contract, but have no effect on transfers pursuant to that contract. As a result, in such cases one is not obliged to perform such contracts, but having performed cannot recover money or other property transferred.

The first factor is illegality. Although for obvious reasons of public policy no one can be obliged by any contract to commit a crime or other anti-social act, or to pay for its commission, nevertheless no action lies in unjustified enrichment to recover money paid, or the value of benefits conferred, under such a contract. If I pay you £100 to commit a crime I cannot recover it even if you do not commit it;[1] again, if I sell you goods illegally on credit I can recover neither the price nor the goods themselves;[2] yet again, a pledge of goods to cover an illegal debt is valid, and cannot be got back without paying off the debt.[3] Admittedly in some cases money paid under an illegal contract can be recovered as unjustified enrichment; for instance, where a landlord breaks the law by demanding an illegal premium the tenant who pays it can nevertheless recover it.[4] But here illegality of the contract combines with some further feature that tends to devalue consent, such as duress; and it is this feature, it is submitted, that really justifies allowing recovery.

Similar to illegal contracts are gaming contracts, specifically made

---

20 *Bell v Lever Bros Ltd* [1932] AC 161, 101 LJKB 129.
1 *Bigos v Bousted* [1951] 1 All ER 92. Cf *Shelley v Paddock* [1980] QB 348, [1980] 1 All ER 1009.
2 *Singh v Ali* [1960] AC 167, [1960] 1 All ER 269.
3 *Taylor v Chester* (1869) LR 4 QB 309, 38 LJ QB 225.
4 *Kiriri Cotton Ltd v Dewani* [1960] AC 192, [1960] 1 All ER 177. Cf *Shelley v Paddock* [1980] QB 348, [1980] 1 All ER 1009.

'void' by s 18 of the Gaming Act 1845. Although the winner of a bet cannot sue for his winnings, the loser cannot get them back once he has paid them.[5] Commonsense supports this rule; people may lightly make promises such as bets which it would be unfortunate to hold them to, but are less likely to be so reckless when it comes to payment.

Lastly, and rather more controversially, minors' contracts are treated in the same way. A minor contracting to buy shares in a company, for instance, is clearly not bound by his contract; but once he has paid for and got the shares he cannot recover what he has paid, even if he is willing to give them back.[6] Again, a minor may not be bound by a contract to write a book and transfer the copyright in it to a publisher; yet once he has done so and transferred the copyright to the publisher he cannot undo the transaction.[7] This is odd; if the contractual obligations of a minor are defective (as presumably they are) because we regard his consent as not very relevant because of his youth, then minority should equally give grounds to impugn payments of money or transfers of property. Indeed, the law reflects this in at least one case; a mortgage by a minor to secure a debt he is not liable for is itself defective.[8]

So much for illegal, gaming and minors' contracts. By contrast, when a contract is defective because of mistake – which is a factor that clearly does go to impugn consent – restitution is generally available to the mistaken party. How far it is available depends, as one might suspect, on the nature of the mistake. If it is serious enough to prevent real agreement from arising at all (a where A contracts with B thinking he is C, C's identity being vital to the contract,[9] or the parties are at cross-purposes as to precisely what they are contracting about) restitution is full and drastic. Money paid is recoverable in full, unconditionally. The value of services rendered can be claimed. Property transferred can be recovered (this latter remedy not being specifically provided for, but following from the rule that a purported transfer of property pursuant to a void contract is itself void).[10]

Oddly enough, however, in this case no restitution is available to the party who is not mistaken, though this may lead to injustice. In *Boulton v Jones*,[11] for instance, A supplied goods to B, who used them. Because B thought he was contracting not with C but with A (the question of

---

5   *Bridger v Savage* (1885) 15 QBD 363 at 367, per Bowen LJ.
6   *Steinberg v Scala (Leeds) Ltd* [1923] 2 Ch 452, 92 LJKB 944.
7   *Chaplin v Leslie Frewin (Publishers) Ltd* [1966] Ch 71, [1965] 3 All ER 764.
8   *Thurstan v Nottingham Permanent Benefit Building Society* [1902] 1 Ch 1, 71 LJ Ch 83, CA; affd, [1903] AC 6, 72 LJCh 134, HL.
9   Cf *Said v Butt* [1920] 3 KB 497, 90 LJKB 239.
10 *Hardman v Booth* (1863) 1 H & C 803, 1 New Rep 240, is a particularly good example.
11 (1857) 2 H & N 564, 27 LJ Ex 117.

identity being vital) he escaped liability to pay anything; as a result, A having supplied goods to B in good faith was left with a claim neither to the goods themselves nor to payment for them.

Where a contractual obligation is defective because of a less drastic kind of mistake (as when A sells B a house that both wrongly think to have vacant possession at the time[12]), or where one party to a contract relies on the misrepresentation of the other to annul a contract, the same result follows on principle; restitution is allowed. But here, because of the convenient theory that the contract is not 'void' but 'voidable' (that is, it is valid but may, as a matter of discretion, be annulled in equity) relief is available not as of right but only if reasonable; and then it is often given subject to terms. For example a person 'buying' a thing that turns out to be his anyway can recover what he has paid, but only if he credits the seller with the money innocently spent by the latter on maintaining it.[13]

(ii) Benefits rendered pursuant to contracts later terminated

This leaves the second question of restitution in contract, benefits conferred under a contractual obligation not defective from the start, but later terminated. Such termination may result either because one party is released from his obligations owing to breach of contract by the other; or because all obligations under a particular contract are discharged by frustration.

A. RESTITUTION WHERE A CONTRACT IS TERMINATED BY BREACH. As will appear in Ch 14, certain breaches of contract by one party entitle the other to throw up his own obligations; if that other does so, that effectively puts an end to the contract. As to whether restitution is available in these cases, it depends on who is seeking it; the contract breaker or the innocent party.

We take the contract breaker first. Here the law differentiates contracts for the sale of goods and contracts to render services. A seller delivering some but not all of the contract goods can claim pro rata for what he has delivered;[14] but, by contrast, a renderer of services can claim payment only if he completes those services and can claim nothing if he merely renders them in part. So a builder who abandons a job half done (owing, say, to insolvency) can recover a reasonable sum for materials supplied, but not for work done.[15] The rule relating to

---

12 The sort of mistake epitomised in *Grist v Bailey* [1967] Ch 532, [1966] 2 All ER 875, and *Solle v Butcher* [1950] 1 KB 671, [1949] 2 All ER 1107.
13 *Cooper v Phibbs* (1867) LR 2 HL 149, 16 LT 678.
14 Sale of Goods Act 1979, s 30(1).
15 *Sumpter v Hedges* [1898] 1 QB 673, 67 LJQB 545. The Law Commission, in its Report No 121, has recommended reversal of this rule.

services is harsh; the assumption behind it, that a contract to pay for services in full when completed impliedly excludes any obligation to pay in part if they are not completed, is at best tendentious.[16] Significantly, in cases such as employment and leases of land where periodical payments are the rule, the contractual presumption has been reversed by statute; by s 1 of the Apportionment Act 1870, such payments are deemed to accrue from day to day, and thus to be claimable pro rata, even if the performance they are promised in exchange for is only partially rendered.

What of the party not in breach? He, by contrast, is (as might be expected) much more generously treated when seeking restitution; in particular, the rule precluding restitutionary recovery for partially rendered services does not apply to him. A builder abandoning the site with the job half done can recover nothing for services rendered; but a builder wrongly thrown off the site can recover a reasonable sum.

B. RESTITUTION WHERE CONTRACTS ARE TERMINATED BY FRUSTRATION. Where a contract is annulled by being frustrated, obviously no question arises as to who was in breach of contract; ex hypothesi neither party is. As a result, there is no reason for restitution not to be generously available; and, in general, it is.

We begin with money paid. At common law this was recoverable if, the contract having been frustrated, the consideration totally failed and the payer got nothing in return (for instance, if a buyer paid in advance for something that it then became illegal to deliver[17]). But this is now academic, since s 1(2) of the Law Reform (Frustrated Contracts) Act 1943 allows recovery of all sums paid even in the absence of such failure. The only limitation on this right is that expenditure by the payee in and about the contract can be deducted from any prepayment he has to return. So if a half-finished house is struck by lightning and the contract to build it frustrated, the client can recover any prepayment, but the builder may retain a sum representing his expenses to date (though, of course, he can retain such expenses only up to the amount of the prepayment).

As for goods delivered under a frustrated contract, both at common law and under the 1943 Act the person delivering them has a claim for their value. So, if a contract to sell 10,000 tons of soya beans is frustrated when 5,000 tons have been delivered, the seller can claim the value of the 5,000 tons while the buyer can recover any prepayment.[18]

---

16   Many breaches of contract in such cases are, moreover, quite innocent; for instance, when the contractor becomes insolvent. And it is difficult to see why the mere fact of such a breach should so drastically penalise the insolvent's creditors.

17   *Fibrosa Spolka Akcyjna v Fairbairn Lawson Combe Barbour Ltd* [1943] AC 32, [1942] 2 All ER 122.

18   Different rules apply, however, in certain cases of sales of goods; Law Reform (Frustrated Contracts) Act 1943, s 2(5) (c).

The difficulty comes with services. Section 1(3) of the Law Reform (Frustrated Contracts) Act 1943 allows a claim for a 'just sum' for services rendered; but it limits any award to the amount by which the recipient benefits from those services (the so-called 'valuable benefit'). And, by s 1(3) (b), the 'valuable benefit' is measured as after the frustrating event, not before. So the builder of a house burnt down shortly after completion recovers nothing under this head; a burnt-down house is no benefit to the site-owner.[19] Whether this is just is doubtful. The argument is attractive in that services should be, as it were, at the 'risk' of the recipient (as regards events destroying their proceeds) from the moment they are rendered, and that from then on he should have to pay for them whatever happens. The present law, moreover, distinguishes oddly between contracts (such as building contracts) concerned primarily with the *result* of services, and those concerning the rendering of services as such. Few would argue, for instance, that an interior decorator should recover nothing for a job partly done and then frustrated merely because the decoration was in very bad taste and added nothing to the value of the premises concerned.[20]

The restitutionary solutions imposed by the 1943 Act are not universal. They can, by s 2(3), be excluded by contrary agreement; and in any case they do not apply to contracts of insurance, or carriage of goods by sea, or contracts of sale frustrated by destruction of the subject-matter.[1] Abstractly, these exclusions can be criticised as anomalous. In practice, contracts of insurance and carriage of goods by sea often describe exhaustively what happens in the event of frustration anyway,[2] so little injustice is done.

(iii) Benefits rendered in non-contractual situations where consent is defective

A. BENEFITS RENDERED BY MISTAKE. Outside contractual situations, English law has no coherent general theory covering recovery for benefits rendered by mistake. The extent of restitution depends on the sort of benefit involved, even though in practice some degree of restitution is allowed in most cases.

Money paid by mistake. This is the most straightforward case; if A pays B £100 because of a mistake he can prima facie recover it.[3] It does not matter whether the mistake goes to motive (as where A wrongly thinks

---

19 Cf *Appleby v Myers* (1867) LR 2 CP 651, 36 LJCP 331 (decided at common law); *BP (Exploration) Ltd v Hunt (No 2)* [1979] 1 WLR 783, varied [1981] 1 WLR 232, CA. The CA decision affd [1983] 2 AC 352, [1982] 1 All ER 125, HL.
20 See *BP v Hunt*, above, [1979] 1 WLR 783 at 803, per Goff J.
1 S 2(5).
2 It goes without saying that the restitutionary rights given by the Law Reform (Frustrated Contracts) Act 1943 can, like any other restitutionary rights, be ousted by contrary agreement.
3 *Kelly v Solari* (1841) 9 M & W 54, 11 LJ Ex 10.

he owes B £100) or intent (as where A intends to pay C but mistakes B for C); nor whether A paid because he thought he was *obliged* to pay B the money or because of some collateral error.[4] Nor need the payee have induced, or been responsible for, the mistake. The mistake, it is suggested, must merely be such that a reasonable man in the recipient's position would have realised what the assumption was that underlay the payment. (Otherwise, if I made a gift to my nephew because I did not realise I had just suffered a grievous loss on the Stock Exchange, I should be able to recover the gift on discovering the truth; which would be bizarre.)

So much for the straightforward pecuniary obligation to repay money paid by mistake. More controversially, it seems that the mistaken payer can alternatively achieve the same result by invoking the law of property. In effect, money paid by mistake, while in law belonging to the payee, in equity belongs to the payer, for whom it is held by the payee on constructive trust.[5] The reason for this rule is clear; for it means that if, while still having the money paid by mistake, the payee becomes insolvent, the payer is a preferred creditor. It is, however, doubtful whether such a rule does justice; moreover, it is, to say the least, a little odd that a payment intended to pass ownership in what is paid, both in law and in equity, should be held not to do so merely because the payer acted under mistaken motives.

Property transferred by mistake. Property transferred by mistake is in general recoverable; but, in contrast to money paid by mistake, the machinery of recovery depends on what sort of mistake is involved. If the mistake went to intent, so the plaintiff did not intend to transfer the property to the defendant at all (as where goods are delivered to the wrong house) no title passes and the plaintiff recovers what he has transferred – or its value – simply because it is his. On the other hand, if the mistake is less drastic and goes merely to motive, as where the milkman mistakenly delivers twice to the same house, then title does pass.[6] Nevertheless, it seems the value of what was transferred can be recovered, at least if it is accepted by the recipient. One instance is covered by statute, since s 30(3) of the Sale of Goods Act 1979 provides that, where a seller of goods over-delivers, the buyer if he accepts the excess must pay for it at the contract rate. But it is suggested that that simply reflects a similar principle applying at common law anyway.

Services rendered by mistake. We have already covered services rendered

---

4   Thus a bank can recover mistaken payment of a countermanded cheque, even though it would not have been obliged to make the payment anyway – *Barclays Bank Ltd v W J Simms Son & Cooke (Southern) Ltd* [1980] QB 677, [1979] 3 All ER 522.

5   *Chase Manhattan Bank NA Ltd v Israel-British Bank (London) Ltd* [1981] Ch 105, [1979] 3 All ER 1025.

6   Unless by the reasoning in the last paragraph the person to whom the second bottle is delivered holds it on constructive trust for the person delivering it.

under a defective contract. Where services are rendered in other cases, it seems that the recipient must pay a reasonable price for them if (a) he accepts them, and (b) he has reason to know that, were the true facts known, the services would not have been rendered gratuitously. The classic case is *Upton-on-Seven RDC v Powell*,[7] where a fire brigade that had been called out on behalf of a farmer put out a fire in his barn, thinking wrongly that they were bound to do so for nothing. In fact, since the barn was outside their 'area', they were not; as a result they successfully claimed payment from the farmer. The result looks perverse, since at the time the fire was put out the plaintiffs did not intend to charge nor the farmer to pay; but it is not really. The parties were mistaken, and if a mistake may release a person from an obligation he thinks he is under[8] there is no reason why it should not be able to impose on him an obligation he thinks he is not under by discounting a factor that would otherwise negative such an obligation.

Services must normally be accepted if the person rendering them, however mistakenly, is to be able to claim payment for them. The window cleaner who inadvertently cleans the windows of the neighbouring house cannot sue the owner of it, however much his services may have benefited him.[9] Since this is so even if the householder would not be prejudiced by having to pay for the service (because, for instance, he would have had his windows cleaned anyway) the reason for this rule can only be the strand of individualism running through English law; positive obligations, such as to pay for services rendered, should not be imposed except on those who have done at least something to bring them on themselves.[10]

This may be so. However, there is much to be said, where the plaintiff acted by mistake, for replacing the principle of individualism with a rather narrower one; only actual prejudice to the defendant should preclude his being obliged to pay for such services. On this reasoning, where windows were cleaned inadvertently belonging to the wrong house, the householder would have to pay for the service if he would have had them cleaned anyway, but not otherwise. On occasion, indeed, the lack of acceptance of a service is not regarded as conclusive. A bona fide possessor of a thing who innocently improves it is, as we have mentioned, not bound to give it up to the owner until paid for his improvements.[11] An analogous, though more limited, principle applies to the possessor of land. If, thinking the land his own, and with the acquiescence of the owner (who thus becomes responsible, if negatively,

---

7   [1942] 1 All ER 220.
8   Eg *Solle v Butcher* [1950] 1 KB 671, [1949] 2 All ER 1107.
9   Cf *Forman & Co Pty Ltd v The Ship Liddesdale* [1900] AC 190, 69 LJPC 44.
10 Similar reasoning seems to lie behind the rule that a person cannot be contractually
    bound by acquiescence – eg *Felthouse v Bindley* (1862) 11 CBNS 869, 31 LJCP 204.
11 Torts (Interference with Goods) Act 1977, s 6.

for his mistake) he spends money on improving it, he obtains a right to either a conveyance of the land itself, or such other right as will give effect to his expectations.[12]

B. BENEFITS RENDERED INVOLUNTARILY. *Benefits rendered under duress*. Like mistake, duress not only vitiates contract; given that it also goes to impugn consent, it not unexpectedly grounds a restitutionary claim in respect of benefits conferred in general. As with mistakes, the extent of restitutionary recovery varies with the circumstances.

The legal effect of physical duress – the gun to the head – is straightforward. Services rendered in such cases, it would seem, ground a restitutionary claim; money or property transferred can be recovered through the law of property since duress prevents title to them passing anyway (the robber does not become owner of the wallet even though in a sense I consent to give it to him to avoid worse consequences).

The difficulty is with other, less drastic, sorts of duress, some of which, while not preventing title to property passing, nevertheless clearly ought to ground restitutionary recovery. Partly the problem is what degree of pressure ought to be necessary to impugn a transaction, since the difference between voluntary and involuntary conduct is a matter of degree. Clearly criteria such as that a person's 'will' must be 'overborne' are only speciously objective and merely beg the question. In fact the only way the law can approach this problem is by treating it as a value judgment; what sorts of pressure ought to be regarded as *justifiable* forms of pressure? Broadly the answer reached by the law is that the following pressures are not justifiable.

First, threats of tort or breaches of contract. Payment extorted as the price of fulfilment of an already binding contract can be recovered;[13] similarly, for obvious reasons, with payments made under threats (say) to destroy property.

Secondly, there is a broad category best referred to as abuse of relationships of trust or dependence. Equity discounts consent obtained by playing on the confidence of those known to be ignorant or simply very stupid;[14] similarly, by the doctrine of 'undue influence', it may annul transfers between those falling into certain categories, such as solicitor and client, or priest and proselyte, or banker and customer, unless they are proved not to have been obtained by misuse of the relationship.[15]

---

12   *Dillwyn v Llewellyn* (1862) 4 De G F & J 517, 31 LJCh 658. It is not clear why the restitutionary jurisdiction is narrower with relation to land. Perhaps it is because mistakes as to title are rarer with land than with chattels anyway. Many US jurisdictions, where land titles are less secure, are more generous with restitutionary recovery.

13   See, eg, *Re Hooper & Grass' Contract* [1949] VLR 269, [1949] ALR 1005.

14   Eg *Fry v Lane* (1888) 40 Ch D 312, 58 LJ Ch 113.

15   Eg *Wintle v Nye* [1959] 1 All ER 552, [1959] 1 WLR 284 (in fact concerning a will, but the principle is the same); *Allcard v Skinner* (1887) 36 Ch D 145, 56 LJ Ch 1052; *National Westminster Bank plc v Morgan* [1983] 3 All ER 85.

It has been attempted to synthesise these cases under broad principles such as 'inequality of bargaining power';[16] but such compendious phrases can mislead. This one is a case in point. It sits ill with the view that it is impropriety, not imbalance, that vitiates transactions. True, in some cases, for instance gifts, the distinction wears thin; impropriety may be inferred very easily from any relative inequality as between donor and donee and thus the transaction annulled. But this is not always so. A trader who, desperate to raise money, creates a very disadvantageous mortgage over his property is not entitled to relief,[17] even though this is surely a case of inequality of bargaining power. At least in business transactions, impropriety remains necessary to upset them; and lawful business pressure, however much inequality of bargaining power it may show, remains firmly justified.[18]

C. BENEFITS RENDERED BY COMPULSION OF LAW. As a general principle, if A is forced by law to do something to benefit B, he can recover the value of that benefit from B. A surety forced to pay a debt can recover from the principal debtor what he has paid. A lessee assigning a lease remains responsible for rent and for breaches of covenant committed by his successors; but if forced to pay, can recover the payment from the person who was really responsible – that is, his successor or assignee.[19] The thinking parallels that behind duress; if A has involuntarily benefited B he can recover whether the compulsion came from B himself or from the State.

Normally the benefit rendered by A will be the discharge of a money obligation of B's; but there is no reason why it necessarily should be. If A is legally bound to render services to B or put his property at his disposal (to take an obscure example, one is obliged to allow firemen to enter one's land to put out a fire on neighbouring land[20]), he should equally have a claim for the benefit conferred.

To be liable under this head, A must have been compelled by law to benefit B. But compulsion may take various forms; going beyond liability to be sued for a debt, it includes the criminal law (it is a criminal offence to impede a fireman in our example) or liability to

---

16 The *locus classicus* is Lord Denning MR's judgment in *Lloyds Bank Ltd v Bundy* [1975] QB 326, [1974] 3 All ER 757.

17 As in *Alec Lobb (Garages) Ltd v Total Oil GB Ltd* [1983] 1 All ER 944, [1983] 1 WLR 87.

18 In *Lloyds Bank Ltd v Bundy* itself, above, the bank concealed, if only by silence, the true nature of the transaction. There was, therefore, a degree of impropriety as well as simple inequality.

19 *Moule v Garrett* (1872) LR 7 Exch 101, 41 LJ Ex 62.

20 Fire Services Act 1947, s 30. Very occasionally, statute binds a person in this way and also provides a remedy against the person benefited: see, eg, Merchant Shipping Act 1894, s 513.

other sorts of legal processes (such as distress, where A's goods are liable to be seized in order to enforce B's obligation).[1] Provided it practically compels A to do what he does, it should suffice. However, A must not only have been forced to benefit B: he must have been forced to do so *directly*, and not merely incidentally. Moreover, at least where discharge of obligations is involved, the obligation must be one that B, rather than A, ought to have discharged. The requirement of directness means that a lessee forced to pay rent owed by an assignee can recover it from the assignee but not from a sub-lessee of the assignee whose interest the payment happens to save from forfeiture.[2] To illustrate the second requirement, a surety forced to pay a debt can recover it from the principal, but not from a sub-surety who promised to pay if *he* did not – even though the latter is, by the surety's payment just as clearly released from his obligation to pay as is the former.[3]

Contribution. A similar principle to the one just described, applies to concurrent obligors and those concurrently liable for a loss. A concurrent debtor paying the whole debt can recover proportionately from his co-obligors; similar with one co-contractors performing the contractual obligation in full. By statute,[4] moreover (replacing more limited common law and equitable rules), where several people are concurrently liable for the same loss, anyone paying more than his rateable share can recover contribution from the others. Although this rule applies whatever the basis of the liability – contract, tort, trust or a combination – it is obviously most significant in accident cases, where an accident is caused by the fault of several persons. As to what is each person's rateable proportion, this varies according to what sort of claim is involved. With concurrent debtors and concurrent contractors where one person performs for all, all must contribute equally. With concurrent liability for losses, the distribution of the ultimate burden is not equal, but instead is on a much more flexible basis, taking into account largely the comparative fault of the various parties in bringing about the loss.[5]

(c) THE DOCTRINE OF BENEFIT AND BURDEN

In certain cases, the acceptance of property or of the benefit of some

---

1   Eg *Exall v Partridge* (1799) 8 Term Rep 308, 3 Esp 8.
2   The best explanation, it is suggested, for the puzzling case of *Bonner v Tottenham and Edmonton Permanent Investment Building Society* [1899] 1 QB 161, 68 LJQB 114, though not the reason given by the court deciding the case.
3   Cf *Craythorne v Swinburne* (1807) 14 Ves 160.
4   Civil Liability (Contribution) Act 1978.
5   Of course, one may have to apportion between one held liable for negligence and one held liable without fault. This not easy, and in practice can only be done in a rough-and-ready way.

obligation has attached to it, as it were, some correlative liability of duty. One example, which we touch on elsewhere, is restrictive covenants affecting land; in certain circumstances obligations to use land in a certain way are attached to the land itself so that one cannot become owner of the land without also becoming subject to them. But the doctrine goes further. A, for instance, may allow B to mine under his land, B promising in return to restore the land to its original condition. Now, if B could assign to C his rights to mine but leave C free from the obligations to restore, C would in effect be unjustifiably enriched; as much as if he had been allowed to take something of A's without paying the full price for it. As a result, by the doctrine of 'benefit and burden', C, if he becomes assignee of B's rights, automatically becomes liable to B's duties as well.[6] A complete list of cases where this doctrine applies is beyond our scope; suffice it to say, it applies mainly in the area of mining rights and occasionally to other obligations attaching to the use of land.[7]

5. Defences to a claim of unjustified enrichment

Even if a potential claim is within one of the recognised categories of unjustified enrichment, certain features may still negative it; they serve to justify, in exceptional cases, enrichment that would otherwise be unjustified.

(a) OFFICIOUSNESS

Where A renders a benefit to B, we have seen that in some cases lack of free acceptance does not bar a claim; for instance, where public policy was involved, or where the benefit was rendered by compulsion. Yet even here B's liability is qualified, since A must show not only that his act benefited B, but also that he himself did not act 'officiously': that is, that he did not knowingly interfere without good reason. So if B owes his bank £5,000, A cannot simply by guaranteeing the debt and then paying it off as he is bound to, get the right to sue B for £5,000.[8] If, on the other hand, A were a business associate of B's with an interest in B's solvency, then the result might well be different. Again, a maritime salvor's claim will fail if he acted in the knowledge that another potential salvor, better able to do the job, was standing by and willing to help.

6 *Tito v Waddell (No 2)* [1977] Ch 106, at 304–307, [1977] 3 All ER 129 at 293–296, per Megarry V–C.
7 See, additionally, *E R Ives (Investments) Ltd v High* [1967] 2 QB 379, [1967] 1 All ER 504; *Halsall v Brizell* [1957] Ch 169, [1957] 1 All ER 371.
8 *Owen v Tate* [1976] QB 402, [1975] 2 All ER 129.

However, voluntary acceptance of a benefit negatives officiousness. However officiously unrequested goods are sent on approval, if accepted they must be paid for. For this reason, and because in most cases under English law restitutionary liability to pay for services still depends on free acceptance anyway, the concept of officiousness is not as important as it might seem.

(b) CHANGE OF POSITION

This question normally arises in respect of a restitutionary claim to recover money paid (though presumably it need not). What if, between receipt and claim, the recipient has spent the money, or otherwise detrimentally relied on being able to keep whatever benefit has been conferred on him? One's first instinct is to ask why it should make any difference; I must pay a debt, or damages for breach of contract, whether or not I have changed my position in the meantime. But, in the typical case of money paid by mistake, there is a difference; the claimant himself rendered the benefit, and thus, innocently or otherwise, induced the recipient's false sense of security. And a plaintiff's claim against a mistaken defendant is always weaker where the plaintiff himself induced the mistake than where he did not. (Compare the case of promissory liability; mistake does not necessarily negative the liability of a contracting party, but misrepresentation, or mistake induced – even innocently – by the person seeking to enforce the contract, invariably does). As a result, it now seems, at least where money is paid by mistake, that it cannot be recovered once the recipient has relied (by, for instance, spending it on something he would not otherwise have bought) on the payment being justified.[9] An earlier view, that some specific representation (apart from that contained in the payment itself) by the payer was necessary so as to bring in the principle of estoppel, now seems untenable.

Of course this does not mean that change of position is, or should be, a defence to all actions based on unjustified enrichment. The House of Lords, when in *Ministry of Health v Simpson*[10] it allowed a personal claim by an unpaid beneficiary of an estate against the person receiving assets that should have gone to him, refused to reduce the claim because the recipient had spent some of the money. This is right; the claimant had not himself been responsible for the recipient's false sense of security, nor had he paid the money himself. But, of course, this

---

9   *Barclays Bank Ltd v W J Simms Son & Cooke (Southern) Ltd* [1980] QB 677, [1979] 3 All ER 522.
10   [1951] AC 251, [1950] 2 All ER 1137. Oddly enough, however, when the plaintiff relies on an equitable proprietary right to recover against third parties, then the defendant has a more extensive defence of change of position: *Re Diplock, Diplock v Wintle* [1948] Ch 465, [1948] 2 All ER 319.

argument only applies in the comparatively rare cases where the benefit in respect of which the claimant claims was rendered to the defendant by someone other than the claimant.

(c) AGREEMENT

Enrichment may be justified by agreement. A buyer of goods who prepays can prima facie recover his payment if he does not receive them; not so, however, if (as in a standard c.i.f. contract) he agrees that from the time of purchase that the goods are at his risk and thus the seller can keep the price even if they do not arrive.[11] Similarly, where a doubtful claim is compromised, any money paid is paid to end the argument, and on the implied (and effective) condition that it is not to be recoverable even if the claim turns out to have been misconceived after all.

(d) CONTRACT

It is obvious that restitution is ousted by a valid contract inter partes; if I sell property at an undervalue I cannot complain that the buyer has been unjustifiably enriched. Oddly enough, however, contract may also oust restitution even between those not parties to it. As an abstract proposition, if A renders a benefit to B under a contract between himself and C, A cannot then complain that B was unjustifiably enriched. Thus a repairer, A, may repair a car brought to him by X which X stole from B; still, even if unpaid by X, he cannot sue B for the improvement to the car. Indeed, he cannot even refuse to give the car back to B until paid. True, B is enriched and this (assuming X is bankrupt or untraceable) is at A's expense; nevertheless, A repaired the car under a contract with X, and it is to X alone that he can look for payment.[12]

The principle also applies where A renders benefits to B so as to discharge a contractual obligation owed to B by a third person, C. Assume C owes B £100, and gives him a cheque for that amount. A, C's bank, pays the cheque forgetting that there are not sufficient funds in the account to meet it. A cannot recover the £100 from B as money paid by mistake; it was received by B in discharge of a valid obligation owed by C; that means that any enrichment of B is, in the circumstances, not unjustified.[13]

---

11 *Comptoir d'Achat et de Vente du Boerenbond Belge SA v Luis de Ridder Ltda, The Julia* [1949] AC 293, [1949] 1 All ER 269.
12 *Tappenden v Artus* [1964] 2 QB 185, [1963] 3 All ER 213, implies this proposition. Not all legal systems accept the doctrine of justification by contract: French law, for instance, is sometimes prepared to give restitution where A benefits B under a contract with C and C then becomes insolvent.
13 This is implicit in *Barclays Bank Ltd v W J Simms Son & Cooke (Southern) Ltd* [1980] QB 677, [1979] 3 All ER 522. There, however, the claim succeeded, since the cheque had been countermanded and so payment of it by the bank did not discharge its customer's obligation.

Chapter 11

Promissory obligation

This chapter deals with the creation of obligations by promises; when, and how far, may a promisor be made to carry out his promise, or be liable in damages for not doing so? This, of course, is a large subject, and it is proposed to deal with it in two stages.

First, given that obviously no system of law can enforce all promises, there is the question of which promises do give rise to legal obligation, and in what circumstances they do. What *form*, for instance, must a promise take; does it matter, for example, whether it is in writing? What *circumstances* are necessary to make a promise binding; thus, does it make any difference whether the promise is gratuitous, or has been relied on by somebody else? Assuming a promise is binding in principle, who can enforce it against whom; that is, who are *parties* to the obligation it creates?

The second part of this chapter concentrates not so much on when promises create obligations, but on the sort of obligation they create. In particular, it deals with the interpretation of promises (especially contractual ones); the sort of liability they create (is it strict, or does it depend on fault?); and the extent to which one party's obligation under a contract is conditional on due performance by the other party.

As might be expected, this chapter concentrates much on the law of contract; but it is both wider and narrower. To begin with, promisory obligation may arise from other sources than contract; trust, for instance, or even tort. Secondly, here we only deal with the *creation* of obligations by promise. The extent to which promise can modify or nullify obligations, while formally part of the law of contract, is covered by Chs 13 and 14, which also deals with certain factors, such as impossibility, which go to limit or negative promissory obligation.

1. What promises give rise to legal obligations?

This question is unfortunately one that cannot be answered in the abstract; there are no universal rules covering all sorts of promises. In fact, broadly the law seems to distinguish at least four different types of promise, to which different rules may on occasion apply. Promises may be (i) *unilateral*, to pay for a benefit as and when received (as where A promises B £500 if B recovers A's stolen jewellery); (ii) *bilateral*, to exchange benefits (A promises to sell, and B to buy, his house next month; (iii) *gratuitous* (A promises to give B £500); or (iv) *warranties* – undertakings that some state of affairs exists (or has existed, or will exist), or that X will do something (for example, a guarantee that a car has covered only 20,000 miles.)[1]

Not only do promises vary; so also do the degrees to which they are enforceable. They may thus be enforceable only to the extent that a promisee relying on them may recover his loss; or alternatively, more generously, in that the promisee may recover the benefit he would have got had the promise been kept. We return to these distinctions elsewhere.

(a) THE FORM OF AN ENFORCEABLE PROMISE

(i) Seriousness

To be binding, a promise must be – or rather, *seem* – seriously intended;[2] this goes equally for the law of contract, which requires an 'intent to create legal relations', and also for other sources of promissory obligation, such as the law of trusts, where equally purely informal arrangements are not enforced. However, in business transactions serious intent is now strongly presumed.[3] Traditionally there is a contrary presumption for other promises, for instance within the family, but that is now rather weak. Appreciation of house prices and thus most families' assets, not to mention increased break-up of families, has ensured increased concentration on individual, rather than dynastic, interests even within the family.[4]

(ii) Promises and agreements

Sometimes the law enforces promises as such, whether or not the promisee has positively accepted their benefit. A promise under seal[5] to pay X £100 is enforceable by X even though X knows nothing of it; and a declaration of trust (which, as we shall see, has many of the effects of a gratuitious promise to transfer property) is treated similarly.

1 Strictly speaking, a warranty is very doubtfully a promise at all, since it does not concern the future action of the 'promisor.' But it is an acceptance of responsibility for a state of affairs, which is nearly the same thing; and it is convenient to treat it as if it were a promise.
2 *Balfour v Balfour* [1919] 2 KB 571, 88 LJKB 1054; cf, in respect of equitable ogligation, *Re Hamilton, French v Hamilton* [1895] 2 Ch 370, 64 LJ Ch 799.
3 *Edwards v Skyways Ltd* [1964] 1 All ER 494, [1964] 1 WLR 349.
4 See *Pettitt v Pettitt* [1970] AC 777 at 816, [1969] 2 All ER 385 at 408, per Lord Upjohn; and at pp 822–823, 413–414, per Lord Diplock.
5 For the meaning of 'sealing', see *First National Securities v Jones* [1978] Ch 109, [1978] 2 All ER 221.

Generally, however, except in the case of gratuitous promises, a promise is enforceable only when the promisee has done something to show acquiescence. In legal terms, an 'offer' must be 'accepted', and the promise turns into agreement. This is not for doctrinal reasons, but for convenience. If A agrees to sell B 1,000 tons of soya beans, there must be a deadline after which neither side can seek alternative suppliers or customers; again, if A offers a £100 reward to find his lost dog, there must be a 'point of no return' after which he cannot withdraw his offer or change its terms. This is why it is traditional to analyse the formation of a contract into offer and acceptance.

OFFER. Only an offer intended, when accepted, to give rise to legal relations immediately can be validly accepted; an 'invitation to treat', or intimation that one might be prepared to do business on certain terms, cannot. Distinguishing the two can be delicate. Although the details are too complicated to be covered here,[6] suffice it to say that the law tends against inferring an offer in the strict sense in the absence of clear intention. Advertisements for functions, for example, and price tags fixed to goods in shops, are construed merely as 'invitations to treat'. One relies on them at one's peril and cannot claim even for wasted expenditure if they turn out misleading.[7]

ACCEPTANCE. Until accepted, an offer can be withdrawn; hence the importance of being able to time acceptance precisely. Now, the law starts by saying an offer is accepted when the offeree's agreement is communicated to, and received by, the offeror. This rule is not a logical necessity, but can be justified on the ground that contract implies agreement, and parties do not agree unless they know they do. Hence it applies even where parties are not face to face, as where a contract is concluded by telephone or telex.[8] (Anomalously, where a contract is made by exchange of letters, the acceptance takes place when and where the accepting letter is posted, even if it never reaches the offeror.[9] But this exception yields to any contrary intention in the offer, and recently courts have emphasised its peculiarity by readily inferring such intention).

But this rule requiring communication to the offeror is not absolute. An offeror may vary the means of acceptance; he can dispense with the need for communication to him, and indeed, so far as his own (but not the offeree's) liability is concerned, with the need for overt acceptance altogether. With unilateral contracts, moreover, such as offers of

---

6   See, eg, G. C. Cheshire & C. H. S. Fifoot, *The law of contract*, 10th edn, 27 f.
7   Arguably were the advertisers at fault there might be a remedy for negligent misrepresentation.
8   Cf *Entores Ltd v Miles Far East Corpn* [1955] 2 QB 327, [1955] 2 All ER 493.
9   *Adams v Lindsell* (1818) 1 B & Ald 681. Contrary agreement is easily found, as appears in *Holwell Securities Ltd v Hughes* [1974] 1 All ER 161, [1974] 1 WLR 155.

rewards and the like, he is prima facie deemed to waive the requirement of communication. My offer to X of £100 to find my lost dog is accepted when he starts to look for it, whether or not he tells me he has done so.[10] Similarly with other contracts where expecting notice of acceptance would be quixotic; thus if I buy a ticket for something from a slot machine, the owner of the machine is deemed to make an offer to me by providing the machine, which I accept by the act of putting my money it. At this moment the contract is complete; thereafter it is too late to try to insert new terms into it.[11]

When discussing questions of offer and acceptance, it is tempting to think of all contracts as formed in this way. In fact this is often not very helpful. Membership of a club, for instance, is a contract between each and every member, comporting (inter alia) the obligation to pay subscriptions, and so on;[12] but the offers and acceptances presumably resulting when a new member joins the existing club leave the mind boggling. Indeed, the assumption on which the theory of offer and acceptance is based, that in any contract there must be one time at which all obligations arise, none arising earlier or later, can itself cause injustice. With contracts, such as large building contracts, that take months to negotiate, with heavy expenses on both sides, it is not obvious that either side ought to be allowed to withdraw, however unreasonably, at any time before final signature, without any responsibility for expenditure thus caused to be wasted by the other party.[13]

(iii) The form of expression of a promise
There are few requirements of form as such for promissory liability. An oral promise, or an implied undertaking (boarding a bus implies a promise to pay the fare), is as binding as anything in writing. The only general restriction is that pure inaction cannot create such an obligation; you cannot oblige me to buy your car simply by writing to me offering to sell it and saying that failure to reply will be deemed acceptance.[14] Of course, some specific requirements of form exist. Contracts of guarantee, for instance, must be in writing;[15] as must promises to repay credit owing under the Consumer Credit Act 1974.[16]

---

10   See *Carlill v Carbolic Smoke Ball Co Ltd* [1893] 1 QB 256, 62 LJQB 257, *Daulia Ltd v Four Millbank Nominees Ltd* [1978] Ch 231 at 239, [1978] 2 All ER 557 at 561, per Goff LJ.
11   Cf *Thornton v Shoe Lane Parking Ltd* [1971] 2 QB 163, [1971] 1 All ER 686.
12   Cf *Clarke v Dunraven* [1897] AC 59, 66 LJP 1; *Harrington v Sendall* [1903] 1 Ch 921, 72 LJCh 396.
13   German law has a useful principle that unreasonable refusal to contract, having raised reasonable expectations in another, may be a tort and thus engender liability for the other's losses.
14   *Felthouse v Bindley* (1862) 11 CB(NS) 869 indirectly decided this point.
15   Statute of Frauds (1677), s 4.
16   Consumer Credit Act 1974, s 61.

Most importantly, contracts for the disposition of an interest in land must, by s 40 of the Law of Property Act 1925, have 'some memorandum or note thereof' in writing, 'signed by the party to be charged' – a similar, though slightly less onerous, requirement.

This latter requirement, however, is less significant than it looks, merely providing buyers and sellers of land with opportunities to change their minds after agreement in principle. This is because even a completely oral contract for the sale of land is enforceable, provided it has been performed – at least in part – by one party thereto so as to show unequivocally that it existed (the doctrine of part performance').

So if I convey land to you under an oral contract I can recover its price; again, if A acts unequivocally on a promise by B that, if A will act as his housekeeper, B will give her his house, A can specifically enforce this promise whether or not it is evidenced in writing.[17] She is not forced simply to recover the value of her services as representing B's unjustified enrichment.[18]

(iv) The requirement of certainty

To make a person liable to fulfil a promise, it must be clear, not only *that*, but *what*, he has promised. English judges, however, while they accept that agreements are ineffective if too vague to be understood even with the aid of reasonable exogesis, nevertheless indulge as far as possible businessmen's habits of imprecision; they go far in judiciously extracting sensible meanings from meagre sources. A contract without a price agreed is deemed to be for a 'reasonable price';[19] very vague specifications for goods sold have meanings teased out of them.[20] Only impossibly imprecise agreements, referring to 'normal terms' that do not exist, or (unspecified) 'hire purchase terms',[1] remain entirely unenforceable. (Indeed, there is something to be said for extending enforceability even further; if the seller of a lorry 'on hire purchase terms' refuses to deliver it at all, arguably he ought to be liable for the buyer's wasted expenditure, if for nothing else. Unfortunately this would entail obliging the parties to bargain in good faith to settle the point of vagueness, for otherwise either could escape liability simply by rejecting any terms offered by the other. And the obligation to bargain in good faith, while not impossible, is unknown to English law).

---

17   *Wakeham v Mackenzie* [1968] 2 All ER 783, [1968] 1 WLR 1175. Cf *Steadman v Steadman* [1976] AC 536, [1974] 2 All ER 977.
18   Which claim also seems available to her: see the Canadian case of *Deglman v Guaranty Trust of Canada* [1954] 3 DLR 785.
19   Sale of Goods Act 1979, s 8(2). True, a contract to sell 'at a price to be agreed' is ineffective, but this is because here the parties have simply failed to agree on anything at all.
20   As in, eg, *Hillas & Co Ltd v Arcos Ltd* (1932) 147 LT 503.
1   *G. Scammell & Nephew Ltd v Ouston* [1941] AC 251, [1941] 1 All ER 14.

Outside the law of contract, it appears the requirement of certainty is less stringent. In the law of constructive trusts, for instance, as we see in the next section, a cohabitee improving another's house (say) on the understanding that he or she will thereby obtain an interest in it, is given whatever interest will best do justice in the light of the expectation; yet in many such cases the antecedent agreement could hardly be less precise or explicit.[2]

(b) SUBSTANTIVE REQUIREMENTS FOR PROMISSORY OBLIGATION

Odd though it may seem, the justification for making promises legally enforceable is not that they are as such morally binding – even though on occasion they may be. Rather, it is suggested, the matter is one of social convenience, admittedly with certain assumptions about moral autonomy added. Thus a contract between two corporations is clearly – and rightly – enforceable, even though no moral obligation can arise because corporations cannot themselves have moral rights or duties. The justification for enforcing the contract is simply that in general commerce is a good thing. Again, whether a bare promise by A to give B £100 creates any moral obligation of itself is doubtful. Yet the law is surely right to allow such promises to be made and (provided they are under seal) to enforce them; if people wish facilities to bind themselves in this way, there seems little point in not allowing them to.

It follows from what he have just said, that there is no reason for the law to enforce *all* promises, but only those where, for some reason, enforcement is specifically justified. Now, the promises that English law chooses to enforce fall into three categories. First, there are cases where something ('consideration') is given, promised or done in return; secondly, there are promises that have been relied on by another; and lastly, cases where neither consideration nor reliance is present, but where certain forms are observed by the promisor.

(i) *Promises where the promisee receives something in return: the doctrine of consideration*
Promissory obligation developed up to the sixteenth century around a number of common individual transactions (sale, provision of services for payment, and so on) most of which in the nature of things involved the promisor getting, or having got, something for his promise. Small wonder, therefore, that when (by a procedural shuffle) a general rule of promissory liability grew up around the action of assumpsit, it included a requirement that the promisee receive some quid pro quo. That

---

2 Why? Perhaps the reason is that many of the above contractual examples involve executory liability, where little harm is done by non-enforcement; whereas non-contractual forms of such liability more often tend to neutralise unjustified enrichment, with correspondingly greater incentive not to deny a remedy.

explains the present rule that consideration allows a promise to be enforced; though it does not, of course, justify it.   For that one can only say, in a rough and ready way, that in general those who pay for promises deserve better to be able to enforce them than those who do not; even though, as might be expected, this justifies only the doctrine as a whole, and not all its individual aspects.

The consideration allowing a promise to be enforced is traditionally dubbed some 'benefit to the promisor' or 'detriment to the promisee'; or, more informatively, something done, given or promised by the promisee to the promisor. Examples elucidate theory. One must pay for goods sold and delivered because the delivery is consideration for the promise to pay; again, a promise to sell one's house in future is binding immediately because the buyer's promise to accept and pay for it is consideration for the vendor's promise to convey it. The rule seems to be, that, provided (a) the promisee's consideration was asked for by the promisor; and (b) the promisee was responsible for supplying it, that suffices to make the contract enforceable. It does not matter whether the promisor benefits objectively, nor what the consideration is worth. A manufacturer supplying 'gifts' in exchange for packet tops from his product which he immediately throws away still does so for consideration;[3] again, a decorator painting my house in execrable taste so as actually to reduce its value still provides consideration for my promise to pay him. Nor does it matter that providing the consideration incidentally benefited the promisee himself: a promise to pay X £1000 if he earns more than £25,000 in 1984 is still made for good consideration.

The promisee must be in some way responsible for supplying the consideration. A promise to pay X £1000 if a small company he is managing director of makes profits of over £25,000 is supported by consideration; but not a promise to pay him £1,000 if an unconnected company does so, or if he breaks his leg. These are merely conditional, but gratuitous, promises. The distinction is narrow; a typical borderline case is a promise to pay X £5,000 per year if and as long as he is not working.[4]

CONSIDERATION: THE PROBLEM OF ACTS REQUIRED BY LAW. Assume X agrees to pay Y £100 if Y continues to work for Z for a month (which Y is contractually bound to do anyway); or agrees to pay him £1,000 to induce him to deliver goods he is bound to deliver to X anyway; or a father promises his son £100 if he does not smoke cannabis (which is a criminal offence) for a year. In one sense Y's doing the act benefits X (since, apart from X's promise, it would not have been done); in another it does not, since Y was obliged to do it anyway. Logically

---

3   *Chappell v Nestlé Ltd* [1960] AC 114, [1959] 2 All ER 701.
4   See *Wyatt v Kreglinger Ltd* [1933] 1 KB 793, 102 LJKB 325.

promises such as these ought to be regarded as supported by consideration; if X regarded performance by Y as valuable to him, it should not matter whether he was right or not, nor whether Y was bound to do it anyway. In fact English law treats logically only the first of these cases, where Y is doing what he is already bound to do as against a third person.[5] Performance of duties imposed by the criminal law, or by contract with the promisor, are anomalously regarded as not good consideration.[6]

Sometimes, it is true, this rule produces the right answer. If A threatens not to perform his contract with B unless B promises £1,000 extra, B's promise should be unenforceable; similarly, much can be said for preventing performance of one's duties under the criminal law becoming a saleable commodity. But this is for quite separate reasons; B's promise in the first case is extracted by a form of duress that ought not to be countenanced,[7] and the second case can be justified simply on grounds of public policy.[8] As it is, the rule that says performance of existing duties (except vis-à-vis third parties) can never be consideration upsets perfectly innocuous transactions; thus, indefensibly, in a building contract, if the site owner promises the building contractor extra payment to deal with unforeseen difficulties, that promise is unenforceable if it happens that the contractor was by the original contract bound to deal with those difficulties anyway.

CONSIDERATION AND EXCHANGE. Consideration must be given *in exchange* for a promise, not simply *because* of it. Thus in *Combe v Combe*[9] a husband promised his divorced wife an annuity. She as a result did not sue him for maintenance. Now, had the husband promised her the annuity 'if she did not sue him', the promise would have been enforceable on normal principles; as it was, however, her forbearance to sue was merely the result of that promise, which therefore was gratuitous and thus unenforceable. A fortiori, where A does something in ignorance of a promise by B to pay him for doing it, what he does is not in exchange for B's promise, and therefore cannot be consideration for it.[10] The consideration, moreover, must be given in exchange for the promise,

5   *Shadwell v Shadwell* (1860) 9 CBNS 159, 30 LJCP 145.
6   This is accepted to be the effect of cases such as *Stilk v Myrick* (1809) 2 Camp 317, 6 Esp 129 and *Collins v Godefroy* (1831) 1 B & Ad 950, 1 Dowl 326.
7   See *The Siboen* [1976] 1 Lloyds Rep 293.
8   This was realised in *Ward v Byham* [1956] 2 All ER 318, [1956] 1 WLR 496, where two members of the Court of Appeal manufactured an element of consideration that the promisee was not already bound to provide in order to circumvent the rule.
9   [1951] 2 KB 215, [1951] 1 All ER 767. See too *Wigan v English and Scottish Law Life Assurance Association* [1909] 1 Ch 291, 78 LJ Ch 120.
10 This is one explanation for the rule that a person fulfilling the conditions of a reward cannot claim it if he acted in ignorance of it: see the Australian decision in *R v Clarke* (1927) 40 CLR 227.

not vice versa; hence, in general, promise must precede consideration, and 'past consideration' will not suffice. So a grateful promise by a person rescued to pay his rescuer £100 is unenforceable.[11] But there is an exception for one kind of promise; a promise to pay for services rendered (or goods supplied) is enforceable even if made after the event, provided the plaintiff clearly did not intend to act gratuitously.[12] In fact this is not a very drastic exception. Even without the promise there would, as we saw in Ch 10, have been an obligation to pay a reasonable price under the rules of unjustified enrichment; all the exception does is to substitute the agreed price for the reasonable one.

(ii) Promissory liability based on reliance
Consideration is a *general* ground for validating a promise; any promise supported by it is prima facie enforceable. This is not true of reliance; however much a promise by A (say) to pay B £100 is relied on, that of itself is not enough to give B any right to sue A. Nevertheless, reliance plays a large part in the law of obligations. First, the person suffering loss through relying on another's promise (for instance, by increasing his expenditure in expectation of a gift) has a stronger claim than one merely suffering disappointment. Moreover, although reliance is not a general ground of enforcement, nevertheless the cases where promises *are* enforceable on this ground are numerous and important enough to warrant regarding it as a separate ground of liability. These cases we now deal with in turn.

A. PURPORTED GIFTS OF LAND. At first sight, this example, which moves out of the law of contract into equity, looks like part of the law of property. If A, the owner of a piece of land, purports (without the proper formality) to give it to B on B building a house on it – or on B doing any other act in reliance on the purported gift – then B, on fulfilling the condition, obtains an equitable right to have A convey the land to him.[13] Now, since in practice there is little difference between a purported future gift and a promise to give in the future, we have here effectively enforcement of such a promise on the ground of reliance.

Although no doctrine similar to this has been applied to property other than land, there is no reason why it should not be. A might purportedly give, say, shares to B if B paid the costs of exercising a rights issue; if he did, arguably B should have a right to have the shares properly conveyed to him.

B. CONSTRUCTIVE TRUSTS OF LAND AND SIMILAR INSTITUTIONS. Assume A and B live together in A's house; B contributes substantially to the

---

11   Cf *Roscorla v Thomas* (1842) 3 QB 234, 11 LJQB 24.
12   See the old case of *Lampleigh v Brathwait* (1615) Hob 105.
13   See, eg, *Dillwyn v Llewellyn* (1862) 4 De G F & J 517, 31 LJ Ch 658; *Pascoe v Turner* [1979] 2 All ER 945, [1979] 1 WLR 431.

household in cash, kind or work. As such these contributions give rise to no claim based on unjustified enrichment;[14] apparently because here donative intent is assumed. (Though, where married couples are concerned, on divorce s 24 of the Matrimonial Causes Act 1973 gives the court wide discretion to divide their property, taking into account, inter alia, just such contributions). But where B's cash contribution is substantial – where, for instance, to enable A to pay the mortgage instalments he pays for improvements – then it may more readily be inferred to have been given in exchange for an interest in the property.[15] Again, though no similar presumption applies to services, nevertheless if an arrangement, express or implied, can be shown that they should give rise to an interest in the property, effect will be given to it. In both cases A will hold the property on constructive trust for B to the extent necessary to effectuate B's interest. The net effect of these rules is that the ostensibly proprietary institution of the constructive trust enforces the express or implied promise of A to give B an interest in his house.

Similarly, too, with arrangements to give a person a lesser right than ownership or part ownership of property. Assume A pays for an extension to B's house on the understanding that he will be allowed to live in it for life. If B refuses subsequently to let him into the house, the law could simply allow A to recover his expenditure from B on the basis of unjustified enrichment;[16] instead, however, equity intervenes to give A whatever interest in the land (such as a life interest) will best give effect to the original understanding.[17]

c. 'EQUITABLE ESTOPPEL'. Put briefly, the doctrine of equitable estoppel is that a person promising not to exercise a legal right he already has loses that right if the promise has been relied on and it would thereafter be inequitable to allow the right to be exercised. In the leading case, a landlord promised not to issue a notice to quit to his tenant if the latter did certain repairs. After the tenant had begun the repairs, a purported notice to quit in breach of the promise was held ineffective.[18] Now, to some extent this doctrine also applies to promises to act. If A, a landowner, promises B, a neighbour, to give him a right of way over his land (effectively, that is, not to exercise his legal right to exclude B) and B relies on the promise, he can force the grant of the right of way.[19] More recently, in *Amalgamated Investment and Property Co Ltd v Texas Commerce International Bank Ltd*[20] A, having guaranteed a loan from B to

14 *Pettitt v Pettitt* [1970] AC 777, [1969] 2 All ER 385; *Burns v Burns* [1984] 1 All ER 244.
15 *Pettitt v Pettitt* [1970] AC at 795, [1969] 2 All ER at 390, per Lord Reid.
16 As it did in *Dodsworth v Dodsworth* (1973) 228 Estates Gazette 1115.
17 *Inwards v Baker* [1965] 2 QB 29, [1965] 1 All ER 446.
18 *Hughes v Metropolitan Rly Co* (1877) 2 App Cas 439, 46 LJQB 583.
19 *Crabb v Arun DC* [1976] Ch 179, [1975] 3 All ER 865. Cf *E R Ives (Investments) Ltd v High* [1967] 2 QB 379, [1967] 1 All ER 504.
20 [1982] QB 84, [1981] 3 All ER 577.

C, later undertook to treat the transaction as if it had involved a loan actually made to D, C's subsidiary. B, having relied on A's assurance, successfully sued A on the guarantee when D defaulted.

Nevertheless, not all promises to act are enforceable in this way. In *Combe v Combe*,[1] as we saw, a gratuitous promise to pay a wife an annual sum was held unenforceable despite the latter's reliance on it by not suiting for maintenance; equitable estoppel did not apply (it was said) on the picturesque, if enigmatic, ground that it could be used as a shield but not as a sword. The difficulty, of course, is to see to what extent the courts are prepared to use the doctrine to enforce positive promises.

It is suggested that the distinction towards which they are groping, albeit not in so many words, is a subtle one, between promises aimed at *changing* existing legal relationships, and those aimed at creating *new* obligations. The former are prima facie enforceable on the basis of reliance alone; the latter require consideration. If this distinction is indeed the right one, it would not only preserve the pattern of the old law; it would also be sensible. It is rarely unjust to say that people rely on promises of gifts and other gratuitous benefits at their own risk; by contrast, it is very inconvenient if bona fide alterations of existing legal relationships are held ineffectual merely because all the advantage happens to be on one side.[2]

D. BREACH OF PROMISE, COUPLED WITH FAULT. The other case where reliance causes liability for breach of promise is advanced tentatively: it is submitted that, as a general principle, the *negligent* failure to keep a promise engenders liability to anyone suffering damage by relying on the promise. What matters is fault, and that the promise has been relied on; if the promisor gives notice in good time that he will not keep his promise, so the promisee has the chance to make alternative arrangements, then there should be no liability.

Assume, for instance, that A undertakes gratuitously to insure B's house; if he negligently fails to do so, without having warned B in time to make alternative arrangements, he is, it is submitted, liable to B if the house later burns down uninsured. One old case decided this;[3] despite later doubts,[4] it is suggested that recent developments in the law of tort, if anything, confirm it. The requirements of liability for

---

1 [1951] 2 KB 215, [1951] 1 All ER 767.
2 Roman law had a useful similar doctrine that supplementary agreements altering existing obligations *(pacta adiecta)* were enforceable by agreement alone, even though agreements creating such obligations would not have been. See Buckland, *Textbook of Roman Law*, 3rd edn, 528.
3 *Wilkinson v Coverdale* (1793) 1 Esp 75.
4 See *Argy Trading Development Co Ltd v Lapid Developments Ltd* [1977] 3 All ER 785, [1977] 1 WLR 444, where on similar facts the plaintiffs lost. But in that case it was never pleaded that the defendants had negligently broken their undertaking, so the authority is hardly very strong.

inadvertently caused loss are present; negligence, foreseeability of the plaintiff and no good social reason to deny liability. More to the point, a general liability for culpable failure to carry out even a wholly gratuitous promise would be only beneficial. Not only do other systems of law recognise such liability; the fact that the promise was gratuitous in origin is reflected in that the promisor who withdraws in good time is not liable,[5] and in that even where he does not withdraw he is excused if his failure to act as promised was not his fault.

(iii) Enforcement of other gratuitous promises
The person who loses by relying on a promise has a good case for sympathy; disappointment aside, he who merely fails to gain what he thought he would (as where a promised present of £100 fails to materialise) has a much weaker one. But the law of contract exists largely to give facilities to those wanting to use them; and if persons want facilities to bind themselves to gratuitous promises, there is little reason for the law to refuse to provide them.

Two sorts of pure gratuitous binding promise exist in English law. One is the straightforward contract under seal, which can be used for any sort of promise under seal, which can be used for any sort of promise. The formal requirements of this are surprisingly simple; provided a document is signed, has space for a seal (no actual seal is needed) and provided the person signing it somehow separately indicates his intent to be bound by it, that suffices.

The other form, in name a transfer of property but in effect hardly distinguishable from a promise to transfer something in future, is the declaration of trust. If I declare myself trustee of my house (or car, or shares) for X, I retain legal title but X obtains equitable title and thence the right to an immediate conveyance by me, on demand, of legal title to him.[6] True, X's right is ostensibly proprietary; it is specifically enforceable, may prevail in insolvency and may even obtain against third parties (other than bona fida purchasers); but none of these features is inconsistent with such a right fitting more closely into the law of obligations than that of property.[7]

(c) THE PARTIES TO PROMISSORY OBLIGATION

(i) Who can enforce the obligation?

A. PRIVITY OF CONTRACT IN GENERAL. A promise, by its nature, is made to someone, for the benefit of someone. Those people may not be the same;

---

5 Once again, compare Roman law: one who agreed gratuitously to do something for another was liable in damages under the *actio mandati* if he did not; but he was not liable if he gave due warning. Buckland, *Textbook of Roman Law*, 3rd edn, 514.
6 *Saunders v Vautier* (1841) Cr & Ph 240, 10 LJ Ch 354.
7 Instructively, French law deals with this problem as part of the law of contract.

if A promises B to pay C £100 the promise is made to B but for C's benefit. Now, English law could have said that anyone to whom, or for whose benefit, a promise had been made could enforce it; but it did not. Instead, it insists that only the person to whom the promise was made can enforce it. Moreover, it limits enforcement even more narrowly, since for these purposes only a person who has actually provided consideration counts as a promisee. So the contract by A with B to pay C £100 is unenforceable by C if C has provided no consideration, even if C is mentioned in that contract as a party and has signed it.[8] (B, of course, may enforce the contract, provided *he* has provided consideration; indeed, if it is the right sort of promise he can even get an order of specific performance.[9] Unfortunately, with other sorts of contract, his right to claim damages is of little use to him, since the House of Lords has refused to hold that, by a refusal of A to pay C, he has suffered more than nominal damage[10]).

This is a notoriously restrictive view. Continental codes, and much American State law, specifically provide for the enforcement of promises by the third parties for whose benefit they were made. In fact, however, the injustice caused by the English rule (and indeed the difference between the results reached by it and other systems) is rather small. First, there are several exceptions to the rule that only a promisee providing consideration can enforce a promise. Secondly, and more importantly, other concepts, such as equity or even tort, may provide a needed remedy where contract does not.

B. EXCEPTIONS TO, AND EVASIONS OF, PRIVITY OF CONTRACT. A few exceptions to privity of contract are barefacedly admitted as doctrinally indefensible but practically convenient. Bankers' commercial credits, for instance, involve a bank, in consideration of being put in funds by its customer, promising to pay an equivalent sum to a third party; the latter, it is always assumed, can sue the bank directly, though no-one seems quite clear why.[11]

Further, it is not surprising that the law of trust, which combines promissory elements with freedom from some of the more annoyingly technical rules of contract, should play its part.

To begin with, the benefit of an enforceable promise, being a sort of property, can be held on trust. Contracting parties, indeed, can validly stipulate for rights arising under a contract to be held on trust for a third party; if they do, the third party can insist that the contract be enforced for his benefit. Thus if A promises under seal to pay B £5,000, the benefit of the promise to be held on trust for C, C can force B to

---

8   *Dunlop Pneumatic Tyre Co Ltd v Selfridge & Co Ltd* [1915] AC 847, 84 LJQB 1680.
9   *Beswick v Beswick* [1968] AC 58, [1967] 2 All ER 1197.
10   *Woodar Investment Ltd v Wimpey Construction (UK) Ltd* [1980] 1 All ER 571, [1980] 1 WLR 277.
11   See, eg, *Urquhart Lindsay & Co Ltd v Eastern Bank Ltd* [1922] 1 KB 318, 91 LJKB 274.

enforce A's promise for his benefit.[12] Again, if vendor and purchaser of a house agree that the buyer's right to the price shall be held as to two per cent for the estate agent, the agent can take the benefit of that promise.[13] Unfortunately, however, English courts will not infer an intent to create such a trust merely from evidence that a contractual promise is intended to enure to the benefit of a third party. Thus a contract of insurance entered into for a third party's benefit is at common law unenforceable by him[14] (though here, statute has intervened). Instead, specific intent to create a *trust* must be shown; with respect, a silly and quixotic requirement, since at least to a layman the difference between intending to promise for a third party's benefit and intending to promise for the promisee's benefit but to make a trust of that promise for the third party is evanescent.

There are, however, other cases where equity intervenes more effectively to allow enforcement of promises by third parties. One is the doctrine of 'completely constituted trusts'. If A transfers property to B on trust for C, a 'completely constituted trust' arises and C becomes owner in equity of what was transferred; in effect, B's promise to A to hold the property on behalf of C is enforceable by C. Furthermore, in one case even a *promise* by A to transfer property to B on trust for C is enforceable by C. If A's promise to B is in consideration of a marriage and C is either a party to that marriage or the issue of it, then he is entitled to sue A for specific performance to enforce A's promise to transfer the covenanted property to B on trust for him. But this extension of promissory liability is limited to such cases; in others, unless it is specifically shown that B's right to sue A was held on trust for C, C is left without a remedy unless A actually fulfils his promise to B.[15] C is here caught by the maxim that 'equity will not assist a volunteer'.[16]

Yet a further example of effective equitable intervention comes in the law of constructive trusts. It arises where A gives B a thing, or more often land or a house, on the understanding that B will give it to C or use it for C's benefit. Here, other systems of law might give C the right to the thing on the ground that B's promise to A was intended to benefit C. English law cannot do this, but achieves the same result by translating promise into property (that is, constructive trust) and

---

12 *Fletcher v Fletcher* (1844) 4 Hare 67, 14 LJ Ch 66.
13 Cf *Les Affréteurs Réunis SA v Leopard Walford (London) Ltd* [1919] AC 801, 88 LJKB 861.
14 *Re Sinclair's Life Policy* [1938] Ch 799, [1938] 3 All ER 124; cf *Re Schebsman ex p Official Receiver, Trustee v Cargo Superintendent (London) Ltd* [1944] Ch 83, [1943] 2 All ER 768. The statute is the Third Parties (Rights against Insurers) Act 1930.
15 *Pullan v Koe* [1913] 1 Ch 9, 82 LJ Ch 37; *Re D'Angibau, Andrews v Andrews* (1880) 15 Ch D 228, 49 LJ Ch 756.
16 In certain cases, indeed, it seems that not even B can sue A to enforce the contract: see, eg, *Re Price* [1928] Ch 579, 97 LJ Ch 423.

saying that B holds what was transferred to him on trust for C. Thus in *Binions v Evans*[17] A conveyed a cottage to B on the basis of B's undertaking to let C (A's ex-employee) live there for life rent-free. It was held that B's acceptance of the obligation to respect C's rights, though made to A and not to C, nevertheless created a trust in favour of C. A parallel doctrine appears in the rules relating to 'secret trusts'. By these rules in their most basic form, if A leaves property to B by will, and B promises to return to hold it for, or give it to, C, then C obtains the right to the property when A dies and B receives it. (Analogous thought also underlies the doctrine of 'mutual wills'; by this doctrine in simple form, if A and B each bequeath property to each other on terms that the survivor will in turn bequeath it to C when he dies, C obtains a contingent right to the property as soon as it is left by will subject to the condition that he is to get it on the death of the survivor of A and B.[18])

By contrast with equity, the law of tort does little to extend promissory liability to third parties (though it does a great deal to allow third parties to sue for loss inadvertently caused; as where an occupier owes a duty to his contractual visitors in contract, and virtually the same duty to his other visitors in tort). But even here, the contribution of tort is not insignificant. First there is the liability, already mentioned, for culpably breaking a promise that has been relied on. This principle seems to apply as much to non-promisees as to promisees. Thus in *Junior Books Ltd v Veitchi Co Ltd*[19] the subcontractor who broke his contract with his main contractor on a building site and installed a floor very badly was held liable for the loss suffered by the building owner, even though he had no contract with him. Secondly, in cases where the law of tort extends to allow recovery of gains foregone, rather than loss suffered, it may be very relevant to promissory liability. Thus in *Ross v Caunters (A Firm)*,[20] a solicitor who carelessly drew up an invalid will was held liable to the beneficiary who failed to inherit as a result; a solution that could equally have been reached, were it possible, by saying that the solicitor's promise to be careful, while made to the testator, was made also for the benefit of the intended legatee.

C. WHOM DO PROMISSORY OBLIGATIONS BIND? If a contract made by A with B cannot benefit C, a fortiori it should not be able to bind him or adversely accept his rights. Indeed, English law begins by saying just this. Nevertheless, there are at least two cases that, although they

---

17 [1972] Ch 359, [1972] 2 All ER 70. *Lyus v Prowsa Developments Ltd* [1982] 2 All ER 953, [1982] 1 WLR 1044, could also be explained on this ground.
18 Eg *Re Green, Lindner v Green* [1951] Ch 148, [1950] 2 All ER 913. Cf *Ottaway v Norman* [1972] Ch 698, [1971] 3 All ER 1325.
19 [1983] 1 AC 520, [1982] 3 All ER 201.
20 [1980] Ch 297, [1979] 3 All ER 580.

ostensibly involve other areas of the law, such as tort or property, nevertheless in practice lead to an agreement between A and B affecting C.

First, there is the economic tort, mentioned in Ch 8, of knowingly participating in a breach of contract between strangers; this, if it does not formally infringe privity of contract, at least subverts it.[1]

Secondly, there is the question of obligations respecting the use of property. If A, a landowner, agrees with B, a neighbour, not to use his land in a certain way (such as not to build on it) and then sells the land to C, C is in certain cases bound by the agreement.[2] Similarly, if A agrees in a specifically enforceable contract to sell his land to B, and then sells it to C, there are circumstances where B can force C to sell the land to him on the terms of the original contract with A. Now, both these cases are traditionally explained as involving not contract but property, and thus are simply exemplifying the principle that property rights, unlike those under a contract, bind third parties. But this is not very convincing. There is nothing proprietary, except the name, about a right to prevent land being used in a certain way, or to demand its conveyance on payment of the price. The real reason why in such cases rights are conferred on third parties is not that they are proprietary, but rather that such enforcement is desirable for other reasons, such as the effective protection of amenity, or the security of contracts for the sale of land.[3]

It may sometimes be possible for obligations respecting the use of personal property to bind third parties. According to the old case of *De Mattos v Gibson*,[4] if the seller of a chattel is obliged by contract not to use it in a particular way, so that an injunction would issue to stop him doing so, then anyone else buying that chattel with knowledge of that restriction on use may be similarly restrained. Now that case and the principle it represents have been variously followed and doubted;[5] but never overruled. It is difficult to see its legal basis, but one possibility is this. Arguably there could be constructed a general rule that a contract to use property, or ot to use it, in a certain way, if enforceable specifically (that is, by injunction or specific performance), can be

1 As was observed by Coleridge J in his dissenting judgment in *Lumley v Gye* (1853) 2 E & B 216 at 246, the case that established liability for participating in a breach of contract.
2 At common law, if he has notice of the agreement (see *Tulk v Moxhay* (1848) 2 Ph 774); now, by the Land Registration Act 1925, or the Land Charges Act 1972, if it is registered.
3 Thus the 'constructive trust' said to arise from a specifically enforceable contract for the sale of land bears little resemblance to any normal form of trust – see D. Waters, *The Constructive Trust*, Ch 2.
4 (1858) 4 De G & J 276, 28 LJ Ch 165.
5 Compare *Lord Strathcona SS Co Ltd v Dominion Coal Co Ltd* [1926] AC 108, 95 LJPC 71, with *Port Line Ltd v Ben Line Steamers Ltd* [1958] 2 QB 146, [1958] 1 All ER 787.

enforced against all those taking the property with notice of it. This would not only allow effective enforcement of such limits on use; it would also provide a common juridical basis for *De Mattos v Gibson* and for the rule that a specifically enforceable contract of sale binds the thing subject to it in the hands of a purchaser other than the original contractor.

Lastly, on occasion statute makes contracts bind third parties. By s 1 of the Bills of Lading Act 1855, for example, the buyer of a cargo at sea who takes a transfer of a bill of lading is bound by (and can enforce) the contract of carriage as if it had been made with him in the first place.

2. The content of promissory liability

(a) TERMS OF A CONTRACT, EXPRESS OR IMPLIED

No promise covers all eventualities; the nature of speech is such that some events are always unprovided for. Nevertheless, the law of contract starts with a restrictive attitude to implied terms. A term will not be inserted into a contract because it is desirable or even reasonable, but only if it is very obvious; a clear oversight, or a term an officious bystander would say should be included 'of course'.[6] Now this attitude, much criticised, is often right. Supplementing a hard-bargained contract between businessmen (or many other kinds of agreement) beyond the needs of 'business efficacy' (as one judge put it[7]) may well frustrate intentions; reasonable or desirable terms may easily contradict the actual nature of an agreement. It may, for instance, be convenient for members of a trade union to agree, in their contract of membership, to abide by the general principles agreed by the TUC; but that is no justification for treating them as though they do.[8]

In any case, the traditional view of the law as very restrictive towards implied terms is deceptive. Some terms are very easy to imply; for example (reflecting a move towards a general liability for negligence) an obligation to take care in providing a service.[9] Much more importantly, though, most contracts are standard: sale, employment, carriage of goods and so on: and to that extent, though the law of contract is amorphous enough on principle to let parties agree what they like, there is a law of separate contracts, each different

---

6   The image is McKinnon LJ's in *Shirlaw v Southern Foundries (1926) Ltd* [1939] 2 KB 206 at 227, [1939] 2 All ER 113 at 124.
7   *The Moorcock* (1889) 14 PD 64 at 68.
8   *Spring v National Amalgamated Stevedores and Dockers Society* [1956] 2 All ER 221, [1956] 1 WLR 585.
9   *The Moorcock*, note 7 above; *Liverpool City Council v Irwin* [1977] AC 239, [1976] 2 All ER 39.

type with its own special terms.[10] In these cases of virtually standard contracts, terms usually found in contracts of a given sort are easily implied; whole books, for instance, have been written about the obligations implied by the terms 'CIF' or 'FOB' in a sale contract. Conversely, terms unusual in the sort of contract involved are very difficult to imply; as where, in a contract of employment, an employee sought to establish an implied obligation on his employer to indemnify – or at least insure – him against the consequences of his own negligence.[11]

Of course, fashions change in the law of contract. It should be noted, for instance, that in business contracts there are signs of a more liberal attitude towards implied terms – in particular, increased willingness to imply terms if necessary to avoid spectacularly inequitable results.[12]

(b) THE DEGREE OF PROMISSORY LIABILITY – FAULT OR NO FAULT?

Contractual liability in English law varies; some is independent of fault, while some is based on negligence, as we saw in Chs 5–7. Promissory liability, however, is in general strict; where a person promises to deliver 10,000 tonnes of soya beans by 1 July, or undertakes that a car has covered only 20,000 miles, he is liable for breach of those promises whether or not he was at fault.[13] Of course, strict liability is not absolute liability; the doctrines of impossibility and frustration, dealt with in Chs 13 and 14 below, draw much of its sting.

(c) CONDITIONAL PROMISES

As we mentioned in the previous section, promissory liability, though strict, is rarely absolute. Not only is it subject to mitigating doctrines such as frustration; but further, at least to some extent, nearly all promises are conditional, whether or not they are explicitly so. To take a trivial example, a seller's promise to deliver goods is conditional on the buyer's being ready and willing to pay the price. Now, this section deals with a particular kind of conditionality; how far are one person's obligations under a contract dependent on what the other party does? Since this is a question with no unique answer, to which the solution

10 *Shell (UK) Ltd v Lostock Garage Ltd* [1977] 1 All ER 481 at 486 f, [1976] 1 WLR 1187 at 1195 f, per Lord Denning MR.
11 *Lister v Romford Ice and Cold Storage Co* [1957] 1 All ER 125 at 143, [1957] AC 555 at 594, per Lord Tucker.
12 See especially *Staffordshire Area Health Authority v South Staffordshire Waterworks Co* [1978] 3 All ER 769, [1978] 1 WLR 1387.
13 It is not entirely clear why English law took this theoretical stance. Perhaps it was because the primary remedy for any breach of contract is damages, not specific performance (see below, Ch 17); it is always possible to make someone pay damages for not doing the impossible even though one cannot order him specifically to do so.

depends on what sort of promise is involved, we deal in turn with three cases: (i) promises to pay for things supplied or services rendered; (ii) promises to act in a particular way; and (iii) warranties – promises about a particular state of affairs.

(i) Promises to pay for goods supplied or services rendered

Promises in this class are (in the absence of contrary agreement) treated starkly and simply; they are conditional on performance of the other party's obligation in full, and on that alone.

That they are conditional on full performance is superficially obvious. A builder who contracts to do certain alterations to my house for a given sum clearly cannot claim the agreed payment unless and until he finishes the job; a seller of a quantity of goods until he has delivered all of them. Three further aspects of the rule, however, are less obvious.

First, as most contractual obligations cannot be performed unless the other party co-operates, a person who contracts to accept goods or services but then wrongfully refuses to accept them does not, even though he has acted wrongfully, have to pay the price. A buyer of goods, for instance, who refuses to accept them is therefore liable to the seller for damages (if the latter has suffered any) but not for the price.[14]

Secondly, while *full* performance of contractual obligations is a necessary condition of the right to be paid the price, *perfect* performance is not. So a builder who completes a job, but does it very badly, can claim the price of his work (subject of course to his own liability in damages for breach of contract);[15] whereas the builder who does only part of the job, but does it perfectly, cannot claim payment at all. As may be imagined, however, the distinction between full but bad performance and partial but good performance is narrow; particularly as the courts have on occasion confused the issue still further by treating some kinds of very defective performance as so drastically bad as not to amount to performance at all.[16]

Thirdly, the rule that contractual payment is conditional on full performance is varyingly mitigated by the possibility of recovery for part performance based on the principles of unjustified enrichment. Where services are rendered, the rule is, as we have seen in Ch 10, harsh; a person who, in breach of contract, fails to render services in full has no claim at all for the services he has rendered. This accentuates the difference between partial performance and full but defective performance; since it means that, whereas the builder who completes the job but does so badly obtains the price for the work subject to damages for breach of contract, the builder who does only

---

14   *R V Ward Ltd v Bignall* [1967] 1 QB 534, [1967] 2 All ER 449.
15   *Hoenig v Isaacs* [1952] 2 All ER 176, [1952] TLR 1360.
16   *Vigers v Cook* [1919] 2 KB 475, 88 LJKB 1132, is a grisly example.

part of the job recovers nothing at all. The obligation to pay for goods
supplied, by contrast, is differently treated. Here there is no problem of
partial performance, because an action does lie in unjustified
enrichment for a part consignment of goods sold and delivered, even
where the seller is in breach of contract. Unfortunately, sales of goods
raise a quite separate problem; that amounts to performance of a
contract for the sale of goods, so that the seller can claim the price
rather than merely damages for non-acceptance? Generally, as we have
said, the goods must have been actually accepted; thus a buyer who
rejects them, albeit wrongfully, is not liable for their price. But there
are exceptions. If ownership in goods has already passed, the seller by
merely tendering them performs all this obligations; hence here he can
claim the price even though the buyer refuses to accept them.[17] Again,
once the *risk* of loss of goods has passed to the buyer, the latter must
pay the price without more if the goods are subsequently destroyed.
This is seen particularly clearly where goods are sold on 'CIF' terms;
here the seller's obligation is simply to send the buyer shipping
documents relating to goods afloat, and once he has done that,
whatever happens to the goods themselves is the buyer's affair alone.[18]

Performance of contractual obligations is not only a *necessary*
condition of the right to be paid; it is also, as we said, *sufficient*. This is
very relevant in the few cases where one party can perform his contract
with the other without the other's co-operation, since it means that,
once having ordered a service and promised to pay for it, a person may
remain liable to pay for it even though later he changed his mind and
countermanded the order. His liability in these cases is not limited to
paying damages to the other party. Thus in *White & Carter (Councils)
Ltd v Macgregor*[19] the defendants ordered from the plaintiffs extensive
poster advertising of their business, but shortly after countermanded
the order. The plaintiffs nevertheless went ahead and executed the
commission; having done so, they were held able to claim the full price.
Admittedly the House of Lords, seeing that the result was a little
bizarre, said that only a contractor with a 'legitimate interest' could
thus claim the price of unwanted services; but if (apparently) there was
such an interest in *White & Carter*, it is difficult to see where there would
not be.

(ii) Promises to act in a certain way
We now turn from promises to pay for performance, to promises to
perform as such. In what way are those promises conditional? To

17 Sale of Goods Act 1979, s 49(1).
18 See, eg, *Manbré Saccharine Co Ltd v Corn Products Co Ltd* [1919] 1 KB 198, 88
    LJKB 402.
19 [1962] AC 413, [1961] 3 All ER 1178. But if later cases such as *Clea Shipping Corp v
    Bulk Oil International Ltd, The Alaskan Trader* [1984] 1 All ER 129.

begin with, a contract itself may expressly or impliedly make one party's obligation depend on a particular event; for instance, where a contract to sell a house is expressed to be 'subject to satisfactory survey'. Such cases of express conditions aside, however, a much more important question is when the act or omission of one party to a contract can excuse the other party from his own duty to perform. (Normally, this involves the question when a breach of contract by one party excuses the other; but it need not. A film star's prolonged illness may excuse an impresario's termination of her employment just as much as her abandoning the set.)[20]

Once again, we start with the terms of the contract. If it expressly makes A's obligation conditional on some performance by B, that is an end of the matter. This often so; to take one of countless examples, a charterparty of a ship will often provide that if the charterer fails to pay hire on time the owner's obligation to keep the vessel at his disposal ceases.[1] (Statute, of course, may limit on social grounds the right of one party to shrug off his obligations merely on the ground of some minor or unavoidable act by the other party. A landlord, for instance, cannot validly stipulate for a right to cancel a lease simply because of some minor breach by the tenant; he must first give the tenant a chance to remedy the breach, if possible.)[2] Conversely, contract may prevent a factor excusing a party to the contract from his obligations even though that factor normally would do so; a contract of sale, for instance, may provide that substandard goods (which the seller is normally entitled to reject) are to be accepted and the price instead reduced accordingly.

The difficulty comes in cases where the contract says nothing about what factors may excuse one party from the obligations to perform; and here, fashions of interpretation have varied. Older cases took a very abstract approach. Each side's obligations under a contract were divided into a number of terms, and each term categorised as one whose fulfilment either was, or was not, essential to the other party's obligation. (Such terms were sometimes characterised, for brevity's sake, as 'conditions' and 'warranties' respectively). This approach is well illustrated in the sale of goods, where it still remains in force because the law was codified by statute as early as 1893. Here, in the absence of contrary intent, goods not conforming to contract specification or not up

---

20 *Poussard v Spiers & Pond* (1876) 1 QBD 410, 45 LJQB 621. Statute may, of course, on social grounds prevent termination of a contract for reasons that are not a party's fault. A hire-purchase agreement, for instance, may not be terminated merely because the hirer dies – see the Consumer Credit Act 1974, s 86.

1 *Scandinavian Trading Tanker Co AB v Flota Petrolera Ecuatoriana, The Scaptrade* [1983] 2 All ER 763, [1983] 3 WLR 203, decided that, if that was what the contract said, there was nothing the courts could do about it.

2 Law of Property Act 1925, s 146.

to standard (not of 'merchantable quality') can be rejected however small their shortcomings, for any reason or no reason.[3]

More recently, however, in contracts governed by common law rather than codified by statute, courts have said that one party's obligation to perform is conditional simply on the other party's reasonable performance *as a whole* of his obligations; only if the performance is so seriously defective as to deprive the other party of substantially the whole of the benefit he contemplated getting from the contract, does it justify his refusing to perform his own obligations. So, to take a notorious example, any charterparty obliges the vessel owner to provide a 'seaworthy' vessel; neverthless, not every footling example of unseaworthiness will justify the charterer in throwing up the charter[4] (though it will, of course, give rise to a claim for damages).

This approach, which is now widely accepted,[5] seems at first sight obviously more sensible. Yet still more recently the true complexity of the question has been realised. Contracts vary; and in certain kinds of commercial transaction, where instant decisions have to be made in the absence of detailed information, then clear-cut rules, even arbitrary ones, as to what breaches will allow the other party to withdraw are rather more appropriate. As a result, the House of Lords has recently become more willing in cases of this kind to infer an intent that some kinds of stipulations are to be true conditions of the other party's liability, such that any breach of them at all will allow him to throw up the contract.[6]

With acts not amounting to breaches of contract but nevertheless allowing obligations to be escaped (as in the example given earlier of the sick film star), the test has apparently always been that now generally applied to other stipulations; was the other party deprived of a substantial part of the benefit of the contract?[7]

THE NEED FOR REPUDIATION. Of course, even assuming A's obligation to perform *is* conditional on B's own performance, B's own failure to perform does not mean that A has to take advantage of it in order to repudiate his own obligations; A may want merely to claim damages (if any) for what B has done, but beyond that to perform his own side of the contract in the normal way, and keep both parties' obligations alive. This matters. Assume B delivers the first of two instalments of

---

3 See Sale of Goods Act 1979, ss 10–14; and see *Re Moore & Co & Landauer & Co* [1921] 2 KB 519, 90 LJKB 731 for a drastic example.

4 *Hong Kong Fir Shipping Co Ltd v Kawasaki Kisen Kaisha Ltd* [1962] 2 QB 26, [1962] 1 All ER 474.

5 *Reardon-Smith Lines Ltd v Hansen-Tangen* [1976] 3 All ER 570, [1976] 1 WLR 989 is a good example. See too *Cehave NV v Bremer Handelsgesellschaft mbH, The Hansa Nord* [1976] QB 44, [1975] 3 All ER 739.

6 *Bunge Corpn v Tradax SA* [1981] 2 All ER 513, [1981] 1 WLR 711.

7 See, eg, *Poussard v Spiers & Pond* (1876) 1 QBD 410, 45 LJQB 621.

coal to A, and it is so defective as to allow A to reject it and throw up his future obligations. If A does so, he loses the right to demand the second instalment (since B's obligation to deliver it is in turn dependent on A's readiness to accept it); but if A waives his right to be accused from his own obligations, and accepts the first instalment, then B's obligation to deliver the second instalment remains in force. (There is some doubt as to whether the rule we have just described applies to a contract of employment. If it does, it means that an employer, even when dismissed in breach of contract, is still able to claim benefits coming to him as 'employee', such as redundancy payments, since he need not accept his dismissal as putting an end to his own obligations as employee. It is submitted that the better authority here, however, is that employment contracts are here no different from other contracts.)[8]

However, the matter may be more complicated. A breach of contract by B may not only release A from his own obligations, but give him for practical reasons no choice in the matter. If an electrician, while rewiring a house, carelessly burns it down, there is nothing the owner of the house can do to keep the contract alive; the electrician's own obligation to continue with the job is conditional on there being still a house to re-wire – which there is not.

Whether a person has exercised his right to be released from his own obligations owing to the other party's breach is a question of fact; though the courts are slow to say he has waived his right until he knows of the breach and has had some chance to make a decision. With sales of goods, the rule is more finely developed: acceptance of the goods after having had the opportunity to inspect them and find out that one could reject them, suffices.[9]

FURTHER GENERAL POINTS ON CONDITIONAL OBLIGATIONS. It is generally the coming into effect of future obligations, not the continuation of those already in effect, that is conditional on the behaviour of the other party to the contract. This is an obscure expression; an example will clarify it. If an employee is dismissed, his obligation to turn up every day and report for work no longer applies: it is an obligation arising from day to day, which ceases to arise on dismissal. But the employee's duty not to reveal his employer's trade secrets continues in effect; it arose at the beginning of his employment and the fact that other obligations cease to arise has no effect on it.[10]

Further, a note on conditions and reasonableness. If, on the interpretation of a contract, A's obligations are truly conditional on

8   *Hill v CA Parsons & Co Ltd* [1972] Ch 305 at 313–314, [1971] 3 All ER 1345 at
    1349–1350, per Lord Denning MR; *Thomas Marshall (Export) Ltd v Guinle* [1979]
    Ch 227 at 239–240, [1978] 3 All ER 193 at 202, per Megarry V–C.
9   Sale of Goods Act 1979, ss 34(1), 35.
10 *Thomas Marshall (Export) Ltd v Guinle* [1979] Ch 227, [1978] 3 All ER 193.

proper performance by B, A's right to rely on that is unconstrained. Thus a buyer may reject goods not corresponding to contract even though in fact the goods tendered were just as good as if they did comply with it for the seller's purposes, and even though the real reason for rejection was that the price had fallen;[11] again, it does not even matter whether, at the time performance was rejected, the person rejecting it did not know of the factor that justified him in doing so. An employer who dismisses an employee ostensibly from malice but later discovers the employee had been stealing anyway, commits no breach of contract.[12]

ANTICIPATORY BREACH. This is an odd doctrine, where by if a breach of contraci would entitle the other party to refuse to perform, it is wrongful not only to commit that breach, but also to express an intention to do so. So in *Hochster v De La Tour,*[13] where A promised to employ B in the future and then said he had changed his mind before the date set for the start of employment, B recovered damages immediately without waiting to see whether A did employ him after all when the time came. This is, to say the least, odd. A possible justification is that, where A prospectively refuses to abide by his side of a contract, B must be allowed forthwith to consider himself released as well, and one way to do this is to say that A's refusal is itself a breach of contract. But such a device is clumsy. The same result could be achieved more neatly and satisfactorily by saying that a statement of intent not to abide by a contract in future was not itself a breach of that contract but nevertheless did entitle the other party, if he is so wished, to refused to perform.

The victim of an 'anticipatory breach' can, if he wishes, ignore the statement of intent not to perform.[14] If he does, the parties are in the same position they would have been in had the offending statement of intent never been made.

(iii) Promises that something is the case
In general, promises of this sort are not conditional on performance by the other party at all. Thus, it is submitted, a customer who had refused to pay for a car sold to him would retain the right to sue the seller for damage suffered because the car was defective, despite his own breach of a fundamental term of the contract.

---

11 Eg *Bowes v Shand* (1877) 2 App Cas 455, 46 LJQB 561; *Re Moore* [1921] 2 KB 519, 90 LJKB 731. The results can be so drastic that courts are astute to construe rights to reject performance as limited to where there is reasonable ground to do so. See, eg, *The Hansa Nord* [1976] QB 44, [1975] 3 All ER 739.
12 Cf *Maredelanto Compania Naviera SA v Bergbau–Handel GmbH, The Milhalis Angelos* [1971] 1 QB 164, [1970] 3 All ER 125.
13 (1853) 2 E & B 678, 22 LJQB 455.
14 *White & Carter (Councils) Ltd v Macgregor* [1962] AC 413, [1961] 3 All ER 1178 illustrates this point graphically.

(d) CONTROL OF CONTRACTUAL TERMS: UNEQUAL EXCHANGES

Depending on (i) how seriously it regards the individual's right to decide what is good for him; and (ii) how far it is prepared to let astuteness and acute commercial pressure prevail as commercial weapons, it is a function of the State, to at least some degree, to control unequal bargains. Now, English law starts out from what looks like uncompromising freedom of contract. In general, no bargain is struck down *merely* because it is unequal (though there are exceptions[15]); instead, something more, some over-reaching, unconscionable activity, or improper pressure, is necessary. In practice, however, this distinction is not a very significant one, since inequality may itself compellingly show overreaching or some other factor that *does* affect obligation. Freedom of contract, in other words, is a method of approach, not a legal result.

What will, therefore, negative promissory obligation is unjustifiable influence or pressure. Unjustifiability is of course necessary: no-one impugns the sale of the assets of a near-insolvent company at a knock-down price, since here the commercial pressure exercised by the buyer, while effective, is justified. Thus we are left with the legal value judgment (as appeared in the last chapter on equivalent matters in unjustified enrichment); what level of coercion, or use of superior intelligence, is tolerated as a means of inducing promises?

We start predictably. Unlawful pressure, threats of violence or damage to property, or of torts or breaches of contract, are unjustified and negative promissory liability in the same way, and to the same extent, as they ground an unjustified enrichment claim. After all, the law can hardly condone unlawful pressure by enforcing contracts induced by the use of it.[16] But, as might be expected, impermissible pressure goes beyond the unlawful, largely because of the equitable doctrine of 'undue influence'. This includes abuse of a practically dominant position. If I threaten to institute serious criminal proceedings against you, or a relative of yours, I cannot enforce the promise you make to induce me not to do so.[17] The right to prosecute does not exist as a lever to induce promises. Similarly, enforcement of a promise resulting from blackmail (such as a threat to reveal, without good reason, a promisor's criminal past) would, in the unlikely event of action being brought on it, be refused.

---

15 Eg the Consumer Credit Act 1974 allows any credit transaction to be reopened if the rate of interest is 'grossly extortionate' – see s 137.

16 See, however, the decision of the Privy Council in *Pao On v Lau Yiu Long* [1980] AC 614, [1979] 3 All ER 65. Here Lord Scarman said, extraordinarily, that a threat to break a contract was commercial pressure, and that those who took a 'commercial' decision to give in to it could not complain, unless their 'will' was 'overborne'. This excursus into the metaphysics of voluntariness is difficult to understand; perhaps the best interpretation of it is that, by a suitably unequivocal act, the right to avoid a contract for economic duress may be waived.

17 *Williams v Bayley* (1866) LR 1 HL 200, 35 LJ Ch 717.

Certain forms of pressure are justified in some respects, but not in others. Superior financial power, for example, can be used for only some purposes. Thus a recording company, who in effect hold the power to make or break a musician's career, can presumably use that power to make him accept uncomfortably low royalties, but not to force him to accept severe restrictions on his professional life, such as whom he is allowed to work for and where he can published what he produces.[18]

So much for the controls on the use of pressure. 'Undue influence', however, also puts controls on the use of superior intelligence or astuteness – extending, that is, the idea of deceit as well as that of duress.

Thus if A can exercise considerably influence over B, for instance being his adviser in financial matters, then transactions between them which might be tainted by that relationship are not binding unless it is shown that B in turn exercised independent judgment, or at least was independently advised. Many relationships presumptively involve such control and influence so as to bring about these legal consequences. Thus promises between priest and proselyte, trustee and beneficiary, solicitor and client and parent and child may be impugned unless it is shown either that the promisor was in fact morally independent, or if he was not that he received independent advice.[19] Similarly, even in the absence of any particular relationship between promisor and promisee, if control de facto is shown, the same result applies. Indeed, this latter principle extends rather further. Gross disparities in intelligence may make the use by one party of superior astuteness unjustifiable; a small, but significant, line of cases shows transactions being upset on this basis alone.[20]

It is sometimes said, as with unjustified enrichment, that all these cases really represent one doctrine; a contract is unenforceable if the result of 'inequality of bargaining power'.[1] The suggestion is as misleading here as it is in connection with unjustified enrichment. To begin with, it does not explain the idea of justification: why, in other words, in the case of the property of the insolvent company being bought up very cheaply, the use of what can only be described as 'inequality of bargaining power' is justified and unexceptional. It is

---

18 *A Schroeder Music Publishing Co Ltd v Macaulay* [1974] 3 All ER 616 at 623 f; [1974] 1 WLR 1308 at 1315–1316, per Lord Diplock.

19 See eg *Lloyds Bank Ltd v Bundy* [1975] QB 326, [1974] 3 All ER 757; *Allcard v Skinner* (1887) 36 Ch D 145, 56 LJ Ch 1052; *Lancashire Loans Ltd v Black* [1934] 1 KB 380, 103 LJKB 129. Some of these cases concern transfers of property, but the principle is the same.

20 Eg *Fry v Lane* (1888) 40 Ch D 312, 58 LJ Ch 113. Disparity in value is also an established ground for refusing specific performance of a contract.

1 Notably by Lord Denning MR in *Lloyds Bank Ltd v Bundy* [1975] QB 326 at 329, [1974] 3 All ER 757 at 765.

difficult, moreover, to describe the misuse of an influential position such as that of spiritual adviser as involving 'inequality of bargaining power', rather than as a taking unfair advantage of another's disinclination to argue, which is rather different. In short, unless it is regarded merely as shorthand, the term 'inequality of bargaining power' tends to obfuscate rather more than it illuminates; it makes the question of when a transaction should be upset seem simple, but only at the cost of obscuring several of the vital issues.

Part II

Chapter 12

Liability through others: Concurrent liability

JOHN LOCKEY
DOWNING COLLEGE
CAMBRIDGE CB2 1DQ

1. Liability through others

The view we have expressed so far, of contractors personally signing contracts and being liable on them, tortfeasors being made to pay damages themselves for torts that they in person have committed, and the like, is convenient but over-simplified. Life is more corporate and impersonal than that. Contracts are signed, payments made and money received not by principals themselves for the most part, but by others acting (or purporting to act) on their behalf. Liability in tort means effectively liability for torts committed by someone else, such as one's employees. As a result, liability through others is a much more important part of the law than it looks at first sight.[1]

Now, assuming that one person is to be liable for what someone else has done, there are three ways to go about producing this result. The first, particularly appropriate where liability is based on fault, is personal liability pure and simple; if an employer, for instance, fails adequately to supervise his employee and the latter as a result causes damage to the plaintiff, then the employer is liable on ordinary fault principles.[2] This goes without saying, and we go no further with it. Secondly, there is attribution; in certain circumstances, the law can look at what A has done, treat B by a fiction as though he had done it, and act accordingly. The act of an agent, for instance, acting on behalf of his principal in concluding a contract, is attributed to the principal. Thirdly, and most simply, the law may take A's act and simply impose liability for it on B, without going so far as to attribute the act itself to B; an employer, for example, is liable together with his employee, for acts committed by the latter in the course of his employment, if such acts would have made the employee himself liable in tort.

---

1 Nor should it be forgotten that corporations are effectively unable themselves to sign contracts or commit torts, which means in general they can only ever act through others.

2 A neat example is *Robin Hood Flour Mills Ltd v N M Paterson & Sons Ltd, The Farrandoc* [1967] 2 Lloyds Rep 276. A similar principle appears in trusts – eg *Learoyd v Whiteley* (1887) 12 App Cas 727, 57 LJ Ch 390.

(a) VICARIOUS LIABILITY

Vicarious liability involves the third principle mentioned above, that of making one person liable for a breach of obligation committed by another. Its basis is simple; if B, while acting on A's behalf, commits a tort against C in the course of doing so, A is liable to C for that tort, even though not personally at fault. The liability is joint: C can sue either A or B, though in practice he will always sue A, since A is more likely (either because he is more financially stable, or because he is insured against liability) to meet any judgment. The justification for vicarious liability is social. Typically an employer will be liable for negligence committed by an employee against a third person; the result of this liability is that, in general, incompetence in the operation of A's business becomes what it should be: a cost of the business.

To take the requirements for vicarious liability in turn.

(i) A tort committed by B
First, the doctrine is limited to tort. For a person to be bound by a contract entered into on his behalf by another, the rather different rules of agency apply; these we deal with later on. Secondly, there must be a tort committed by B: it is not enough that, had A done what B did, A would have committed a tort. Thus an estate agent is not liable in deceit when an employer makes an innocent misstatement which the employer knows is false; the employee himself committed no tort which the employer can be vicariously liable for.[3]

(ii) Particular relationship between A and B
Only specified relationships engender vicarious liability. One is where A renders gratuitous services to B for B's benefit, as by 'ferrying' his car from X to Y.[4] But this head of liability is not very important. It applies only where A is acting purely for B's benefit and not his own; thus the House of Lords has refused to extend it to cases where A voluntarily entrusts a thing, such as a car, to B and B commits a tort in connection with it.[5] Such liability might be useful, but it is not for the courts to introduce.

Far more important is the relationship of employer and employee, when it comes to engendering vicarious liability. The chief difficulty here is distinguishing employees, for whom there is vicarious liability, from independent contractors, for whom there is (generally) not. Often straightforward (the difference between the employed van-driver and the independent haulage firm is obvious), the distinction can be enigmatic. It seems to consist not so much in the difference between

3   *Armstrong v Strain* [1952] 1 KB 232, [1952] 1 All ER 139.
4   *Ormrod v Crosville Motor Services Ltd* [1953] 2 All ER 753, [1953] 1 WLR 1120.
5   *Morgans v Launchbury* [1973] AC 127, [1972] 2 All ER 606.

being told what to do (independent contractor) and in addition being told how to do it (employee),[6] as in the matter of financial risk. An independent contractor trades – and risks – on his own account, often for instance providing his own equipment; whereas an employee does so on his employer's account.[7] In any case, despite initial attractiveness, the distinction between employee and independent contractor as generators of vicarious liability is difficult rationally to defend. Merely because an employer takes less financial risk vis-à-vis an independent contractor, this is no reason to make him take less risk in respect of what that contractor does to anyone else. Nor is the argument convincing that only an employee works for his employer's profit and therefore only he should make his employer liable; for even a non-profit-making organisation or public authority can (rightly) be vicariously liable. In short, there is much to be said for the argument that, if vicarious liability exists to ensure that anyone injured by incompetence connected (in the widest sense) with X's business is compensated by X, the precise relationship between X and the person doing the damage ought to be irrelevant. (Perhaps, however, where the employer is acting in a private, rather than a business, capacity the present rule ought to be retained. There would be something bizarre in holding the taxicab's fare liable for negligence committed by the driver, for instance, even though presumably the employer of a chauffeur ought to bear the risk of his negligence).

The rule that one cannot be liable for the acts of an independent contractor is in any case not absolute. In a few cases, the relationship of employer and independent contractor is sufficient to give rise to what is effectively an extension of vicarious liability. The most important case is that of employer's duties to their employees to ensure their safety; broadly, where the maintenance of a place of work, or the provision or maintenance of equipment, is involved, then the employer is liable for the negligence of any independent contractor engaged to do the job.[8] (Indeed, in respect of equipment there is a statutory vicarious liability on the employer for negligence even in the course of the *manufacture* of equipment.[9]) Other examples of liability for the acts of independent contractors are less significant. But they include operations on land that happen to cause damage to neighbouring occupiers, and operations on the highway. So if I carry out building works on my land

---

6   Few employers of very skilled persons, such as systems analysts or crane drivers, would be able to tell them how to do their jobs; yet the relationship is still that of employer and employee.

7   *Ready-Mixed Concrete South East v Ministry of Pensions and National Insurance* [1968] 2 QB 497, [1968] 1 All ER 433; though cf *Ferguson v John Dawson & Partners (Contractors) Ltd* [1976] 3 All ER 817, [1976] 1 WLR 1213.

8   *Wilsons & Clyde Coal Co Ltd v English* [1938] AC 57, [1937] 3 All ER 628.

9   Employers' Liability (Defective Equipment) Act 1969, s 1.

that normally would not interfere sufficiently with my neighbour to make me liable to him, but by the fault of the building contractor they do, I am liable to my neighbour.[10] Similarly, if I employ an apparently competent contractor to repair part of my property that happens to overhang the highway, apparently I am liable to anyone injured as a result of his negligence.[11]

(iii) Tort committed in the course of the relationship

Assuming a given relationship gives rise to vicarious liability, it does so only in respect of acts done in the course of that relationship; more particularly, an employer is liable only for acts done 'in the course of employment.' This means two things. First, the opportunity for the employee to commit the tort must result from the fact of his employment;[12] secondly, the tort must have something to do with what the employee is employed to do. Both must be satisfied for vicarious liability to arise. For instance, a garage is liable to its customer if his car, having been left there, is stolen by the nightwatchman employed to guard it; but not if it is casually stolen by the petrol pump attendant.[13] In the latter case the opportunity arises from the employment but the tort has nothing to do with it. Of course, precisely what an employee is employed to do can be minutely and casuistically analysed. A driver forbidden to pick up passengers who nevertheless does so, causes an accident and injures an outsider as well as the passenger makes his employer liable to the first but not the second; he was employed to drive, but not to carry passengers.[14] Except in so far as it defines what a person is employed to do, however, the mere fact that an employer has forbidden something does not of itself preclude vicarious liability.[15]

At first sight surprisingly, but in fact not illogically, there can be vicarious liability for deliberate wrongdoing, such as theft or assault, as much as for negligence. Of course, it will be more difficult to argue such wrongdoing is within the course of employment; but there is no reason why (to take the facts of the leading case) a solicitor should not be liable if his clerk, employed to oversee his clients' affairs, instead takes the opportunity to defraud one of them.[16]

10   See *Matania v National Provincial Bank Ltd and The Elevenist Syndicate* [1936] 2 All ER 633, 106 LJKB 113.

11   *Pickard v Smith* (1861) 10 CBNS 470, 4 LT 470.

12   We refer to 'employment' for the sake of argument. The same principle applies in cases where one is vicariously liable for the fault of those whom one does not employ.

13   Cf *Morris v C W Martin & Son Ltd* [1966] 1 QB 716, [1965] 2 All ER 725.

14   Cf *Twine v Bean's Express Ltd* (1946) 175 LT 131, 62 TLR 458, and *Rose v Plenty* [1976] 1 All ER 97, [1976] 1 WLR 141.

15   *Limpus v London General Omnibus Co* (1862) 1 H & C 526.

16   *Lloyd v Grace Smith & Co* [1912] AC 716, 81 LJKB 1140; cf *Morris v C W Martin & Son Ltd* [1966] 1 QB 716, [1965] 2 All ER 725.

(b) THE THEORY OF VICARIOUS LIABILITY

The thinking behind vicarious liability as just described, is that if an employee commits a tort in the course of his employment, the employer is liable for it; the duty, and the tort, is the employee's, the liability is shared between employer and employee. Now, another way to achieve the same result would be to shift the emphasis; to forget the wrong of the employee and put the employer under a *personal* duty to see that care is taken, theft avoided, and so on. Often in practice this will make no difference; if I can sue the employer of a bricklayer who drops a brick on me, I am not concerned whether the bricklayer's liability is attributed to the employer, or whether the employer is liable for his own breach of duty. But there would be advantages in the theory of a personal duty. First, a higher duty could be placed on employer than on employee, with consequential benefits in loss distribution; indeed, the employer could be made liable on occasion even if the employee were not[17] – something presently impossible. Secondly, by concentrating on the personal duty of the employer one could divert attention from the precise relationship between employer and employee and more easily expand the class of cases where there was liability for the acts of independent contractors, which it has already been suggested would be desirable. Indeed, it is interesting to note that the liability of an employer to his employees, which includes liability for the acts of independent contractors, is predicated on a personal duty owed by the employer himself.

(c) LIABILITY FOR OTHERS IN NON-TORTIOUS OBLIGATIONS

When we turn from tortious to non-tortious obligations, the theory appropriate to tort, that an employer is liable for a tort committed by his employee, ceases to apply. Instead two other means are available to make one person liable for acts of another. One is agency, dealt with below. The other is the concept of a personal duty to see that care is taken, which is here the rule rather than (as in tort) the exception. As a result, where a duty to take care arises out of contract, there is liability for the fault of independent contractors. If A, a builder, in altering B's house employs C, an independent plasterer, he is liable for any negligence of C in carrying out the job.[18] Again, the contractual duty of a carrier by sea, laid down by art III of the Hague Rules appended to the Carriage of Goods by Sea Act 1971, to show 'due diligence' to provide a seaworthy ship, comports liability for the fault of independent contractors as well as servants.[19] A similar principle applies, moreover,

---

17 Cf *Staveley Iron and Chemical Co Ltd v Jones* [1956] AC 627, [1956] 1 All ER 403.
18 Cf *Francis v Cockrell* (1870) LR 5 QB 501, 10 B & S 950; *Stewart v Reavell's Garage* [1952] 2 QB 545, [1952] 1 All ER 1191.
19 *Riverstone Meat Co Pty Ltd v Lancashire Shipping Co Ltd* [1961] AC 807, [1961] 1 All ER 495.

to liability consensual but not contractual, such as that of a bailee; so, for instance, a haulier who warehouses goods and hires a security firm to guard them is liable when the latter does not do so properly.[20]

(d) AGENCY

Agency involves attribution of one person's act to another. If P (the principal) authorises A (the agent) to do an act in his name, the act is treated as though it were P's. Superficially similar to vicarious liability, in that it involves making one person liable for what someone else has done, agency is in fact different in at least five ways. The theory is different; agency involves attribution of A's acts, not merely his liability, to P. Further, agency as a doctrine is justified as a matter of convenience, not social policy. It does not involve concurrent liability; typically, if A contracts on behalf of P, P is liable whereas A is not. An independent contractor may be an agent, even though he cannot normally engender vicarious liability. And agency in general may confer rights as well as imposing duties on the principal.

Further, agency, unlike vicarious liability, applies to all sorts of legal liability, and indeed to all legal acts. Thus not only is P bound by a contract concluded by A on his behalf; if he authorises A to receive money in his name, the money once paid to A is deemed to have been paid to him; and even torts can be committed through an agent. Thus if A authorises B, his employee, to tell deliberate lies on his behalf he will be liable in deceit to those duped both vicariously and by the rules of the agency. But liability in tort for the acts of an agent is not very significant, because agency is prima facie limited to authorised acts, and few actually authorise others to commit torts on their behalf (whereas, as we have seen, unauthorised acts may clearly engender vicarious liability). As a result the law of agency is largely concerned with contractual and similar liability and related matters.

Authority in agency

The rules of agency apply where P *authorised* A to act in his name. The simplest case is where P's authority is expressed or plainly implied (as an example of the latter, a small company, by appointing a managing director, impliedly authorises him to guarantee on its behalf the debts of an associated company).[1] Difficulties only arise where some element is lacking; where A deals with a third party, T, *without* P's authority but in his name, or where A deals with T in his *own* name but without P's authority.

---

20   *British Road Services Ltd v Arthur V Crutchley & Co Ltd* [1968] 1 All ER 811, [1968] 1 Lloyd's Rep 271.
  1   *Hely-Hutchinson v Brayhead Ltd* [1968] 1 QB 549, [1967] 3 All ER 70.

A. WHERE A ACTS WITHOUT AUTHORITY. First, is P bound by what A has done? Prima facie the answer is no. However, T, the person with whom A dealt, may be able to invoke the doctrine of 'ostensible authority'. By this, if P has in any way made T believe that A has authority to act on his behalf, he is bound by A's act as though A did have authority. Often regarded as an aspect of the technical rule of estoppel, that a person making a representation on which someone else relies to his detriment cannot in subsequent legal proceedings be heard to deny that representation (the representation in question being that A has authority from P), the rule of 'ostensible authority' is better justified on broader grounds; that is, that a person should not in legal proceedings be able to take advantage of a mistake on the part of another which, however innocently, he himself is responsible for.[2] Examples of ostensible authority are many. To take just one, a company appointing a company secretary impliedly represents that he has authority to do all the things that a company secretary normally does; his authority may actually be more limited, but third parties dealing with him are not bound by those limits unless they know of them.[3]

Ostensible authority relies on P being responsible for making T believe A has his authority. Occasionally, however, P is bound even though A does not have his authority and he has not implied that he has. For instance, P may have benefited from A's action; thus where A borrows money from T on P's behalf and uses it to pay off debts owed by P to X, T can sue P for the money lent.[4] Strictly speaking, the basis of T's claim is not agency but the doctrine of subrogation mentioned in Ch 16; nevertheless in effect an unauthorised transaction is enforced against P. Again, a person may be bound by operation of law by what someone else has done whether he agrees to be or not. For example, by s 56 of the Consumer Credit Act 1974 a dealer in goods has authority to commit a person lending to the purchaser of those goods to certain obligations in respect of them despite any contrary agreement.

Even where A deals with T with no authority at all from P, so that T has no remedy against P, T is not completely without redress; there is a very strong implication that, where A contracts on behalf of P, he warrants that he does have authority from A. If he does not, he is in breach of that warranty, and the result of this is that prima facie T has the same remedy against him that he would have had against P.[5]

So much for whether P is bound by transactions entered into in his name without his authority; in general he is not. On the other hand, he

2 Compare the rule in contract that even an innocent misrepresentation disables the misrepresentor from enforcing the contract obtained thereby.
3 *Panorama Developments Guildford Ltd v Fidelis Furnishing Fabrics Ltd* [1971] 2 QB 711, [1971] 3 All ER 16.
4 See, eg, *Bannatyne v MacIver* [1906] 1 KB 103, 75 LJKB 120, below, Ch 16.
5 *Collen v Wright* (1857) 8 E & B 647, 27 LJQB 215.

can enforce them if he wishes, provided they were undertaken explicitly on his behalf, if he adopts ('ratifies') them within a reasonable time.[6] Of course, having ratified them he is also bound by them in the normal way; he cannot take the benefit of a contract entered into in his name without accepting the burden. In fact this situation is very like the case where X contracts with Y thinking that Y is Z; X's mistake means that he is not bound by the contract unless he agrees to be, but he can nevertheless ratify the contract and enforce it in the normal way, provided he accepts its burdens.[7]

B. WHERE A ACTS IN HIS OWN NAME AND NOT IN P'S. If A deals with T in his name and not in P's, one might have thought that, even though A acted with P's authority, the contract could only be with A and not with P. Not so, however: by the doctrine of the 'undisclosed principal' P can both enforce and be sued on any obligation created by A. Even though T thought he was dealing simply with A, effectively both P and T have an option to enforce the contract as though it were made in P's name. (T, however, since he thought he was contracting with A, may alternatively sue him on the contract).

This seems odd at first. English law so emphasises personality generally in contracts as to vitiate promissory obligation where the promisor did not know who the promisee was; why the laxer attitude here? The answer appears to be pragmatic; the 'undisclosed principal' rule is not in fact unfair.

It is not unfair to P: he gets what he bargained for, since he authorised the transaction in the first place. The fact that T thought he was dealing with A is hardly reason to prevent him suing P.

Nor, in practice, is it unfair to T to allow P to sue him. True, it seems hard, since he thought he was contracting with A; but this is deceptive. Had A not contracted with P's authority, he nevertheless could have *assigned* to P the benefit of any obligation undertaken by T; in that case T could not have complained of being sued by P. Now, allowing an undisclosed principal to sue merely short-circuits this process; in effect, provided A contracted with P's authority in the first place the need for actual assignment is dispensed with. Such an explanation of why the undisclosed principal ought to be allowed to sue explains two peculiar rules applying to him. First, just as (as pointed out in Ch 16, below) the assignee of the benefit of an obligation takes 'subject to equities', an undisclosed principal cannot obtain any better rights than his agent had. Thus if T agrees to pay £100 at a time when A owes T £30, P as A's undisclosed principal cannot sue T for more than the balance of £70.[8] Secondly, just as a contractual obligation cannot be assigned if

---

6   *Keighley Maxsted & Co v Durant* [1901] AC 240, 70 LJKB 662.
7   Cf *Mackie v European Assurance Co* (1869) 21 LT 102, 17 WR 987.
8   *Rabone v Williams* (1785) 7 TR 360n.

the identity of the promisee is vital to it, so also in such cases the doctrine of the undisclosed principal ousted. So if a theatre owner refuses to admit me I cannot send a friend to buy a ticket for me and then claim entry as an undisclosed principal.[9] However, just as most contractual rights are assumed to be assignable, so also the doctrine of the undisclosed principal is presumed not to be ousted unless a contrary intention is clear.[10]

A person is liable as an 'undisclosed principal' only where he has given *actual* authority; subject, however, to one anomalous and indefensible exception. Where P appoints A his agent for some general purpose, but specifically limits his authority in some respect (for example, if a buyer for a chain store is told to buy no item costing over £100 without specific permission) P nevertheless remains liable if A exceds that specific limit even if A deals with T in his own name.[11] This is very peculiar; P neither authorised the contract nor led T to think he had; as a result it is not particularly just to hold that P is bound by it. The argument that, by analogy with vicarious liability, which allows an employer to be liable for forbidden torts committed in the general course of employment, the law of agency should make a principal liable for forbidden *contracts* entered into in the course of employment, is entirely unconvincing. The reason for extending vicarious liability to forbidden acts – that those involuntarily injured by incompetence in the running of a business ought to be compensated by that business – simply does not apply to contracts voluntarily entered into by third parties.

(e) ACTS ON BEHALF OF COMPANIES

Companies litigate, act, oblige and are obliged; yet in the nature of things, being abstract entities, they cannot do the acts, such as signing documents or driving a car, that are normally necessary to trigger obligations. In practice there is not much of a paradox here. In general vicarious liability and agency fill the gap well; contracts are signed by agents of companies on their behalf, their lorries driven (often badly) by their employees. So normally references to a company's obligations mean obligations made or broken through others. But this is not always so. Certain wrongs can be committed by companies as such; negligent omission, for example, or passive breach of contract. Much more importantly, however, some liabilities cannot be incurred vicariously. A carrier by sea, for example, is liable for losses caused by

---

9   *Said v Butt* [1920] 3 KB 497, 90 LJKB 239, (though cf *Dyster v Randall* [1926] Ch 932).
10 Most instructive is *Fred Drughorn Ltd v Rederiaktiebolaget Transatlantic* [1919] AC 203, 88 LJKB 233.
11 *Watteau v Fenwick* [1893] 1 QB 346, 67 LT 831.

fire on board only if he himself was negligent: his servants' fault will not do.[12] Other obligations depend on something being done that cannot be done through an agent; thus a business tenant can, under the Landlord and Tenant Act 1954, demand a renewal of his lease at a market rent only if he himself 'intends' to use the premises in a certain way. The law could have said that companies were simply unable to do things requiring this sort of personal rather than vicarious action; but it did not. Instead, the rule is that acts (and negligence) of very senior management in a company done on its behalf are treated as the acts of the company itself and not simply acts of servants and agents done in its name.[13] This useful fiction, vitally separate in theory from agency and vicarious liability, is in fact a sort of hybrid between the two. As with agency, it involves the fiction that an act of A was 'really' was done by B, whereas in fact it clearly was not; as in vicarious liability, on the other hand, it seems to make no difference whether the act of the senior management concerned was forbidden, or even criminal.

2. Concurrent obligations

It goes without saying that more than one person can be liable on an obligation, or cause loss by breach of one. A and B together can contract to pay C £100; two drivers can together negligently cause an accident killing a pedestrian; two trustees can be concurrently liable for one breach of trust. In all these cases, subject to not very significant exceptions,[14] liability is *solidary*; each obligor is liable for all the sum promised or damage caused, and, having paid the sum or damages, can sue anyone else liable for contribution of the proportion that the latter ought to have paid.[15] With obligations in tort, where solidary liability is perhaps most significant, the result is straightforward and just; the accident victim can sue anyone responsible in any way for the accident, who will be liable in full and then must himself (if he can) establish liability to contribute on behalf of someone else.

TYPES OF CONCURRENT OBLIGATION

English law recognises two kinds of concurrent obligation. Concurrent contractual obligation, such as a promise by A and B to pay £100, can

---

12   Merchant Shipping Act 1894, s 502; Hague Rules, Art IV(2) (b) (in Schedule to Carriage of Goods by Sea Act 1971).
13   See, eg, *Lennards Carrying Co Ltd v Asiatic Petroleum Co Ltd* [1915] AC 705, 84 LJKB 1281; *Bolton Engineering Co Ltd v Graham & Sons Ltd* [1957] 1 QB 159, [1956] 3 All ER 624.
14   Notably collisions at sea governed by the Maritime Conventions Act 1911.
15   See Civil Liability (Contribution) Act 1978, s 1.

be *joint* or *joint and several*; the distinction being the intriguingly scholastic one whether the parties intended one obligation to pay £100 to bind both A and B, or two separate obligations, one binding each of them, but so that C is not to recover more than £100 in total. Similarly, wrongdoers may be liable *jointly*, with both being responsible for a single event causing damage; or *severally*, where both contribute to the same damage but not through a common event. Examples of joint wrongdoers are two trustees held liable for a single breach of trust because both participated in it; an employer vicariously liable for his employee's tort; or publisher and printer of a particular libel. By contrast, two drivers independently (and negligently) colliding with a third at the same moment are several wrongdoers.[16]

The distinction between these two sorts of concurrent liability does no credit to the law, since there is no rational ground for applying different rules to concurrent obligors in these varying situations. The law recognises this, and the differences between different sorts of concurrent obligors are diminishing. The only one that matters for our purposes[17] concerns extinction of liability. In the case of all concurrent contractors, and of joint tortfeasors (but not several tortfeasors or anyone concurrently liable for breach of trust) release of one obligor releases all the others automatically. As a result, a person owed £100 by A and B jointly who releases A in exchange for £50 cannot then sue B for anything. This rule, serving only to snare unwary creditors, is justifiable only on the rarefied argument that a joint obligation is, in some metaphysical sense, indivisible, and any release of it must therefore ipso factor release all those liable on it.[18]

Standing alone, the rule just mentioned would make life intolerable for those negotiating settlements with one of a number of obligors, since the essence of settlement is that it involves the cancellation of an obligation in exchange for some sort of payment. It is therefore palliated by a complementary rule, that although a *release* of one joint obligors releases all, a covenant not to sue him does not.[19] This distinction is in fact insubstantial; at least to a layman, the difference between releasing one's debtor and promising not to sue him can only be described as bewildering. However, the very insubstantiality of the difference gives the courts an opportunity to do substantial justice by inclining to construe settlements as covenants to sue rather than

16 See *The Koursk* [1924] P 140, 93 LJP 72.
17 An earlier difference, that judgment recovered against one joint obligor discharged the others even if (owing, say, to insolvency) it was not satisfied, has been abolished by statute: see now Civil Liability (Contribution) Act 1978, s 3.
18 Logic suggests that this rule should not apply to joint and several contractors, who are not bound by one single obligation. One can only answer that the law is here not logical.
19 *Hutton v Eyre* (1815) 6 Taunt 289, 1 March 603.

releases, especially where the creditor clearly intends not to forego any rights he may have against the others who are concurrently liable to him.[20]

20   *Solly v Forbes* (1820) 2 Brod & Bing 38, 4 Moore CP 448.

Chapter 13

Factors negativing obligation

This chapter deals with a number of different factors, in themselves rather disparate, that nevertheless have in common the fact that they may negative an obligation that would otherwise exist; namely mistake, duress, necessity, impossibility, illegality and general considerations of public policy.

1. Mistake

Not surprisingly, mistake is important as a negativing factor mainly where promissory obligation is involved. Promises claim their title to oblige, if at all, by consent; but the argument from consent is that much weaker if the person sought to be bound acted under a mistake. Now, English law has no very coherent theory of when a mistaken promisor can invoke his mistake in order to escape liability, since the growth of this part of the law has been pragmatic rather than planned; nevertheless, general principles can be teased out of the law more straightforwardly than it might seem.

(a) MISTAKE INDUCED BY THE PROMISEE

We start with perhaps the simplest way mistake can affect obligation. A promisee who himself *induces* the promisor's mistake by some misrepresentation cannot enforce the promise (unless the promisor, having found out the true facts, elects to be bound). This is normally expressed as the proposition that misrepresentation is a ground to annul a promise in equity. It does not matter how innocently the promisee acted, or whether he knew what he said was not true; it is sufficient that he was responsible for the mistake for the law to provide that he, if anyone, should suffer. So a seller of a car who persuades another to agree to buy it by misrepresenting it, however innocently, as a 1980 model when it is not, cannot enforce the contract. A fortiori, of course, if he deliberately deceived the buyer. Misrepresentation, moreover, in this context may include a half-truth;[1] this is important,

---

1   This is the best explanation of *Sowler v Potter* [1940] 1 KB 271, [1939] 4 All ER 478.

given the fact that at least in some cases a person is not prevented from enforcing a contract merely because he acquiesced in the promisor's mistake, provided he did not actually induce it.

It is sometimes said that misrepresentation, at least as to peripheral matters such as the age of a car, make a contract merely voidable – that is, valid until avoided by the representee. To a limited extent this is true; in a contract of sale, for instance, property in goods passes even though the contract was induced by misrepresentation, until the misrepresentee takes steps to annul the transfer.[2] But with regard to promissory liability, misrepresentation avoids a contract from the start; it is always a defence to an action on a contract that the plaintiff's misrepresentation caused the defendant to enter into it, whether or not the defendant ever took any steps to avoid it.[3]

(b) MISTAKES SHARED BY PROMISOR AND PROMISEE

We now move to the case where mistake is not induced by one party, but shared by both. A agrees to sell his car to B when both parties wrongly believe it is a 1980 model; or when, unknown to either, it has been irreparably damaged the minute before. Now, in most such cases, unless one party specifically took the risk in the contract of what happened (eg by promising that the goods sold still existed, or guaranteeing that the car was indeed a 1980 model) both parties are relieved from their obligations; but how they are relieved, and how far, varies in different cases. Statute occasionally makes the matter clear; by s 7 of the Sale of Goods Act 1979, for instance, a contract to sell goods which have perished is made 'void'. More generally, though, in a very few cases of extremely serious mistake (such as where A sells B an annuity on C's life, neither realising that C is dead and the annuity worthless[4]) the common law does the same as s 7 of the 1979 Act and simply exonerates both parties completely from liability.

However, very few mistakes are serious enough to bring the rule just mentioned into effect. They do not include the general run of mistakes, nor many other mistakes that one might think vital, such as the mistaken belief by the seller and buyer of a painting that it is an Old Master.[5] Yet denying any remedy at all here takes sanctity of contract much too far; parties do not, simply[6] by contracting agree to take the

---

2   So if A deceives B into selling a car which A then sells to C, title to the car passes to A and thence to C. See *Lewis v Averay* [1972] 1 QB 198, [1971] 3 All ER 907.

3   Eg *Redgrave v Hurd* (1881) 20 Ch D 1, 54 LJ Ch 113.

4   *Strickland v Turner* (1852) 7 Ex Ch 208.

5   This is the result of *Bell v Lever Bros Ltd* [1932] AC 161, 101 LJKB 129 which actually involved an attempt to recover money paid, rather than to be exonerated from a promise to pay it.

6   The parties may, of course, contract to bear any risk of mistake they like, as in *McRae v Commonwealth Disposal Commission* (1951) 84 CLR 377, below.

risk of mistakes this drastic turning out to their disadvantage. As a result, equity transcends the common law by exonerating parties to a contract rather more easily; it is sufficient if they are under a mistake serious enough (as with the example of the picture just mentioned) to make it unfair to enforce the contract as it stands. Thus a contract to let a house will not be enforced if both parties are mistaken as to the maximum legal rent; nor a contract to sell a house if both parties are wrong in thinking that it contains a sitting tenant.[7]

So much is straightforward. Unfortunately matters are a little more difficult. Clearly a party should not have to *perform* a contract entered into as a result of both parties being seriously mistaken; but what if he has spent money meanwhile thinking the contract was valid? If the mistake is serious enough to make the contract void at common law, there is ex facie nothing that he can do. English law does not allow a contract to be kept alive for the purpose of recovering wasted expenditure but not for the recovery of damages for failure to perform it. The only way to avoid injustice here is by judiciously manipulating the terms of the contract itself. In the instructive Australian case of *McRae v Commonwealth Disposals Commission*,[8] for instance, the defendant purportedly sold the plaintiff scrap metal merchants a non-existent wrecked ship; the plaintiff wasted a large amount of money looking for it where the defendant said it was. The Australian High Court countered the defendant's argument that the contract was void and therefore he could not be liable for that wasted expenditure, by finding an implied undertaking by the defendant that the wreck *did* exist and then holding the defendant liable for breach of it.

In most cases, however, where parties to a contract are not sufficiently drastically mistaken to make the contract void at common law, justice is easier to do. This is because the right to be relieved from such contracts is equitable and thus discretionary; therefore it is always open to a court to refuse to give relief to a party unless he compensates the other at least for the expenditure wasted by him. Hence in *Cooper v Phibbs*[9] a person who contracted to buy property that turned out to be his own after all, was given relief, but only on terms that he compensated the person who purported to sell it to him for expenditure made by the latter in good faith on the property.

(c) OTHER MISTAKES

Most difficult are cases where the promisor's mistake is neither shared nor induced by the promisee; where A agrees to buy a car that he thinks is a

---

7   *Solle v Butcher* [1950] 1 KB 671, [1949] 2 All ER 1107; *Grist v Bailey* [1967] Ch 532, [1966] 2 All ER 875.
8   (1951) 84 CLR 377.
9   (1867) LR 2 HL 149, 16 LT 678. Relief was similarly given on terms in *Solle v Butcher*, note 7 above.

1980 model but which B, the seller, knows is not; or where A intends to offer £1,500 for the car but inadvertently offers £2,000, which is accepted. Now here the law logically, but a little arbitrarily, distinguishes two kinds of mistake; mistake as to the *terms* of the transaction, and other mistakes as to the surrounding facts (which we shall call mistakes as to *motive*).

Mistake as to terms

Mistake as to the terms of the transaction means mistake over what the parties are agreeing, or what thing they are agreeing about. It includes the slip of the tongue, causing an offer of £2,000 instead of £1,500; or two parties dealing at cross purposes, as where, in the heat of an auction, the buyer bids for Lot 138 and has Lot 139 knocked down to him. Here English law on principle refuses to enforce the promise, on the crude, sound and effective ground that there is no agreement that the law can give effect to. So if A offers to buy 12 bottles of wine from B at £75 a bottle B cannot accept A's offer if A obviously meant £75 a case;[10] except in form there is no agreement between the parties at all. To protect the innocent promisee, however, a promisor may only exculpate himself under this rule if the promisee had reason to know he did not mean what he said. If the promisee had no such notice, the promise is enforceable in the normal way, as it would be if the promisor had not been mistaken at all. (Arguably, this protection for the innocent promisee goes too far. There is much to be said for limiting him to claim from the promisor any expenditure made in good faith, or other loss suffered in reliance on the contract, and denying him any claim for lost profits.)[11]

Even against an innocent promisee, however, a promisor may on very rare occasions be able to invoke the principle of 'non est factum' and escape liability. By this principle (which is limited to written instruments) a person signing a document under a very radical mistake as to its nature without negligence on his own part, may be exonerated from liability. Substance and not form matters in deciding whether the mistake is radical enough; apparently, for instance, a deed promising to pay £10,000 differs radically from one promising to pay £2,000, but perhaps not from a deed mortgaging one's house for £10,000.[12] The requirement of no negligence means this plea is very rarely successful and is in practice not very significant; especially as, in all but very few cases, it has been said that signing a document without knowing what is in it, amounts to negligence.[13]

---

10   *Hartog v Colin & Shields* [1939] 3 All ER 566. See *Petelin v Cullen* (1975) 132 CLR 355 in addition.
11   Cf the position of German law: see German Civil Code, para 122.
12   Cf *Saunders v Anglia Building Society* [1971] AC 1004, [1970] 3 All ER 961.
13   *Saunders v Anglia Building Society*, note 12 above, at 1027, 972–973, per Lord Wilberforce.

Mistake as to motive

Mistake as to motive, unshared and uninduced, does not of itself vitiate a contractual promise. A buyer cannot escape his obligations merely because he thought what he was buying was better than it was;[14] a person who tenders £100,000 for a building contract remains bound even if he only did so because he had made an arithmetical mistake in his costings.[15] Now this rule is justified provided the other party does not know about the mistake; contract exists to pre-empt the argument that a person did not act in his own best interests in agreeing to something. Unfortunately the rule is taken further, and protects even a contracting party who knows the other party to be mistaken, on the ground that the law imposes no duty on one to disabuse another of a mistake he is under.[16] This is open to one of obvious objection that it condones fraud, and to the less obvious one that it causes anomaly. We mentioned above that, where both parties contract under a serious misapprehension, the contract may be annulled in equity;[17] if so it is most odd that the contract stands if only one party is mistaken and the other knows it. It means, for instance, that a fraudulent seller who knows goods are defective can enforce a contract to sell them, whereas an innocent seller who shares the buyer's misapprehension cannot.

The rule allowing enforcement of someone else's promise that one knows to have been made because of a mistake is well established; nevertheless it is so unsatisfactory that in a number of cases it does not apply. These include, for instance, certain kinds of contract known as contract 'uberrimae fidei'. Insurance is the most important example; an insured must disclose matters that he knows of that would affect the risk, or the insurer's liability is avoided.[18] Other examples include cases where parties are unlikely to be bargaining at arms' length; family arrangements, for instance, where members of a family agree to share out the property of a member of the family who has just died. Again, equity marks off certain contracts as requiring a positive duty of candour, notably, contracts between those of a 'fiduciary' relation to each other, such as trustee and beneficiary.[19]

Furthermore, the rule that a half-truth counts as a misrepresentation can be manipulated so as to achieve the same result. If, for instance, A

---

14 *Scrivener v Pask* (1866) LR 1 CP 715, Har & Ruth 834, is a neat example. See too *Smith v Hughes* (1871) LR 6 QB 597, 40 LJQB 221.
15 *Imperial Glass Ltd v Consolidated Supplies Ltd* (1960) 22 DLR (2d) 759.
16 This is implicit in *Smith v Hughes*, note 14 above.
17 Because of the rule in *Solle v Butcher* [1950] 1 KB 671, [1949] 2 All ER 1107.
18 *Carter v Boehm* (1766) 3 Burr 1905, 1 Wm Bl 593. In fact contracts of insurance normally put an even heavier duty of disclosure on the insured, so this rule in practice not very important.
19 *Williams v Scott* [1900] AC 499 at 508; *Armstrong v Jackson* [1917] 2 KB 822, 86 LJKB 1375.

requests B to guarantee C's debt to A, A is deemed impliedly to state that there is nothing unusual in the risk C is taking; so if (say) C has a history of non-payment of debts, B may escape from his undertaking on the ground of a deemed misrepresentation.[20] This device the law could have extended to other contracts (for instance, it could quite plausibly have introduced an implied representation into a contract of sale that, to the seller's knowledge, there were no facts that would seriously affect the value of the goods); for better or worse, however, it never did so.

GRATUITOUS CONTRACTS. With gratuitous promises, as where A contracts under seal to pay B £100, authority is scanty, but on principle it seems that mistake as to motive suffices to exonerate him.[1] It certainly suffices to allow the recovery of money paid by mistake, as pointed out in Ch 10, and it would be odd if it were more difficult to impugn a gratuitous promise to pay money than to impugn the payment itself.

(d) MISTAKE AS AFFECTING NON-CONTRACTUAL OBLIGATIONS

One is tempted to dismiss the idea of mistake affecting liability in tort or unjustified enrichment; these forms of liability are not consensual, and hence why should mistake be relevant to them? Moreover, since one cannot be liable for many torts at all unless one acts either deliberately or negligently, in those cases the problem of mistake is taken care of by the criteria for liability, without any need for a separate defence at all.

However, this is not the whole story. There is a very close parallel, applying to other forms of liability, to the rule that one cannot enforce a contract against a person who contracted under a mistake induced by oneself. By the doctrine of estoppel, if A, however innocently, deceives B into committing a tort against him, A cannot complain of that tort if, had the facts been as he said they were, no liability would have been incurred. A, in proceedings against B, is precluded from denying that what he told B is true. Thus if B is about to sell goods that in fact belong to A and A inadvertently says they are not his, A cannot sue B for conversion if he sells them.[2] Similarly with liability to return unjustified enrichment, though here it must also be shown that B somehow altered his position on the faith of what A said. So if I mistakenly pay you money I do not owe you, but expressly tell you that I do owe it to you, then once you have spent it I cannot recover it from you.

---

20   *Lee v Jones* (1864) 17 CBNS 482, 34 LJPC 131.
1   Cf the rule in *Lady Hood of Avalon v Mackinnon* [1909] 1 Ch 476, 78 LJ Ch 300, that a deed giving away property may be cancelled for mistake.
2   *Pickard v Sears* (1837) 6 Ad & El 469, 2 Nev. & PKB 488.

2. The effect of duress

(a) PROMISSORY LIABILITY

We have dealt elsewhere with the question when duress prevents promissory liability *arising*; but can duress ever excuse the breaking of a valid promise? On general principles, it would seem it cannot; a foreign seller of goods is not exonerated from liability for failure to deliver, for instance, merely because his own government forbids him to comply with the contract and threatens to punish him if he does.[3] But, of course, duress of some kinds might frustrate a contract; if, for instance, a dancer's contract to dance at X's theatre is frustrated by the dancer's illness, presumably it would equally be frustrated by threats of personal violence that kept her away. Alternatively, the person prevented from performing a contractual obligation might be able to rely on an implied term; a postman, for instance, threatened with terrorist reprisals if he delivered to a particular address would, presumably, not be in breach of his contract of employment if he refused to do so.

(b) OTHER LIABILITY

Nor, it would seem, is duress any defence as such where non-promissory liability is concerned. Old authority, for example, makes a person liable for trespass to land even if he acted 'for fear of his life and wounding of twelve armed men.'[4] But presumably that rule applies only to cases, such as assault, where liability is not dependent on the defendant's culpability. A motorist forced at gunpoint to park his car so as to obstruct pursuing policemen would hardly be liable to the latter in negligence when they hit it. This would not be because duress was a defence as such, of course, but simply because the motorist would not have been at fault at all.

3. Necessity

When is something that would otherwise be a breach of obligation excused on the ground of necessity? In some cases, notably where liability defends on fault or culpability, necessity is dealt with in the same way as duress; one who acts from necessity simply is not at fault. A fireman acting in the heat of the moment need not make the load on

---

3 *Kleinwort, Sons & Co v Ungarische Baumwolle AG* [1939] 2 KB 678, [1939] 3 All ER 38.
4 *Gilbert v Stone* (1647) Aleyn 35. Cf *Howard E Perry & Co Ltd v British Railways Board* [1980] 2 All ER 579, [1980] 1 WLR 1375.

his vehicle as secure as a lorry-driver in normal circumstances;[5] again, launching a ship directly into the path of another is excusable if done to avoid serious danger to those on shore.[6] What of other liability? At least in tort, there seems to be a vague doctrine that reasonable action to avoid a grave, immediate emergency is excused. The doctrine is vague at least partly because many common situations are specifically dealt with by statute anyway, so the common law rarely itself has to face the issue of principle.[7] The necessity, it seems, can be that of defendant, plaintiff or third parties; the emergency itself may be putative, provided the defendant reasonably thought that it existed. One may thus dam one's own land against an oncoming flood even though the result is inevitably to inundate one's neighbours' land;[8] or even in an extreme case destroy one's neighbour's property to save one's own, as by shooting a dog to stop it worrying one's sheep.[9] Moreover, it goes without saying that one can use reasonable force in self-defence and defence of others against aggression. Equally one can legitimately take steps to preserve others' property, for instance if one finds jewellery unlocked and unguarded.[10] Similarly with protection of the public; it seems demolition of a dangerous building to stop it falling on the highway is justified.[11] Lesser degrees of necessity falling short of immediate emergency are, however, disregarded. It is hackneyed law, for instance, that trespass and false imprisonment are not excused by State necessity,[12] nor taking over someone else's empty house just because one happens to be homeless.[13]

As far as contractual, or rather promissory, obligations are concerned, much must depend on the terms of the individual promise; yet in general, at least where the necessity is that of the other party to a contract or a third person, necessity will often render justifiable what would otherwise be a breach. Thus by the doctrine of 'agency of necessity', an agent may legitimately, in an emergency and lacking instructions from his principal, take steps to preserve the latter's interests; if he does so he is not in breach of contract.[14] As for the interests of third persons, the obligations of a carrier by sea form a good

---

5   Eg *Watt v Hertfordshire CC* [1954] 2 All ER 368 at 371, [1954] 1 WLR 835 at 838, per Denning LJ.
6   *Frances (Owners) v The Highland Loch (Owners)* [1912] AC 312, 81 LJP 30.
7   Eg, s 3 of the Criminal Law Act 1967 allows generally the use of reasonable force 'in the prevention of crime.'
8   *Garrard v Crowe* [1921] 1 AC 395, 90 LJPC 42.
9   See the Animals Act 1971, s 9; for an analogy at common law, see *Cope v Sharpe (No 2)* [1912] 1 KB 496, 81 LJKB 346.
10 *Kirk v Gregory* (1876) 1 Ex D 55, 45 LJQB 186.
11 *Dewey v White* (1827) Mood & M 56.
12 *Entick v Carrington* (1765) 19 State Tr 1029 at 1073.
13 *Southwark LBC v Williams* [1971] Ch 734, [1971] 2 All ER 175.
14 Eg *Tetley & Co v British Trade Corpn* (1922) 10 Ll LR 678.

example; he must normally take the shortest reasonable route to his destination, but is nevertheless not deemed to be in breach of contract if he deviates to save life at sea.[15] However, in the last resort all depends on the terms of the contract, and some contracts impliedly must be taken to exclude the idea of necessity as a defence. Breach of a contract to sell 1,000 tons of soya beans would hardly be excused merely because the seller used the beans to relieve a sudden unexpected famine while they were en route to the buyer.

4. Impossibility

At first sight it seems ridiculous to oblige someone to do (or procure) the impossible; thus the Romans had a doctrine that a contract to do the impossible was simply void. But this is only a half truth. There is nothing ridiculous or illogical in making a person pay *damages* for failure to do the impossible; and perhaps because English law traditionally regards obligations as enforceable primarily by damages rather than specifically, it has never developed a general defence of impossibility. One can thus be liable in tort in certain cases for failure to do the impossible (a learner driver, for instance, is liable in negligence if he fails to live up to the standard of a reasonably experienced, competent driver, even though that it impossible for him);[16] and, of course, in contract. Promissory liability being prima facie strict, one can be liable for failing to deliver a cargo that does not exist; again, if one guarantees that goods sold have a certain quality it is no defence that type could not have that quality. (Of course, if neither party to a contract knows that a promise is impossible to perform – as with a contract to sell goods that have just perished – that may be a reason not to enforce the contract; but the operative feature here is mistake, and not impossibility).

Of course, merely because one *can* be obliged to do the impossible, it does not follow that impossibility never affects any obligation. If liability depends on fault, for example, it cannot amount to fault to fail to do the impossible (provided it is generally impossible, rather than individually impossible to this particular defendant). Similarly, in the slightly different case where a contractual obligation is not impossible at the outset but later becomes impossible, the doctrine of frustration, as dealt with in Ch 14 below, may well exonerate the contracting parties from liability.

15 *Scaramanga v Stamp* (1880) 5 CPD 295, 49 LJQB 674. Cf Carriage of Goods by Sea Act 1971, Schedule, Art IV(2) (1).
16 *Nettleship v Weston* [1971] 2 QB 691, [1971] 3 All ER 581. See also *J Summers & Sons Ltd v Frost* [1955] AC 740, [1955] 1 All ER 870.

5. Minority

There are various reasons for not subjecting minors to the law of obligations in the same way as adults. With promissory obligations, we may regard minors' consent to be bound as less significant owing to lack of judgment; with other obligations, arguably minors should not be subject to them because of lack of moral sense. Now English law generally accepts the former argument, but not the latter; with non-promissory obligations it feels that protection of others' interests is more important than minute enquiry into blameworthiness. Thus a minor may be liable in negligence if he fails to reach the standard of a reasonable person of his age;[17] he may also be liable for any other tort, such as conversion.[18] Similarly he must return unjustified enrichment.[19] (However, as might be expected, where a minor is not liable on a contract, such as to repay money lent, he cannot be made liable indirectly through tort or unjustified enrichment.)[20]

What of promissory liability? Here there is no general theory of liability worth the name;[1] as regards the liability of minors, promissory obligations seem to divide into three categories.

First, there is the general run of promises, on which the minor is not liable; a warranty on goods, for instance, or a contract of guarantee. The minor used to be liable on these promises if he ratified them after majority, but s 2 of the Infants' Relief Act 1874 removes even this ground of enforcement. The protection of the minor is total; it is not even relevant that he pretended to be of full age. On the other hand, it seems that even though a minor is not liable on a contract, the other party to it is; hence a minor may not be obliged under a contract to accept services, but can nevertheless sue the person rendering the services if he does so defectively.

The Infants' Relief Act 1874, by s 1, apparently created a further class of contracts, notably those for the loan of money or supply of goods to an infant, which were 'absolutely void.' However, despite the special treatment received by these contracts, the practical rules relating to them appear to be the same as for contracts in general; that is, they are enforceable *by* the minor but not *against* him.[2]

---

17   *McHale v Watson* (1966) 39 ALJR 459.
18   Eg *R v McDonald* (1855) 15 QBD 323, 52 LT 583.
19   *Stocks v Wilson* [1913] 2 KB 235, 82 LJKB 1145.
20   *R Leslie Ltd v Shiell* [1914] 3 KB 607.
 1   For recommendations for a more coherent scheme, see the Latey Report, Cmnd 3342 (1967).
 2   This is presumably the case; otherwise a minor could not complain when injured by substandard goods supplied to him in breach of 'contract'. *See Godley v Perry Ltd* [1960] 1 All ER 36, [1960] 1 WLR 9, where a minor recovered in such circumstances.

Secondly, there is a small class of contracts that are very closely bound up with the law of property; notably leases of land.[3] Here the property element predominates; the obligation to pay rent on a lease does bind a lessee who is a minor, although the minor can, if he wants, disclaim the lease and its obligations for the future when he comes of age.

Thirdly, a minor is liable on a promise to accept and pay for 'necessaries'. This odd term includes food, clothing, housing and the occasional luxury, provided they are reasonably necessary to maintain the minor's standard of living. At least for necessary goods, however, the minor's liability is only dubiously based on his contract as such, rather than on some principle such as unjustified enrichment, since the liability is to pay a reasonable price, not the contract price.[4] There is some attraction in extending a similar rule to necessary services as well.

By an extension of the rules about necessaries, a minor is also bound by a contract of employment, provided it is not very disadvantageous to him.[5] It goes without saying, of course, that contracts for necessaries are enforceable *by* the minor as well as *against* him.

6. Illegality

Any legal system must allow cases involving crime and, to a lesser extent, sin to form an exception to the normal law of obligations. The reasons for this are, as they must be, partly deterrent; liability in damages for not committing murder or fornication is unthinkable for obvious considerations. But deterrence is not the only reason. The law does not operate in a moral vacuum, and there is no reason why it should not simply declare moral disapproval of some activities by dissociating itself from them. Thus few will be deterred from stealing cars by the knowledge that if they do and their companion in crime negligently drives into a tree they will be denied compensation for negligence; nevertheless we still bar such claims.[6]

Whether any entirely rational scheme for denying liability that would otherwise exist on the grounds of illegality is possible, is open to doubt.[7] The English approach to the matter is certainly complicated

---

3 A lessee of land is apparently considered less as contracting to pay rent for the supply of land, than as having an interest in land inseparably connected with the obligation to pay rent.

4 Sale of Goods Act 1979, s 3.

5 Compare *Roberts v Gray* [1913] 1 KB 520, 82 LJKB 362, with *De Francesco v Barnum* (1889) 43 Ch D 165, 59 LJ Ch 151.

6 Cf *Ashton v Turner* [1981] QB 137, [1980] 3 All ER 870.

7 To put the whole matter to the court's discretion, as with the New Zealand Illegal Contracts Act 1970, merely leaves unanswered the question of how to exercise the discretion.

and sometimes confused; all we can do is try to extract what general principles there are as best we can.

(a) GENERAL CONSIDERATIONS

We start with two general considerations concerning illegality, which seem to affect all obligations, whether promissory or not, whatever their legal basis.

First, the law will not protect an illegal (or immoral) *interest* of the plaintiff. An owner of smuggled goods cannot sue for the insurance on them when they are destroyed;[8] nor are damages available for conversion when goods are seized that the plaintiff was not allowed to possess anyway.[9] Similarly, one cannot recover damages for loss of criminal income, whether one's own or another's.[10]

Secondly, one engages in illegal (or immoral) activity primarily at one's own risk with respect to harm suffered. One robber cannot sue another when he negligently crashes the getaway car and injures him; again, if two men fight illegally, neither can sue the other for any harm done.[11] Yet again, one doubts whether the thief of a car injured because the brakes were defective could sue the owner for negligence in failing to maintain them, nor (despite the Occupiers' Liability Act 1984) whether a burglar could complain who tripped over an obviously loose stair-rod. In contract, a haulier cannot be sued for negligence in damaging goods if the owner deliberately arranged carriage of them in an unlicensed vehicle.[12]

(b) ILLEGALITY IN CONTRACTUAL OBLIGATIONS

Traditionally, it is said that certain kinds of contract are 'illegal', whether as being entered into for an immoral purpose, or as being prohibited by statute, or as being illegal at common law. If, it is said, a contract comes in this category, it is (subject to exceptions) 'void' and nobody is bound by it to do anything. Great energy is then spent determining what contracts are thus 'illegal'. In fact this approach is misguided; illegality affects not contracts as such, but obligations arising under them. Now, we have already dealt with two ways in which illegality can affect contractual (as well as other) obligations; next, we describe two further principles that cover specifically contractual liability.

---

8   *Geismar v Sun Alliance and London Insurance Ltd* [1980] QB 383, [1977] 3 All ER 570.
9   *Malone v Metropolitan Police Comr* [1980] QB 49, [1979] 1 All ER 256.
10   *Burns v Edman* [1970] 2 QB 541, [1970] 1 All ER 886.
11   *Ashton v Turner* [1981]QB 137, [1980] 3 All ER 870; *Murphy v Culhane* [1977] QB 94, [1976] 3 All ER 533. For immorality in this connection, see *Hegarty v Shine* (1878) 14 Cox CC 124.
12   *Ashmore Benson Pease & Co Ltd v Dawson Ltd* [1973] 2 All ER 856, [1973] 1 WLR 828.

First, a person cannot be liable in damages for not committing a wrong; the illegal gun-runner, to take an extreme example, cannot be sued for his failure to deliver as promised. (Nor, incidentally, can he be made liable to return a prepayment on the basis of unjustified enrichment.)[13] The aim is, plainly, deterrence. There are, however, two exceptions to this principle. One is where one of two contractors reasonably relies on the other to make sure no illegality is committed. A householder ordering a building of particular design on his architect's advice that it can lawfully be put up is not prevented from suing the architect in negligence or otherwise when it cannot, even though he may be relying technically on a contract to do something which is unlawful.[14] The other exception is where the plaintiff is not *in pari delicto* with the defendant, in particular where he did not know facts making the promised performance illegal; if, for instance, A agrees to transport B's goods in a van which, unknown to B, is unlicensed, B can sue A for failure to do so.[15] (Here, however, there is a further anomaly; however innocent either party, if the *making* of a contract is illegal, and not only its performance, no action at all can be brought on it.[16] But this category is difficult to understand, and perhaps not surprisingly very few contracts have been held to fall into it. It is therefore not very important).

Secondly, there can be no obligation to pay another for knowingly committing illegality or immorality. This principle extends also to claims for payment for knowingly participating in, or assisting, illegality or immorality; a prostitute cannot sue for the wages of sin, but neither can her landlord sue her for rent on the flat he let to her to earn those wages.[17] But this principle is again limited. It is claims for payment *for* committing illegal or immoral acts that is barred, and some minor transgression committed in the course of doing something unobjectionable will not suffice. Thus a shipowner who at one point slightly overloads his ship is not prevented from claiming his freight for the voyage.[18] Moreover, only *knowing* illegality is covered by this rule. A promise to indemnify X for the damages he has to pay for assault or deliberate deceit is unenforceable; a promise to indemnify him against the consequences of his negligence, criminal or not, is not.[19]

13 Cf *Bigos v Bousted* [1951] 1 All ER 92.
14 Cf *Strongman (1945) Ltd v Sincock* [1955] 2 QB 525, [1955] 3 All ER 90.
15 *Archbolds (Freightage) Ltd v Spanglett* [1961] 1 QB 374, [1961] 1 All ER 417.
16 *Re Mahmoud & Ispahani* [1921] 2 KB 716, 90 LJKB 821.
17 *Pearce v Brooks* (1866) LR 1 Exch 213, 4 H & C 358.
18 *St John Shipping Co Ltd v Joseph Rank Ltd* [1957] 1 QB 267, [1956] 3 All ER 683.
19 *Gray v Barr* [1971] 2 QB 554, [1971] 2 All ER 949. This, in a way, is obvious; if the rule were otherwise, most of the basis of liability insurance would be undermined.

(c) THE AMBIT OF ILLEGALITY AS A DEFENCE

We have talked of 'illegality' and 'immorality' and their effect on
obligations; but what sorts of 'illegality' or 'immorality' are involved?
Illegality is widely understood. It extends to all criminal offences, even
quite technical ones,[20] and to deliberate torts;[1] though apparently, not
to breaches of contract. As for immorality, this covers sexual
promiscuity and any other sexual misbehaviour, but itself also goes
rather further, taking in, among other things, defrauding the Inland
Revenue and trafficking in honours.

7. Public policy

Certain obligations the law refuses to enforce without taking the rather
high moral tone it takes towards criminal and immoral activity in
general. We briefly deal with two such cases.

(a) PROMISES TENDING TO UNDERMINE MARRIED LIFE

A promise to pay X £1,000 'on divorce', or £5,000 p.a. 'while she lives
apart from her husband', is unenforceable as subverting marriage; the
same goes for any other agreement tending to discourage a person from
marrying at all, or tending to undermine an existing marriage.[2] A
similar rule applies to the comparatively innocuous 'marriage brokage'
contract, whereby (say) a matrimonial agency introduces prospective
couples on terms that if they marry a certain sum is payable.[3]

(b) AGREEMENTS IN RESTRAINT OF TRADE

Agreements not to work, trade or compete ('in restraint of trade') are,
prima facie, unenforceable.[4] The rule is justified by a nebulous
antagonism of the common law towards restraints on competition, and
also a paternalistic reluctance to allow a person to contract himself out
of a job.
    Such a rule as just stated, however, cannot be absolute. Especially in
the absence of a general tort of unfair competition (see Ch 8) the
vendor of a business must be able to undertake not to compete with the

---

20   Eg *J M Allan (Merchandising) Ltd v Cloke* [1963] 2 QB 340, [1963] 2 All ER 258.
  1   Such as deceit: *Brown Jenkinson & Co Ltd v Percy Dalton (London) Ltd* [1957] 2 QB 621,
          [1957] 2 All ER 844.
  2   See, eg, *Re Johnson's Will Trusts, National Provincial Bank Ltd v Jeffrey* [1967] Ch 387,
          [1967] 1 All ER 553.
  3   *Hermann v Charlesworth* [1905] 2 KB 123, 74 LJKB 620.
  4   *Vancouver Malt & Sake Brewing Co Ltd v Vancouver Breweries Ltd* [1934] AC 181, 103
          LJPC 58.

purchaser (otherwise no-one would buy the business); employers must
be able to stop ex-employees using their business connections after they
have left to 'poach' their employers' customers. To accommodate these
and other cases, restraints of trade are enforceable, traditionally,
provided they are in the interests both of the parties and of the public.[5]
But this is a Delphic phrase. It can be elucidated by saying that
agreements in restraint of trade are enforceable if, and only if (i) they
are not obtained by one party exerting undue economic pressure over
the other; and (ii) they do not clearly harm outsiders or the public; and
(iii) they are entered into with good reason.

Economic pressure is fairly straightforward as a means of preventing
enforcement of restraints of trade. In *A Schroeder Music Publishing Co Ltd v
Macaulay*,[6] a recording company insisted, rather one-sidedly, that artistes
whose work it published severely limited their right to publish elsewhere,
while itself accepting no obligation to publish anything. The House of
Lords, striking down contracts containing this provision, said that the
superior economic power that had been used to obtain them was one
feature making the restraint of trade that they contained unacceptable. As
for harm done to outsiders or the public, the abstract harm presumably
done by anti-competitive practice as such is not enough. But any further
harm to third parties often suffices; thus the Football League's practice of
severely restricting transfer of players between clubs obviously harms the
players, and as a result any contract incorporating or enforcing it will be
unenforceable as in restraint of trade.[7]

Most important, however, is the subject of what amounts to good
reason to impose obligations in restraint of trade. Such obligations
must serve a legitimate interest; and profitability as such, or (what
often amounts to the same thing) freedom from competition, are
interests but not legitimate ones.

What interests are legitimate? These include (non-exhaustively)
protection of goodwill where a business is sold; the confidentiality of
trade secrets and trade connections (such as customer lists); efficiency
of business in general (as with exclusive distribution agreements); and
professional standards. Provided a restraint of trade goes no further
than necessary to protect some such interest, then it is unobjectionable
and enforceable.

More concretely, restraint of trade problems tend to arise, and to be
dealt with in detail, in four areas of the law; covenants by employees
not to compete, covenants on the sale of the goodwill of a business, the
operation of trade associations, and exclusive distribution arrangements.

5 Eg *Nordenfelt v Maxim Nordenfelt Guns and Ammunition Co* [1894] AC 535 at 565.
6 [1974] 3 All ER 616, [1974] 1 WLR 1308.
7 *Eastham v Newcastle United Football Club Ltd* [1964] Ch 413, [1963] 3 All ER 139.

(i) Covenants by ex-employees not to compete
These are valid to the extent necessary to protect trade secrets and
trade connections, but no further; they cannot legitimately preserve the
employer from competition as such,[8] nor prevent the employee using
the general skills of his trade.[9] Applying this test to individual cases
depends largely on the sort of employment involved; the more skilled,
the more likely that knowledge gained in the course of it represents a
trade secret rather than simply general skill. Again, the more
influential the employee, or the more worldwide the business, the wider
the allowable restrictions on competition.[10]

(ii) Covenants on the sale of goodwill
These are perhaps the most generously treated of all restraints of trade,
and of course may to some extent protect the buyer of a business from
competition as such (since most such clauses put a blanket limit on the
right of the vendor to follow that trade at all within a certain distance
from the premises bought by the purchaser). In general, any reasonable
restraint on the vendor will normally be upheld; even, where necessary,
up to a 25-year ban on competition anywhere in the world.[11]

(iii) The operation of trade associations
Agreements between members of a trade association may be justified if
they may tend to make the industry concerned more efficient as a
whole. Hence, for example, exclusive marketing schemes are not as
such unenforceable.[12] But, once again, all depends on what is
reasonably necessary to achieve this aim. Thus agreements binding a
member of an agricultural co-operative to it for life, or completely
preventing retail chemists selling general merchandise, have been
struck down as too restrictive.[13]

(iv) Exclusive distribution
A contract by a petrol station owner, for instance, to sell only X's
petrol is justified and enforceable – though plainly in restraint of trade
– as increasing distributional efficiency, provided it is not for an
excessively long time.[14] The same goes for an agreement by a manu-

---

8   *Mason v Provident Clothing & Supply Co Ltd* [1913] AC 724, 82 LJKB 1153.
9   *Herbert Morris v Saxelby* [1916] 1 AC 688, 85 LJ Ch 210.
10   Eg *Fitch v Dewes* [1921] 2 AC 158, 90 LJCh 436; *Nordenfelt v Maxim Nordenfelt Guns
     and Ammunition Co* [1894] AC 535, 63 LJCh 908.
11   See the *Nordenfelt* case, note 10 above.
12   *English Hop Growers v Dering* [1928] 2 KB 174, 97 LJKB 569.
13   *McEllistrim v Ballymacelligot Co-op Agricultural and Dairy Society Ltd* [1919] AC 548, 85
     LJPC 59; *Pharmaceutical Society of Great Britain v Dickson* [1970] AC 403, [1968] 2 All
     ER 686.
14   *Esso Petroleum Ltd v Harper's Garage (Stourport) Ltd* [1968] AC 269, [1967] 1 All
     ER 699.

facturer to distribute his products only through a limited number of outlets. But, as with other agreements in restraint of trade, if such agreements put excessive restrictions on a person's activity, they cease to be legitimate. But in fact the approach of the common law to these problems is only of limited relevance. The Restrictive Trade Practices Act 1976 puts severe statutory restrictions on such agreements; even more significantly, Art 85 of the EEC Treaty, already touched on in Ch 8, avoids many sorts of agreements far more extensively than the common law ever did on the grounds that they restrict competition within the meaning of EEC law.

8. The act of the plaintiff

Assume A has broken his obligation to B, but any damage suffered by B is the result of his own deliberate and voluntary act. Even though, but for A's wrong, B would not have suffered any damage, in most cases A's wrong is overborne by B's act. This is true both of promissory liability (if I insure my house against fire, the policy is construed not to protect me if I set fire to it myself[15]) and of other types of liability (I cannot sue you if you negligently advise me to hit an unexploded bomb with a sledge-hammer and I do so, with disastrous results[16]). So much is obvious, and in a sense a fortiori to the rule that consent bars liability.[17]

However, there are limits to the principle. First, B's act must be truly voluntary. If A injures B and later, in a fit of depression brought on by the injury, B commits suicide, that does not bar B's relatives' claim.[18] B's suicide was deliberate; it was not voluntary.

Second, B's act must not be justifiable. This is neatly shown by the so-called 'rescue cases'. Assume A negligently knocks X into a fast-flowing river and B, in a brave but forlorn attempt at rescue, dashes into the river and is drowned. Although one might argue that any claim of B against A should be barred because B brought his danger on himself (and indeed, courts used to accept just this argument), the tendency today is to say that, unless utterly foolhardy, B's act is justified and therefore does not defeat his claim.[19]

Justification, of course, need not be altruistic, though it is in the case just mentioned. Just as the rescuer of *another* can sue, so can the rescuer of *himself*; if a passenger on a train, seeing a collision about to happen, jumps out and is injured, he can recover for his injuries from the person

15 Cf *Midland Insurance Co v Smith* (1881) 6 QBD 561, 50 LJQB 329.
16 *O'Reilly v National Rail and Tramway Appliances Ltd* [1966] 1 All ER 499.
17 Cf *ICI Ltd v Shatwell* [1965] AC 656, [1964] 2 All ER 999.
18 *Pigney v Pointer's Transport Services Ltd* [1957] 2 All ER 807, [1957] 1 WLR 1121.
19 Eg *Haynes v Harwood & Son* [1935] 1 KB 146, 104 LJKB 63.

whose fault was responsible for the collision.[20] A similar rule applies to other obligations as well. If, for instance, I insure goods and then deliberately damage them to avert an insured peril (such as drenching them with water to prevent them catching fire) that does not prevent me claiming the loss from the insurer.[1]

20 *Jones v Boyce* (1816) 1 Stark 493.
1 *Symington & Co v Union Insurance of Canton Ltd* (1928) 97 LJKB 646, 139 LT 386.

Chapter 14

Extinction and modification of obligations

The previous chapter dealt with factors preventing obligations arising at all. This one covers factors that will modify or destroy an obligation once it has arisen.

1. Performance and tender

It goes without saying that any positive obligation, whatever its source, is extinguished by being performed. Similarly, it is suggested, though not so obviously, with mere tender of performance. In a contract for the sale of goods, for instance, a seller who tenders conforming goods and has them wrongfully rejected is not bound to tender them again; the buyer's rejection of them is a breach that puts an end to the seller's obligation.[1] So also in the rare cases where the question arises in tort; if A is under an obligation to deliver goods up to B and he tenders them but they are not accepted, he does not have to take them away and tender them again (though presumably he must allow B to collect them on demand).

2. Subsequent impossibility and frustration

(a) NON-CONTRACTUAL OBLIGATION

Most obligations can be affected by subsequent impossibility; the effect of this factor, however, on non-contractual obligations varies so much according to the facts of the case that it is difficult to draw general principles. Thus an obligation under a trust to use money in a particular way for X's benefit ceases if that becomes impossible – for instance, if X dies; here, equity being a proprietary jurisdiction, the property concerned becomes held on a resulting trust for the settlor.[2] With obligations arising from the law of tort, on the other hand,

---

1 Tender is not, of course, the *same* as performance. A seller of goods who tenders them only to have them wrongfully rejected, for instance, cannot sue for the price of the goods, but only for damages.
2 *Re Abbott Trust Funds, Smith v Abbott* [1900] 2 Ch 326, 69 LJ Ch 539.

excepting those based on fault, impossibility is likely to be irrelevant; one remains liable, for instance, for failing to return another's goods even if prevented by the act of a third person from doing so.[3] (Yet even here there are complications; *legal* impossibility, as where statute forbids the return of property, will clearly override any obligation to return it.)

(b) CONTRACTUAL OBLIGATION

Barring actual illegality, conceivably promises might be taken literally and always enforced[4] whatever happened; but that would clearly be unsatisfactory. Promises, like all utterances, are – as we remarked in Ch 11 – intended and understood subject to unexpressed reservations. Moreover, the unfairness arising from insisting on applying promises to all unforeseen circumstances is obvious. In practice, therefore, it is a question not of whether, but of how far, the law is prepared to modify or extinguish promissory liability in the case of subsequent events.

(i) The doctrine of frustration[5]
The main weapon of English law in this connection is the doctrine of 'frustration', whereby some events ('frustrating events') automatically exonerate both parties to a contract from all future obligations under it.

Such frustrating events include first, literal impossibility of actual performance; as where an artist engaged to paint a picture dies, or the subject-matter of a contract of sale is destroyed, or performance becomes illegal.[6] But this class of frustrating events is limited. In particular, it does not include the fact that one or both parties' motives for entering into the contract may have disappeared even though performance as agreed may be possible. The assumption is that contractors are unconcerned with each others' motives, and therefore the fact that one party's aims in entering into the contract turn out to be unfounded should not affect the other's rights. To take an old example, a contract to hire a taxi to take one to Epsom on Derby day remains binding even if the race is cancelled.[7] A fortiori, a contract remains binding even if it turns out drastically more difficult or expensive to perform than one party thought it would be; a contract to ship goods from the Mediterranean to India is not frustrated when the

---

3　Eg because of threatened industrial action – *Howard E Perry & Co Ltd v British Railways Board* [1980] 2 All ER 579, [1980] 1 WLR 1375.
4　At least in damages; the idea of specifically enforcing an impossible obligation is obviously absurd.
5　For what happens to property transferred, etc, under a frustrated contract, see Ch 10, above, on unjustified enrichment.
6　Eg when war breaks out and the destination of goods to be exported becomes enemy territory.
7　*Herne Bay Steam Boat Co Ltd v Hutton* [1903] 2 KB 683 at 689, per Vaughan Williams LJ.

Suez Canal is closed and the goods have to go twice as far round the Cape of Good Hope.[8]

Secondly, however, in a few cases where a contract is so intertwined with the motives behind it that it makes no sense without them, then the courts have exceptionally been prepared to allow failure of motive to frustrate it. Only this, for instance, adequately explains the decision that a contract for the hire of a room overlooking Edward VII's coronation procession ceased to apply when the procession was cancelled.[9] It is not easy to see how one can know whether there is a close enough connection between contract and motive for this principle to apply; but one can say that such cases have been highly exceptional.

Thirdly, if performance of a contract becomes subsequently illegal, it goes without saying that both parties to it are relieved of their obligation under it.

The principles we have just described show a very restrictive attitude towards frustration and the ability of supervening events to affect existing contractual obligation. It will be interesting to see how long this attitude continues, particularly when compared with the law's increasing acceptance that mistake may negative obligation even though it merely goes to motive, provided only that it drastically upsets the balance between the parties. It is odd, to say the least, that the effect of supervening events on obligation should be so different from that of mistake.

RESPONSIBILITY FOR FRUSTRATION. Just as a person cannot claim for a loss if it results from his own deliberate act, prima facie he cannot invoke the doctrine of frustration to exonerate him if the frustrating event he relies on is his own deliberate act. Death, for example, releases an artist from his contract; suicide, it is suggested, leaves his estate theoretically liable for breach of it. It seems that the act need not even be unreasonable; thus a person agreeing to supply A and B each with 1,000 tons of soya beans, who is prevented by government order from supplying more than 1,000 tons in toto, is liable to A in breach of contract if, even for good commercial reasons, he chooses to allocate the whole 1,000 tons to B. Indeed, he is arguably liable to both A and B in breach of contract if he divides the available supplies equally, so that A and B each receive half their total order;[10] but perhaps this conclusion could be avoided by astutely construing the legislation as impliedly justifying the abatement of individual orders pro rata.

Analogously, a person cannot be exonerated if he relies on a frustrating event due to his own breach of contract. If, for instance, a

---

8 *Tsakiroglou & Co Ltd v Noblee Thorl GmbH* [1962] AC 93, [1961] 2 All ER 179.
9 *Krell v Henry* [1903] 2 KB 740, 72 LJKB 794.
10 Cf *Maritime National Fish Ltd v Ocean Trawlers Ltd* [1935] AC 524, 104 LJPC 88. In many contracts for the sale of commodities allow the seller to allocate available supplies rateably.

film star undertakes not to put herself in unusual danger during the making of a film, she should be liable for breach of contract if she does, is injured and as a result completion of the film is delayed – even though her illness would normally be something for which she was not liable.[11] It is sometimes thought that this principle can be expanded to provide that a person cannot rely on a frustrating event if it is his fault; but it is submitted that this is not the case, and the only fault that precludes frustration is fault amounting to breach of an express or implied term in the contract. Otherwise, whenever death was claimed as a frustrating event, one would be faced with a minute investigation whether the death was the deceased's fault or not.

FRUSTRATION AND THE TERMS OF THE CONTRACT. Frustration as a doctrine is subject to the terms of the contract; the parties can, if they wish, agree that events that would otherwise frustrate the contract, shall not. It is sometimes argued that one should generally infer such an agreement in respect of events foreseeable at the time of the contract, or which the parties actually knew might happen; but this seems too abstract a view, and that such an inference ought to depend on the circumstances of the individual contract. Of course, the list of exonerating events may equally be extended; and indeed many kinds of contracts, for instance for the international sale of commodities, make the common law of frustration seem insignificant because they contain explicit clauses ('force majeure' clauses) that exonerate much more widely for supervening events than the common law would.

The dependence of frustration on the terms of the contract has led to the contention that the basis of the doctrine is merely an implied term, present in any contract unless specifically excluded.[12] But that is implausible. Not only is there no indication what sort of term to imply. Further, a Scottish judge once remarked that a contract to deliver milk to X's house on a given day would be frustrated if a tiger were loose in the vicinity; but to infer into such a contract a term like 'tiger days excepted' would be fantastic. The better view is that frustration is a doctrine imposed by law on the basis of fairness;[13] just as we attach little weight to agreement if due to a mistake, so also we discount it if circumstances have materially altered since.

(ii) Doctrines other than frustration
Frustration is both a limited and a drastic doctrine; limited in the circumstances where it applies, but where it does apply having the

11   Cf *Ocean Tramp Tankers Corpn v V/O Soufracht, The Eugenia* [1964] 2 QB 226, [1964] 1 All ER 161.
12   Eg *Tamplin SS Co Ltd v Anglo-Mexican Petroleum Products Ltd* [1916] 2 AC 397 at 404, per Lord Loreburn.
13   *Denny, Mott & Dickson Ltd v James B Fraser & Co Ltd* [1944] AC 265 at 275, [1944] 1 All ER 678 at 683, per Lord Wright.

drastic effect of terminating both parties' obligations willy-nilly, even if one party wishes to keep the contract alive. Not surprisingly, other, complementary, doctrines have appeared that modify, rather than extinguish obligations in the light of subsequent events.

One is the implied term proper. A contract to sell unlimited quantities of water in perpetuity at a fixed price per gallon is not frustrated merely because water becomes much more expensive; nevertheless, to avoid unfortunate consequences for the seller the Court of Appeal inferred that the contract was impliedly terminable on reasonable notice.[14]

Secondly, it seems some supervening events may excuse what would otherwise be minor breaches of obligation without bringing the whole contract to an end. An actress engaged to play for the season breaks no obligation if, owing to illness, she fails to appear on one night; yet this is not due to frustration proper, since one night's illness clearly does not put an end to the whole contractual relationship.

3. The effect of consent and agreement

(a) CONSENT

The idea that consent condones what would otherwise be a breach of obligation ('volenti non fit injuria'), or can modify an existing obligation, not surprisingly pervades the law. A surgical operation consented to is not an assault; a beneficiary cannot complain of a breach of trust he consented to; a contractor cannot recover damages for a breach of contract he has consented to.[15]

To nullify or modify an obligation, consent, it seems, must have three features. First, it must be expressly or impliedly communicated to the person under the obligation. If I go away hoping someone will steal my car while I am away so I can claim on my insurance, that does not exonerate the person who takes it from liability. Secondly, consent must be free from serious mistake. Thus consent to a breach of trust is operational only if fully informed;[16] consent to an operation is similarly ineffective if the whole nature of the operation is misdescribed. Hence here the surgeon will be liable for battery.[17] Thirdly, there is a difference between knowingly *incurring* a risk and knowingly *consenting* to it. This is especially important in negligence cases. If I cross a street

---

14 *Staffordshire Area Health Authority v South Staffordshire Waterworks Ltd* [1978] 3 All ER 769, [1978] 1 WLR 1387.

15 *Leather Cloth Co Ltd v Hieronimus* (1875) LR 10 QB 140, 44 LJQB 54.

16 *Re Pauling's Settlement Trusts, Younghusband v Coutts & Co* [1964] Ch 303, [1963] 3 All ER 1.

17 *Chatterton v Gerson* [1981] QB 432, [1981] 1 All ER 257.

where drivers are notoriously dangerous and thus know I may be run down, I do not lose the right to sue the motorist who, driving too fast, does so.[18]

It goes without saying that consent may be implied as well as express. If A and B engage on a dangerous enterprise, such as using explosives without proper precautions, neither can sue the other for negligence; consent to the risk is implicit in what they do.[19] Similarly, a visitor to premises where there is a notice exempting the occupier from liability for damage is deemed to consent to take the risk of defects in the premises.[20] Indeed, consent may be given not by the plaintiff at all, but by someone with his authority. If A deposits goods with B on the understanding that B in turn entrusts them to C, in general A is bound by any limitation on C's liability accepted by B.[1]

(b) AGREEMENT

Consent may excuse a breach of obligation; but it has two short-comings. First, it is revocable, and cannot destroy the underlying obligation. If I permit you to come on my land, but before you have entered, revoke my permission, you cannot complain. Secondly, consent provides no means to release conclusively an obligation. If you owe me £100 and I consent to receive only £60 of it, that does not destroy your obligation to pay the other £40, which as a result I can revive at any time later.[2] The function of *agreement*, as against consent, in this connection is to overcome these problems; to enable me to give you permission to come on my land that I cannot simply revoke with impunity, and to release you conclusively of your debt of £40 to me.

Agreement in the form of a deed, or of a contract, with consideration, to which both obligee and obligor are party, is effective to do both these things. In other words, what can create promissory obligation can modify existing obligations as well. Thus if I, in a contract with consideration, release a debt, I cannot then sue for it. Again, if I contract, for payment, to let you on my land in future, I cannot later revoke that permission without at least being liable to you in damages.

Prima facie, indeed, no permission given by contract can be validly revoked at all except according to the terms of that contract. If I submit a dispute to an arbitrator and by contract agree to his publishing his finding even if it defames me, I cannot sue him for defamation even if

---

18   *Smith v Baker* [1891] AC 325, 60 LJQB 683. Cf *Dann v Hamilton* [1939] 1 KB 509, [1939] 1 All ER 59. But the line can be difficult to draw between knowing of a risk and consenting to run it. See *Titchener v British Railways Board* [1983] 3 All ER 770.
19   *ICI Ltd v Shatwell* [1965] AC 656, [1964] 2 All ER 999.
20   *Ashdown v S Williams & Sons Ltd* [1957] 1 QB 409, [1957] 1 All ER 35.
1   *Morris v C W Martin & Sons Ltd* [1966] 1 QB 716, [1965] 2 All ER 725.
2   *Foakes v Beer* (1884) 9 App Cas 605, 54 LJQB 130.

just before he publishes it I withdraw my permission to him to do so.[3] Equally, a cinema owner contracting to let the client see the whole of the performance cannot effectively withdraw the licence half-way through; if he forcibly ejects him he is guilty of assault.[4] There are two exceptions to this principle. One is public policy; however much I am paid to submit to medical experimentation, this will not justify treating me forcibly, however wrongfully I withdraw my consent at the last minute. The other exception is an anomalous but well-established restriction relating to land; contractual licences to come on land are irrevocable only if enforceable specifically, by injunction or specific performance; but not otherwise.[5]

So much for the effects of contracts on obligations. The difficulty arises with attempts to destroy or modify obligations by agreements falling short of contracts. At common law the rule was restrictive. Agreements designed to modify existing legal relations were enforceable only on the same conditions as agreements designed to create new obligations (that is, contracts).[6] Agreements falling short of these requirements were simply ineffective. This rule was well-established, even though it is odd and indefensible outside the sterile logic that all agreements are governed by the law of contracts and therefore all must be subject to the same rules, whatever they are aimed to do. Its effects are unfortunate. An agreement by a creditor owed £100 to accept £50 in full settlement is unenforceable because it is made without good consideration. Equally, an agreement between A and B exonerating C from liability to A (as where owner of goods and carrier agree that a third party, like a stevedore, handling them shall not be liable for negligence) cannot effectively modify C's obligation to A, because C is not a party to it.[7]

In certain cases, however, equity modifies the harshness of the common law rule that only an agreement equivalent to a contract can modify existing obligations effectively. This is done by the doctrine of 'equitable estoppel'. By this, an agreement modifying or negativing an existing obligation may take effect even though (for lack of con-

---

3 This is implicit in *Chapman v Lord Ellesmere* [1932] 2 KB 431, 101 LJKB 376.

4 *Hurst v Picture Theatres Ltd* [1915] 1 KB 1, 83 LJKB 1836.

5 See *Winter Garden Theatre (London) Ltd v Millennium Productions Ltd* [1948] AC 173, [1947] 2 All ER 31; *Hounslow LBC v Twickenham Garden Developments Ltd* [1971] Ch 233, [1970] 3 All ER 326.

6 Compare the Roman law rule that *any* agreement (*pactum*), whatever its form, sufficed to vary existing obligations – Buckland, *Textbook of Roman Law*, 3rd edn, 528.

7 *Scruttons Ltd v Midland Silicones Ltd* [1962] AC 446, [1962] 1 All ER 1. Cf *Port Jackson Stevedoring Pty Ltd v Salmond & Spraggon (Australia) Pty Ltd, The New York Star* [1980] 3 All ER 257, [1981] 1 WLR 138. Unfortunately the House of Lords refused to allow the agreement in that case to take effect as a simple consent to bear the risk ('volenti non fit injuria') not subject to the technical rules of the law of contract. Statute has occasionally reversed the rule against third parties taking advantage of exception clauses in their favour; eg Carriage of Goods by Sea Act 1971, Schedule, Art IV BIS.

sideration, for instance) not satisfying all the requirements of contract; provided (a) it is relied on, or at the very least, accepted by the person seeking to enforce it, and (b) it would be unconscionable to allow it to be disregarded. Hence in the classic case of *Hughes v Metropolitan Rly Co*[8] it was held that a landlord who, having given his tenant six months' notice to quit, undertakes not to enforce that notice if the tenant repairs the premises, must if the tenant takes him at his word, then give him a new period of notice. Again, a seller who, as an indulgence, says he will allow his buyer to pay in a different, depreciated, currency, cannot, once he has been paid, revert to his original right.[9] More remarkably, in *Central London Property Trust Ltd v High Trees House Ltd*,[10] a landlord, having agreed to accept reduced rent during wartime difficulties, was prevented from reverting to the original rent except on reasonable notice (he was also held to have lost any right he might have had to claim the rent previously remitted).

The key is obviously what the requirements of reliance and unconscionability comport, and this is by no means certain. Often the matter will be clear. The tenant in *Hughes'* case, having spent money in reliance on the landlord's undertaking, obviously deserves protection. But this will not invariably be so obvious. Nevertheless, given how anxious businessmen are to know their legal position, one suspects that courts would in practice say it was unconscionable to try to revoke any agreement modifying an obligation, unless either the revocation took place in circumstances (say immediately after the agreement) where it could do no conceivable harm to anyone, or alternatively the revocation itself was affected by mistake or some sort of duress.[11]

Assuming that equitable estoppel exists to give effect to modifications of rights, it still remains to ask, how far does it do so? Must the doctrine give effect to the modification entirely or not at all; or may it, if equitable, do so only partially? If a landlord gratuitously agrees to take reduced rent for five years, can he nevertheless after two years, provided it is equitable, go back to the original rent, even though that involves breaking the agreement? Despite some disagreement over the matter, it would seem that he can.[12] If so, equitable estoppel remains a less potent means of nullifying obligations than contract itself, since there is clearly no power in the courts to allow a party to go back on a *contract* modifying an obligation merely because it would be equitable in the circumstances.

8   (1877) 2 App Cas 439, 49 LJQB 583.
9   *W J Alan & Co Ltd v El Nasr Export and Import Co* [1972] 2 QB 189, [1972] 2 All ER 127.
10   [1947] KB 130, [1956] 1 All ER 256n.
11   As in *D & C Builders Ltd v Rees* [1966] 2 QB 617, [1965] 3 All ER 837.
12   See *Ajayi v R T Briscoe (Nigeria) Ltd* [1964] 3 All ER 556 at 559, [1964] 1 WLR 1326 at 1330, per Lord Hodson. Contra, though, Denning J in *Central London Property Trust Ltd v High Trees House Ltd*, Note 30 above.

(c) LIMITS ON THE POWER TO EXCLUDE AND MODIFY OBLIGATIONS

It is not surprising that social factors may prevent an otherwise valid agreement to modify or limit certain obligations having effect. This means effectively, though not exclusively, consumer protection; restrictions, in particular, on the ability to exclude or limit by agreement the obligations to take care in the provision of services, and in sale of goods contracts to supply goods of merchantable quality, fit for their purpose and up to description.

Until 1967 English law had few controls over such exclusions; no provision, as in German law, that contracts, including consumer contracts, had to be kept in good faith; nor any rule of common law putting certain obligations beyond the power of parties to modify them because such obligations were regarded as too fundamental to be modified at all.[13] True, judges did sterling work in deliberately – often perversely – construing exemption clauses narrowly;[14] in construing contracts as not including them;[15] and in developing an advanced doctrine of conditional obligation ('fundamental breach', referred to later) that clauses in a contract reducing a contracting party's obligation, while valid, were presumed to be conditional on that party performing his main obligation in a way not grossly defective. But these were defective answers, defeasible by clever draftsmen. Since 1967, statute has extensively intervened. The vitiating effect of mis-representation on contractual obligation can now only be excluded in so far as it is reasonable.[16] As against consumers, by the Unfair Contract Terms Act 1977 the obligation to take care in providing services, and when selling goods to provide goods of the right quality, cannot be excluded at all; as against others, the duty can be excluded only in so far as it is reasonable.[17]

An obligation, moreover, is created[18] effectively to provide under a contract the sort of service to be reasonably expected under that sort of contract; exclusion of that term is similarly limited. Yet again, business liability for negligence causing death or personal injury cannot be excluded at all.

Where a term, to be valid, must be reasonable, the courts in deciding whether it is, seem to pay lip-service to the criteria laid down in the 1977 Act (the possibility of insurance against the loss; the degree of

13 Except, perhaps, deceit: see *S Pearson & Son Ltd v Dublin Corpn* [1907] AC 351, 77 LJPC 1.
14 Eg *White v John Warwick & Co Ltd* [1953] 2 All ER 1021, [1953] 1 WLR 1285; more recently, see *Ailsa Craig Fishing Co Ltd v Malvern Fishing Co Ltd* [1983] 1 All ER 101, [1983] 1 WLR 964.
15 Eg *Thornton v Shoe Lane Parking Ltd* [1971] 2 QB 163, [1971] 1 All ER 686.
16 Misrepresentation Act 1967, s 3.
17 Unfair Contract Terms Act 1977, ss 2, 6, 7.
18 Ibid, s 3(2) (b).

choice presented to the 'customer'); in practice they seem to take to heart three factors. First, there is the fact that the onus is on a person alleging a term to be reasonable.[19] Secondly, standard implied terms are not to be departed from without good reason; on occasion, the reason for a decision has merely been that a term normally found in a particular sort of contract has been excluded without apparent justification.[20] Thirdly, limitations on liability are apparently more generously treated than blanket exclusions:[1] the assumption being, perhaps, that few losses in practice are solely the fault of one party to a contract anyway, rather than any sophisticated considerations of, say, economic efficiency.

Other statutory controls on exclusion of liability are a varied group. Consumer protection extends further, for instance, to obligations laid down in respect of hire purchase and consumer credit transactions,[2] and in respect of the building and rebuilding of dwelling-houses; these terms are similarly inexcludible.[3] Other controls have nothing to do with consumer protection, existing (for instance) to protect agriculture by preventing seedsmen excluding liability for misdescribing their seeds,[4] or to protect shareholders in companies by outlawing exclusion of a company director's duty to look to the interest of the company.[5]

Occasionally social considerations have induced the judges themselves to invalidate some forms of exclusion. Probably, for instance, one cannot exclude liability for one's own (as against one's employees') fraud.[6] Indeed, had not statute intervened, the common law would very likely have moved towards some general doctrine of relief against the more obnoxious exemptions from liability. But, for obvious reasons, that question is now academic.

(d) DOCTRINAL REASONS PREVENTING EXCLUSION OF LIABILITY; FUNDAMENTAL BREACH

We have already mentioned in passing the use of 'fundamental breach' as a means to control exclusions of liability. This doctrine is a sophistication of the idea of conditional obligations on the following lines. If (for example) a seller undertakes to supply goods but not to be

19   The presumption comes in the Unfair Contract Terms Act 1977, s 24(4).
20   Eg *George Mitchell (Chesterhall) Ltd v Finney Lock Seeds Ltd* [1983] 2 All ER 737 at 744, per Lord Bridge; see also *Rasbora Ltd v J C L Marine Ltd* [1977] 1 Lloyd's Rep 645 at 651.
1   *Ailsa Craig Fishing Co Ltd v Malvern Fishing Co Ltd* [1983] 1 All ER 101, [1983] 1 WLR 964.
2   Unfair Contract Terms Act 1977, ss 6(1) (b), 7(3a); Consumer Credit Act 1974, s 173.
3   Defective Premises Act 1972, s 6(3).
4   Plant Varieties and Seeds Act 1964, s 17(1).
5   Companies Act 1948, s 205.
6   *S Pearson & Son Ltd v Dublin Corpn* [1907] AC 351, 77 LJPC 1.

liable for certain defects, his obligation is split into two elements; the obligation proper, to supply satisfactory goods, and so on; and terms modifying it. The applicability of the latter is then presumed to be conditional on the former not being broken excessively seriously. So if the seller delivers mildly defective goods he is protected; but if the goods are badly defective then the term exonerating him does not apply, and he is liable. Now, as a wholesome exercise in construction (where some judicial sanctimony in a good cause is in order) this rule is unexceptionable and – in the absence of contrary intent – still applies.[7] Connected with it, however, was a serious heresy which only recently was scotched. On the misguided principle that similar rules must apply to agreements modifying obligations as apply to agreements creating them, the rule just mentioned was combined with the quite separate one that *promissory* obligations under a contract are conditional on substantial performance by the other side.[8] It was then said that any breach by one party (A) which exonerated the other party (B) from his promissory obligations, 'exonerated' B also from any limitations on A's liability. To confuse matters further, this was then said only to happen if B did not (as a person faced with a serious breach of contract by the other party could) elect to keep the contract – with A's right to limit his liability – alive; of if A's breach were so disastrous as to leave B no choice in the matter.[9] Confusion reigned before the House of Lords restored orthodoxy,[10] and restored fundamental breach to its original state: a simple presumption that exonerating clauses are intended not to apply to cases of very serious breach.

(e) DEFECTIVE AGREEMENTS PURPORTING TO ANNUL OR MODIFY OBLIGATIONS

This subject can be dealt with briefly. The same defects in consent as will vitiate promissory liability will equally prevent a contract or other agreement from effectively nullifying or affecting an existing obligation. Duress is one example. In *D & C Builders Ltd v Rees*[11] a builder, nearly insolvent but owed some £500, was threatened by his debtor that, unless he released £200 of the debt, he would not be paid at all and would become bankrupt. He released that sum out of the debt, but his release was annulled. Partly this was because this was a release of a

7 *Suisse Atlantique Société d'Armement Maritime SA v NV Rotterdamsche Kolen Centrale* [1967] 1 AC 361 at 426 f, [1966] 2 All ER 61 at 89 f, per Lord Upjohn.
8 Above, Ch 11.
9 The high water mark of this development was *Harbutts Plasticine Ltd v Wayne Tank and Pump Co Ltd* [1970] 1 QB 447, [1970] 1 All ER 225.
10 By the decision in *Photo Production Ltd v Securicor Transport Ltd* [1980] AC 827, [1980] 1 All ER 556.
11 [1966] 2 QB 617, [1965] 3 All ER 837.

contractual obligation by non-contractual means, ineffective at common law (as we have seen) and not saved by equitable estoppel; it was, however, also because the means by which the release was obtained – a threat of a breach of contract – was duress such as would vitiate any contract anyway.

An alteration of existing obligations obtained by other means that will annul a contract, such as misrepresentation, can, of course, also be upset. Thus if an exporter of soya beans, for example, persuades his buyer to cancel the contract by falsely telling him that Government regulations prevent him from fulfilling it, the cancellation is ineffective and the seller remains liable for breach of contract.[12] Similarly, it is suggested, a release given will be ineffective if at the time both parties were fundamentally mistaken about the surrounding circumstances, such that their mistake would have vitiated any other contract.

---

12 See *André & Cie v Ét's Michel Blanc* [1979] 2 Lloyds Rep 427 (misrepresentation inducing cancellation of contract).

Chapter 15

Causation and contributory negligence

1. Causation

It goes without saying, whatever the basis of liability, that one is not liable for damage to another unless that damage is the result of one's breach of duty. Now in law the concept of causation appears in two rather different forms: one logical, one pragmatic. The logical form can be summarised in the words 'sine qua non'; if the damage would have occurred even if the defendant's breach of duty had not, then the defendant normally escapes liability. The pragmatic form is the principle that, even where as a matter of fact plaintiff's loss resulted eventually from defendant's breach of duty, certain events between the two must nevertheless exonerate the defendant; otherwise liability might be practically infinite.

(a) CAUSATION 'SINE QUA NON'

A wrongdoer – whether tortfeasor or contract or trust breaker – is prima facie not liable for damage that would have happened anyway; as where a hospital fails to diagnose a deadly disease that would in any case have killed the patient before treatment was possible.[1] So much for the basic principle, which is uncontroversial. Even here, there are exceptions.

The most important exception is concurrent responsibility. If two negligent drivers simultaneously hit the same pedestrian, both are responsible in full for the whole of the damage he suffers, even though clearly the damage would still have happened had either driver not been negligent. Indeed, it is submitted that the same principle should extend beyond concurrent *responsibility* to concurrent *cause*, where a wrongful act combines with an innocuous one to cause a loss; for instance, if a careless driver hits a pedestrian at the same time as a careful one, the fomer should be liable to the pedestrian even though

---

1 See *Barnett v Chelsea and Kensington Hospital Management Committee* [1969] 1 QB 428, [1968] 1 All ER 1068 (tort); *The Europa* [1908] P 84 (contract); *Earl Gainsborough v Watcombe Terra Cotta Clay Co Ltd* (1885) 54 LJ Ch 991 (trusts).

the pedestrian would in any case have been injured by the other driver.[2]

Slightly less obviously, it used to be thought that a similar principle applied where two causes of loss were not simultaneous but successive. In *Baker v Willoughby*,[3] the plaintiff loss the use of one leg because it was injured successively by the defendant and X. Although his loss of use after the injury by X would have happened even had the defendant not injured his leg, nevertheless the defendant was held liable for the whole loss, despite the intervening act of X. As Lord Reid observed, the plaintiff and X, having concurrently caused the loss, were therefore both liable in full. However, this reasoning now appears discredited. Recently in *Jobling v Associated Dairies Ltd*,[4] the House of Lords refused a plaintiff whose back was injured, but who three years later was cripped by disease anyway, more than three years' compensation for his injury. The ordinary principles of 'sine qua non', it was said, applied to preclude any further claim: the theory of concurrent liability did not come into it. Whether *Jobling's* case leaves *Baker v Willoughby* intact on its facts is unclear (it can be distinguished because in the earlier, but not the later, case the second injury was tortious[5]); nevertheless, the distinction drawn between concurrent and successive causes is a little odd.

(b) PRAGMATIC CAUSATION; OTHER FEATURES BREAKING THE CHAIN OF CAUSATION

Even assuming the defendant's breach of duty, and damage that would not have happened but for it, certain intervening circumstances will prevent the defendant being liable for the loss. These are circumstances justifying an assertion that, applying 'common sense',[6] the defendant did not 'cause' the loss. The function of causation in this sense is the same as that of 'remoteness of damage' – to prevent too extensive liability. Despite the courts' refusal to commit themselves any more precisely as to what it means (they hide behind unanalytical ideas like 'common sense') three factors seem to dominate this aspect of causation.

First, courts sympathise little with those whose wrongdoing produces unexpectedly bad results: features aggravating damage that

2   *Smith, Hogg & Co Ltd v Black Sea & Baltic Insurance Co Ltd* [1940] AC 997, [1940] 3 All ER 405, suggests this conclusion in respect of one part of the law, notably carriage of goods by sea. Cf *Anderson v Minneapolis Railroad* 179 NW 45 (1920).
3   [1970] AC 467, [1969] 3 All ER 1528.
4   [1982] AC 794, [1981] 2 All ER 752.
5   But why this should be relevant is not clear.
6   A somewhat uninformative criterion advocated by Lord Reid in *Stapley v Gypsum Mines Ltd* [1953] AC 663 at 681, [1953] 2 All ER 478 at 485–486.

would have occurred anyway rarely break the chain of causation. A carrier by sea, for instance, providing an excessively slow and defective ship remains liable for the full loss if his cargo, once delayed, is caught by a further catastrophe, such as the outbreak of war, and suffers further problems.[7]

Secondly, however, a complete change of circumstances – including possibly the passage of a long period of time – separating breach of duty from damage, may justify breaking the link. So if a slightly damaged ship is taken on a strenuous voyage on which it is further damaged so as to need heavy repairs, this subsequent event exonerates those originally responsible for the first damage completely from liability.[8]

Thirdly, there is a specialised instance of the previous case: the doctrine of *novus actus interveniens*. A human act separating breach of duty and damage, provided it is both unforeseeable and quite unreasonable, may cause the original breach of duty to be disregarded. An employee supplied with defective equipment and injured by it cannot complain if he was using it perversely;[9] similarly a motorist causing an accident is not liable for the pile-up resulting when the police bungle the attempt to reach the scene.[10] On the other hand, if A negligently fails to look after B's property and it is stolen, then obviously the thieves' action does not break the chain of causation. Theft, after all, is not unforeseeable.[11]

2. Contributory negligence

Causation is an 'all-or-nothing' idea. Even though the question whether X's act caused Y's damage often reduces in practice to whether it is felt X *ought* to be responsible for the damage, one cannot say 'X caused Y's loss, but only to the extent of 50 per cent.' If what X did caused Y's loss to any extent at all, X is liable in full.

There is an exception, however, where X's act combines with Y's own fault ('contributory negligence') to cause damage to Y. At common law this was no exception at all; Y's own fault either exonerated X completely or had no effect on X's liability at all. But, by s 1 of the Law Reform (Contributory Negligence) Act 1945, the court can now apportion responsibility in such cases according to the comparative fault of X and Y; so if what X did was a cause of Y's injury but Y was also 40 per cent to blame, Y recovers damages

7   *Monarch SS Co Ltd v Karlshamns Oljefabriker* [1949] AC 196, [1949] 1 All ER 1.
8   *Carslogie SS Co Ltd v Royal Norwegian Government* [1952] AC 292, [1952] 1 All ER 20.
9   *Quinn v Burch Bros (Builders) Ltd* [1966] 2 All ER 283, [1966] 2 QB 370.
10 *Knightly v Johns* [1982] 1 WLR 49, [1982] 1 All ER 85.
11 *Stansbie v Troman* [1948] 2 KB 48, [1948] 1 All ER 599.

reduced by 40 per cent. This reduction in damages applies only where it is Y's own fault that combines with X's act; where X and Z's fault combine equally to injure Y, both are – as we have seen – liable in full, and must rely on the right to contribution to ensure that responsibility is eventually apportioned.[12]

However, contributory negligence applies in this way to exonerate the defendant partially in respect of only certain obligations. The Law Reform (Contributory Negligence) Act 1945 refers to the 'fault' of the defendant, a term including any duty of care based on tort or (it is submitted) on contract[13] or – say – bailment. Similarly included are deliberate wrongdoing, such as assault (but, by statute,[14] not conversion or trespass to goods) and cases of strict liability; again, it is submitted, whether such wrongdoing amounts to a tort or to a breach of contract.·Not included, though, is pure promissory liability; one can sue a seller for full damages for failure to deliver goods even if oneself partly at fault in causing the non-delivery.

With strict liability, such as for breach of certain kinds of statutory duty and liability under *Rylands v Fletcher,* comparative fault must obviously be modified, since otherwise a defendant showing no fault would never be liable to a plaintiff showing some. The rough and ready rule here is that, where strict liability faces contributory negligence, damages are reduced by a certain amount, not to nil, but nevertheless by rather more than they would have been reduced had the plaintiff proved negligence.[15]

---

12 Except in the case of certain maritime collisions: see Maritime Conventions Act 1911, s 1.

13 This, however, is doubtful. It is sometimes said, perversely, that contributory negligence defeats any claim based on contract: eg *Sole v W J Hall Ltd* [1973] QB 574, [1973] 1 All ER 1032. But see *Quinn v Burch Bros (Builders) Ltd* [1966] 2 QB 370 at 377–381, [1965] 3 All ER 801 at 806–808, per Paull J. There is no authority whether contributory negligence reduces damages for breach of trust: on principle it should. See G. L. Williams, *Joint Torts and Contributory Negligence*, para 80.

14 Torts (Interference with Goods) Act 1977, s 11(1).

15 *Quintas v National Smelting Co Ltd* [1961] 1 All ER 630, [1961] 1 WLR 401.

Chapter 16

Transfer of obligations

Obligations, or things in action, make up at least as much of many people's wealth as physical things; after all, shares in a company, credit balances at a bank and rights under a trust are all merely legal claims against company, banker or trustee.[1] Hence the importance of dealing, at least in outline, with the rules relating to the transfer (or 'assignment') of things in action.

A preliminary word of caution, however. Most forms of property are clearly either physical things or things in action, but not all. A bailor's interest under a bailment, for instance, or a beneficiary's under a trust, share features of both physical things and obligations, according as one concentrates on the bailor's or beneficiary's ownership or on their rights as against bailee or trustee. Here the law can only classify arbitrarily (classify it must, since different rules apply – for instance when it comes to transfer – to things and obligations). Thus, despite similarities between bailment and trust, it happens that interests under trusts are classified as obligations, whereas the right of a bailor in respect of the thing bailed is classed simply as ownership of the thing. Secondly, this chapter is about the *transfer* of obligations; transactions that transfer the obligee's right against the obligor without the latter's necessary co-operation. Of course there exist other institutions that may have similar effects. If A owes B £100, B may promise to pay to C whatever he recovers from A; or B may release A from his obligation and A then undertake a new obligation to C ('novation'); or A may apparently give C the right, instead of B, to sue him if, with B's acquiescence, he undertakes to pay C.[2] But we are not concerned with these.

1. What obligations can be transferred?

On principle, the answer to this question is simple; prima facie, the benefit of any obligation can be transferred, whatever its basis. It does

---

1 W. Friedmann, *Law in a Changing Society*, Ch 3, eloquently makes the point that any conception of property as limited to tangibles is very inadequate. Indeed, even the most tangible of all property, land, is fairly insignificant unless supplemented by the benefit of an obligation – that is, the obligation of the tenant to pay rent – as many a private landlord has found to his cost.
2 See the odd case of *Shamiah v Joory* [1958] 1 QB 448, [1958] 1 All ER 111.

not matter whether it is contractual, as with a debt, or tortious, as with a right to damages, or equitable, as with an interest under a trust. The exceptions are specific.

First, statute may preclude transfer. The right to receive social security, for instance, cannot be assigned.[3]

Secondly, contractual rights cannot be assigned if the contract under which they arise forbids it; if so, any purported assignment is ineffective. This is an absolute rule, and applies even though assignment can do no possible harm to the obligor. Freedom of contract prevails over the argument that commerce may be hindered with no countervailing commercial advantage to anyone.[4]

Again, some rights are unassignable as being inherently exercisable by one person only; an artist, for instance, commissioned to paint a portrait cannot assign the benefit of that commission to someone else. Similarly, at common law, with contracts of employment: the employee is deemed to regard it as vital who he is employed by, and his employer cannot transfer the right to his services to anyone else.[5] (In fact, employers are largely corporate and employment generally impersonal today; as a result statute and EEC law have now largely emasculated the common law rule.)[6]

Fourthly, certain kinds of obligation can be assigned by act of parties only if there is reasonable ground for so doing; the law distinguishes between obligations that are assignable absolutely, for any reason or no reason, and those assignable only on reasonable grounds. The former category includes debts, rights to specific property, and interests arising in equity under trusts, wills and the like. These are regarded as fair items of commerce. Hence a person can sue as assignee of a debt, for example, even if he took the assignment purely as a speculation, or indeed merely to harass the debtor more effectively.[7] As for the second class of obligations, this consists mainly of claims for damages for a tort or breach of contract. Apparently on the argument that rights of this sort do not exist to be bought or sold like any commodity, and that unrestricted dealings in them might lead to 'maintenance' (that is, third parties meddling in litigation they have no concern with[8]) reasons

3   See, e.g., Supplementary Benefits Act 1966, s 16.
4   *Helstan Securities Ltd v Hertfordshire CC* [1978] 3 All ER 262. The comment at [1979] CLJ 50, that the effect may be to prevent contractors raising much-needed finance on the security of accounts receivable without any countervailing advantage to anyone, is pertinent.
5   *Nokes v Doncaster Amalgamated Collieries Ltd* [1940] AC 1014, [1940] 3 All ER 549.
6   See Employment Protection (Consolidation) Act 1978, s 94, and EEC Directive 77/187. Cf *Pambakian v Brentford Nylons Ltd* [1978] ICR 665 at 672.
7   *Fitzroy v Cave* [1905] 2 KB 364, 74 LJKB 829.
8   Is the fear justified? Scots law seems to allow unrestricted trafficking in rights of action even in tort, with apparently no ill-effects. See, eg, *Cole-Hamilton v Boyd* 1963 SC 1.

for assignment must be shown. What reasons suffice? The best-established is where a right of action is closely connected with some other property being simultaneously disposed of by the assignor; the seller of a damaged car, for instance, can sell with it the right to sue whoever damaged it.[9] A related case is that of an insurer who pays an owner of property for damage done to it; quite apart from his right to be subrogated to any claims the owner may have had, he is entitled to take an express assignment of any rights of action of the owner.[10] But the category of justified assignments is not closed, as the House of Lords' judgment in *Trendtex Ltd v Credit Suisse*[11] in 1981 made clear. For instance, a creditor of X whose only chance of being paid (because X is nearly bankrupt) is to take an assignment of some right of action vested in X and exercise it for his own benefit, is entitled to do so; but not someone who buys the same right of action purely as a speculative transaction. A purely aleatory or gambling interest, in other words, will not justify taking over another's right of action for damages; but any further 'genuine commercial interest' (the words are Lord Roskill's in the *Trendtex* case[12]), such as an interest in the assignor's solvency, will.

Fifthly, the benefit of an obligation cannot be transferred if the obligation does not yet exist. For example, A cannot 'assign' to B his right to his next month's salary before he has earned it; at the time of the purported assignment there is simply nothing to assign.[13] However, this is not a very significant limitation, since, although A cannot assign to B rights that he has not yet got, there is nothing to stop him contracting with B to assign them to B if and when he does get them. Moreover, the law makes this process even easier by two further rules. First, if a person contracts to assign rights as and when he gets them, the effect of that contract is automatically to make B the equitable owner and thus assignee of those rights when they do arise; no further action is required by the assignor. Secondly, a purported assignment of obligations that have not yet arisen is construed as an implied contract to assign them when they come into existence. In general, therefore, the net result of a purported assignment of a future obligation is that the obligation is assigned in equity as soon as it arises.[14]

---

9 Cf *Ellis v Torrington* [1920] 1 KB 399, 89 LJKB 369.
10 *Compañía Colombiana de Seguros v Pacific Steam Navigation Co Ltd* [1965] 1 QB 101, [1964] 1 All ER 216.
11 [1982] AC 679, [1981] 3 All ER 520.
12 [1982] AC 679 at 703, [1981] 3 All ER 520 at 531.
13 But a right is not a future right merely because it cannot be enforced yet. The benefit of an obligation to pay £100 in three months' time is a present right, and can be transferred in the normal way. See *E & J Earle Ltd v Hemsworth RDC* (1928) 44 TLR 605.
14 *Tailby v Official Receiver* (1888) 13 App Cas 523. But the assignment must be for value, since equity will not enforce rights arising from a gratuitous promise.

2. The means of transferring the benefit of an obligation

The assignment of things in action is an unplanned area in English law, straddling common law and equity, property and obligation; hence it is not surprising that there should be not one but four means of transferring the benefit of an obligation. (These are in addition, moreover, to specific statutory means laid down for assignment of the more commonplace intangible rights, such as copyright, shares, or life insurance policies.[15] Nor do they cover negotiable instruments such as promissory notes and cheques; these, together with the obligations they embody, are transferrable by mere delivery if made out to bearer, or by endorsement if made out to anyone else.)[16] The four general means are (a) statutory assignment under the Law of Property Act 1925; (b) assignment in equity by way of contract; (c) assignment in equity by declaration of trust; and (d) equitable assignment pure and simple.

(a) STATUTORY ASSIGNMENT

By s 136 of the Law of Property Act 1925, any obligation, whatever its source, can be assigned by a document in writing, signed by the assignor and communicated to the obligor and (almost certainly) the assignee as well. The assignment only becomes effective when all these stages have been gone through;[17] this matter of timing is extremely important if, for instance, at some time in the transaction the assignor becomes insolvent, since only if the assignment is complete by the time of the insolvency will the assignee prevail over the assignor's general creditors.

There are only two defects in statutory assignment as a means to transfer the benefit of an obligation. First, it can be cumbersome. Secondly, it cannot be used to assign part only of an obligation (eg half of a debt of £500), or to assign by way of security only, rather than outright. These defects, however, mean that assignment in equity, which it is not subject to them, continues to be significant; hence we now turn to the various forms of it.

(b) ASSIGNMENT IN EQUITY BY WAY OF CONTRACT

EQUITABLE ASSIGNMENT IN GENERAL. Even before the introduction in 1875 of the statutory means of assignment now contained in the Law of Property Act 1925, equity – as against the common law – had always provided facilities to assign all sorts of obligations, both legal and

---

15 See, eg, Copyright Act 1956, s 31; Stock Transfer Act 1963; Policies of Assurance Act 1867, s 5.
16 Bills of Exchange Act 1882, s 31(2), (3).
17 *Holt v Heatherfield Trust Ltd* [1942] 2 KB 1, [1942] 1 All ER 404.

equitable. The statutory provisions supplemented, but did not abolish, equitable assignments; hence statutory and equitable assignments survive in parallel. The effect of equitable assignment, whatever form it takes, is the same as that of statutory assignment; that is, the benefit of the obligation becomes vested in the assignee. The only difference is procedural; an equitable assignee of a *legal* obligation enforces it, strictly speaking, not in his own name but in that of the assignor.[18] (It goes without saying, of course, that he enforces it for his own, and not the assignor's, benefit).

ASSIGNMENT BY WAY OF CONTRACT. To turn, however, to assignment by way of contract. The essence of this is that the assignor contracts, for value, with the assignee to transfer to him the benefit of the obligation. Because of the doctrine that a specifically enforceable contract of sale makes the seller a constructive trustee for the buyer,[19] the result is to make the assignee owner in equity of the benefit of the obligation, and thus to give him the right to enforce it. Typically, for instance, an assignor will promise to assign to an assignee the benefit of debts owing to his business as and when they arise, in exchange for a loan or other payment by the assignee. As they each arise the assignor's promise attaches to them and they automatically vest in equity in the assignee.[20] The chief defect of this means of assignment is that it depends on contract, which needs consideration, and thus that it cannot be used for gratuitous assignments.[1]

(c) ASSIGNMENT IN EQUITY BY WAY OF DECLARATION OF TRUST

The benefit of an obligation being a form of property, a person may declare himself trustee of it, as he can with anything else. If he does, the effect is that the person for whom he declares himself trustee becomes equitable owner of the benefit of the obligation and can thus insist on enforcing it for his own advantage. The formalities required for this form of assignment are minimal; the assignor must merely evince an intent to create a trust. The declaration of trust may even be oral, except that in certain cases where an interest under a trust is involved, s 53(1) (c) of the Law of Property Act 1925 requires it to be in writing.[2]

---

18 If the assignor refuses to co-operate then he can be joined in the action as defendant and the assignee still can recover from the obligor; so the point is procedural only.
19 The contract seems to be assumed in all cases to be specifically enforceable.
20 This form of effectively mortgaging future obligations was accepted in *Tailby v Official Receiver* (1888) 13 App Cas 523.
1   See *Re McArdle* [1951] Ch 669, [1951] 1 All ER 905; a contract for past consideration, not being binding, cannot engender an equitable assignment.
2   This is because a declaration of trust by the owner of an equitable interest in a thing may amount, anomalously, to a 'disposition' of that equitable interest within s 53(1) (c) of the Law of Property Act 1925. See P. H. Pettitt, *Equity and the Law of Trusts*, 4th edn, 58.

Nor is consideration necessary for a valid declaration of trust; as a result, this means – as against equitable assignment by way of contract – can be used for purely gratuitous transfers of the benefit of obligations.[3]

(d) EQUITABLE ASSIGNMENT PURE AND SIMPLE

This is clearly the most straightforward means of equitable assignment. The assignor merely says to the assignee that he assigns the benefit of the obligation to him, and that of itself is apparently effective to make the assignee owner in equity of the benefit of the obligation. Were the law logical, indeed, it would be the only sort of equitable assignment; the declaration of trust is a clumsy and rather unnecessary device where intangibles are involved, and the use of a contract to transfer proprietary rights involves a disconcerting confusion between the concepts of obligation and property.

Like the declaration of trust, it is submitted that this method can be effectively used for a gratuitous assignment; consideration, in other words, is not necessary. This is clear where it is an equitable obligation, such as a right under a trust, being assigned;[4] and, though the point is not certain, Atkinson J thought in 1941 that the same went for a legal obligation.[5] Such a view certainly accords with principle; it is only in general *promissory* rights that equity refuses to enforce in the absence of consideration, and here the assignor is purporting to *transfer* the benefit of the obligation, not to *promise* to transfer it. True, there are cases that seem to deny that one can have an equitable assignment without consideration, but they are weak authorities because most of them in fact involve promises to transfer the benefit of obligations, where consideration is necessary.[6]

(e) THE SIGNIFICANCE OF EQUITABLE ASSIGNMENT

Despite the possibility of statutory assignment, equitable assignment remains significant for three reasons. The first we have touched on already; equitable assignment, unlike statutory assignment, allows assignment of part of an obligation, and more importantly provides the only means to assign the benefit of an obligation by way of security. Secondly, there is no need for writing (subject to exceptions already mentioned); whereas a statutory assignment must be in writing. Thirdly, equitable assignment, while to be effective it requires communication

3   This seems the best explanation of *M'Fadden v Jenkyns* (1842) 1 Ph 153, 12 LJ
    Ch 146.
4   *Voyle v Hughes* (1854) 2 Sm & G 18, 2 Eq Rep 42.
5   *Holt v Heatherfield Trust Ltd* [1942] 2 KB 1, [1942] 1 All ER 404.
6   Eg *Clegg v Bromley* [1912] 3 KB 474, 81 LJKB 1081.

to the assignee, requires no communication to the obligor. It can thus be effective immediately between the parties to it – with appropriate consequences if the assignee becomes insolvent – even before such communication takes place (as in the nature of things, eventually it must).

3. The effects of the transfer of an obligation.

(a) THE ASSIGNEE'S RIGHTS ARE NO GREATER THAN HIS ASSIGNOR'S

An assignee of an obligation can, as a general rule, be in no better position as against the obligor than his assignor was. Defects in the original obligation, and counterclaims that would go to reduce the amount the obligor would have had to pay the assignor, equally affect the assignee. They do so, moreover, whether or not the assignee had any reason to know of them; in this sense, caveat emptor applies with a vengeance to the transferee of an obligation. (The analogy here is with the transfer of chattels, where the transferee gets no better title than the transferor had. It is a bad analogy, because the rule relating to assignment of obligations exists to protect the interests of the obligor rather than those of a previous owner of the thing transferred. Nevertheless the analogy is applied).

Thus if X sells a business to Y and assigns his right to sue Y for the price to Z, Y may plead against Z, as much as he could have pleaded against X, the fact that X deceived him into buying the business.[7] Similarly with counterclaims, though here the rule is more complicated. Where a counterclaim arises out of the same transaction as the original claim, it always affects the claim of the assignee. Thus a builder building a house for a customer can assign his right to be paid, but only subject to any cross-claim of the customer for damages for bad workmanship.[8] Where the counterclaim is quite separate, it affects the assignee only if it arose before the obligor had notice of the assignment. A bank,[9] for instance, may normally set off the debit in an overdrawn balance against a credit balance held by the same customer in another account, even if the customer has assigned the credit balance to a third party. But if, having notice of the assignment, the bank allows further drawings on the overdrawn account, it does so at its own risk and these cannot affect the assignee's rights.[10]

---

7   *Lawrence v Hayes* [1927] 2 KB 111, 96 LJKB 658.
8   *Young v Kitchin* (1878) 3 Ex D 127, 47 LJEx 579.
9   It goes without saying that a bank account is in law a debt owed by the bank to its customer (or vice versa) and thus a thing in action.
10   *Roxburghe v Cox* (1881) 17 Ch D 560, 50 LJCh 772.

There are two exceptions to the doctrine that the assignee's rights can be no greater than the assignor's. One is that a contractual obligation may exclude the doctrine and explicity give assignees greater rights than the original contracting party. A policy of life assurance, for instance, may exclude liability to the insured himself if he commits suicide, but say that that exclusion shall not affect an assignee for value. The other exception is negotiable instrument, such as cheques, promissory notes and bills of exchange. Here, broadly any assignee who takes in good faith and for value is a 'holder in due course' and can enforce the obligation whatever the rights of his assignor may have been.[11] This doctrine is justified by commercial practice and convenience, and also by the fact that anyone putting his name to this sort of instrument ought to realise the risks he is taking in doing so.

(b) ASSIGNMENT AND THIRD PARTIES' RIGHTS

Whatever sort of assignment is involved, once the obligor has notice that the benefit of an obligation has been assigned the assignment is valid for all purposes. Equitable assignments, however, we have seen, may take effect without such notice; nevertheless, where notice has not been given the assignee may find his interests postponed to those of certain third parties.

First, the obligor is discharged if, after assignment of the obligation but before he has notice of it, he pays the assignor and not the assignor;[12] an obvious rule, given that the obligor has no means to know of the assignee's rights. (The assignor, of course, must hand over everything he receives to the assignor; otherwise he would be unjustifiably enriched.)

Secondly, if the assignor purports to assign the benefit of the same obligation twice to different persons, the second assignee does not necessarily lose out. Instead, by the rule in *Dearle v Hall*,[13] the first assignee to give notice to the obligor, whoever he is, prevails over the other.

Third, if the assignor becomes bankrupt after assignment but before notice to the obligor, s 38 of the Bankruptcy Act 1914 provides that the benefit of the obligation may still go to his trustee in bankruptcy by the doctrine known as 'reputed ownership.' (This is not very significant, however. The doctrine of 'reputed ownership' does not apply to companies in liquidation as against bankrupt individuals.)

It is easy to see why the obligor should be unable to be affected by

11   Bills of Exchange Act 1882, s 38(2).
12   *Brice v Bannister* (1878) 3 QBD 569, 17 LJQB 722.
13   (1828) 3 Russ 1.

assignments he has had no notice of. It is less easy to see why third parties should benefit from lack of notice to the obligor, as they do because of the rule in *Dearle v Hall* and the rules of reputed ownership. The formal reason is a rather far-fetched analogy between giving notice to an obligor that an obligation has been assigned and transferring possession of goods; where possession of goods has been transferred, this is a public act and ought to be able to affect third parties' rights, whereas if ownership has been transferred but possession has not, then third parties should be able to deal with the transferor of the goods as though he were still owner of them. It is easy to see why the analogy is a bad one; giving notice to an obligor of the assignment of an obligation is not a public act in the same sense as transferring possession of goods is, and so it is hard to see why it should radically affect anyone's rights except for the obligee himself.

4. Transmission of obligations on death

This is not a book about the law of succession; nevertheless, some features of the law of transfer of obligations on death are interesting because of the light they throw on the English law of obligations in general.

The basic rule is contained in the Law Reform (Miscellaneous Provisions) Act 1934, which begins simply enough by providing in s 1 that prima facie the benefit of all obligations owed to a dead person passes to his estate. The only exceptions are statutory. Claims for defamation, for bereavement when a member of one's family is killed, and for money that one would have earned after one's death had one's life not been shortened (claims for 'lost years', dealt with in Ch 17) do not pass.[14] All other claims, without exception and whatever their basis, do.

Though simple and straightforward, this rule is not very satisfactory. It fails to take a vital distinction (drawn, for instance, in Scots law[15]), between claims that go to make up a person's wealth (such as debts owed to him, interests under a trust, or compensation for damage to property), which obviously ought to pass to his estate, and claims for injury to non-pecuniary interests, which ought not to. Admittedly some claims for non-pecuniary interests are specifically (and rightly) excepted; defamation and bereavement, for instance. But this still

---

14 Law Reform (Miscellaneous Provisions) Act 1934, ss 1(1), 1(1A), 1(2) (a).
15 Compare *Stewart's Executrix v London Midland and Scottish Rly Co* 1943 SC(HL) 19 and *Smith v Stewart* 1961 SC 91 with the logically sound but quite misconceived English decisions in *Rose v Ford* [1937] AC 826, [1937] 3 All ER 359 and *Gammell v Wilson* [1982] AC 27, [1981] 1 All ER 578. Both the latter decisions, significantly, had to be reversed by statute.

leaves several other claims, such as for pain and suffering in tort, which cover essentially non-pecuniary interests and thus exist to soothe and not indemnify, passing to a dead person's estate; which, it is suggested, has little plausible claim to them.

Perhaps better in this connection would have been to take a leaf from the book of bankruptcy law, which has drawn a sophisticated distinction between oligations owed to a person which go to make up his wealth and thus ought to pass to his trustee in bankruptcy, and other obligations. The former class includes contractual rights in general;[16] and rights of action in tort, but only in so far as they genuinely affect the bankrupt's property or business, such as for conversion of goods.[17] By contrast, the class of rights that do not pass includes the right to sue for defamation, or for breach of confidence, so long as the damage suffered by the bankrupt is non-pecuniary,[18] and even the right to sue for trespass to land, except as far as actual damage to property is shown.[19] If something like the latter class could have been omitted from the claims surviving to a dead person's estate, the law on that subject would, it is suggested, be a good deal more rational.

5. Transmission by operation of law: subrogation

Subrogation is an assigment of the benefit of an obligation by operation of law, imposed in certain defined circumstances. Assume A, for instance, negligently damages B's car, whereupon B's insurer pays B for the damage. B's insurer could recoup himself against A by taking an assignment of B's right to sue A expressly, but he does not need to. The law itself impliedly transfers B's rights against A to him without the need to do more.

More formally, the principle of subrogation provides that, where X is under some obligation vis-à-vis Y (it does not seem to matter what sort of obligation it is) then in certain cases if Z, a third person, performs that obligation and so releases X from it, the law will impliedly transfer Y's rights to Z (including not only the benefit of the obligation itself, but also any security taken by Y for its performance).

The categories of subrogation are not closed, but they broadly cover three sorts of case.

First, there are cases where the person paying off X's obligation to Y

---

16 Such as the right to damages for wrongful dismissal – *Beckham v Drake* (1849) 2 HLCas 579.

17 *Stanton v Collier* (1854) 23 LJQB 116, 22 LTOS 240; cf *Wenlock v Moloney* (1967) 111 Sol Jo 437.

18 See *Re Kavanagh ex p Bankrupt v Jackson (Trustee)* [1949] 1 All ER 264, 65 TLR 486; cf *Wilson v United Counties Bank Ltd* [1920] AC 102, 88 LJKB 1033.

19 *Rose v Buckett* [1901] 2 KB 499, 70 LJKB 736.

was legally bound to do so; for example the insurer, or a surety paying off the principal debtor's obligation. These examples are not of course exclusive; there is no objection to granting subrogation in other cases where one person is forced to pay a debt that someone else ought to have paid.[20] The object here is of course not simply to obtain recoupment as such, since a person forced to discharge another's obligation can get that under the principles of unjustified enrichment in any case; it is normally to obtain in addition any securities that may have been taken by Y to cover X's obligation.

Secondly, there are cases where X's obligation to Y is discharged by Z not by compulsion but because Z had authority to do so and did not intend to act gratuitously. Typically Z will have acted on the basis of X's promise to reimburse him, but X's promise will have turned out for some reason unenforceable. Thus in *Bannatyne v MacIver*,[1] for instance, the plaintiff provided cash to pay off the defendant company's debts on the basis of a promise of reimbursement that in fact was unauthorised. Although unable to sue on the promise of reimbursement, he was held able to stand in the shoes of those whom he had provided the cash to pay off and enforce their obligations against the defendant company. Similarly subrogation may provide a would-be secured lender with a replacement security if his own turns out ineffective; thus a building society lending money to a minor to buy a house cannot enforce either the loan or the mortgage given by the minor, but can stand in the shoes of the vendor from whom the minor bought the house and exercise his unpaid vendor's lien.[2]

Thirdly, there is a variation of the cases just mentioned where it is not Z who pays off X's obligation to Y, but X himself, using money lent to him by Z. This is obviously only relevant if, for some reason, Z's loan to X is irrecoverable; but, if it is, then prima facie Z is entitled to stand in Y's place and sue X in Y's name. Thus a lender to a child can recover a loan to the child that was used by it to pay for something, such as necessaries, that it was bound to pay for; similarly a lender to a company who could not otherwise recover his loan because the company acted *ultra vires* in borrowing from him, can nevertheless recover to the extent that his loan went to pay off lawful debts of the company.[3] Moreover, if the lender intended to make a secured loan he can be subrogated not only to the debt discharged but also the securities thereby released; not so, however, where he intended to make an unsecured loan, since the doctrine of subrogation should not have the effect of giving a lender better rights than he himself intended to obtain.[4]

---

20   *Re Downer Enterprises* [1974] 2 All ER 1074, [1974] 1 WLR 1460 is a neat example.
1   [1906] 1 KB 103, 75 LJKB 120.
2   *Thurstan v Nottingham Permanent Benefit Building Society* [1902] 1 Ch 1, 71 LJCh 83; affd [1903] AC 6, 72 LJCh 134.
3   Eg *Baroness Wenlock v River Dee Co* (1887) 19 QBD 155, 56 LJQB 589.
4   *Re Wrexham Mold & Connah's Quay Rly Co* [1899] 1 Ch 440, 68 LJCh 270.

These cases of subrogation are not necessarily exhaustive; indeed there is something to be said for some abstract doctrine such as that Z ought to be subrogated to Y's rights against X provided merely he discharged X's obligation to Y and had good reason to do so.[5] (In fact the development of such a doctrine is likely to be slow, at least in England, because technical doctrines make it surprisingly difficult for one person validly to discharge the obligation of another and thus release the latter;[6] and subrogation is possible only where X's obligation to Y has actually been discharged.)

Lastly, rights to subrogation may arise, or be varied, by contract; an insurer, for instance, may stipulate in the contract of insurance for particular rights in respect of claims by the insured.[7]

The affinities between subrogation and assignment are obvious. A right of subrogation arising by contract, indeed, may well be indistinguishable from an equitable assignment of the obligation concerned.[8] Nevertheless, there are significant differences between the two. Assignment is essentially consensual, subrogation primarily (though not exclusively) takes place by operation of law. This thinking matters; it means, for example, that courts are likely to find it much easier to deny subrogation on the ground of public policy than they are to annul an assignment on the same ground.[9] Further, although subrogation is in law a sort of assignment, it is an odd sort of assignment, since what triggers it is an act (payment) that would normally have the effect, not of preserving or transferring the obligation discharged, but simply of extinguishing it. The common law always had difficulty here, saying for instance with maddening (and sound) logic that if a surety paid off a secured debt he could not be subrogated to the security because it no longer existed, having been discharged. It took the Mercantile Law Amendment Act 1856, s 5, to change the law and deem the security to be kept alive. Equity on the other hand wisely sacrificed logic to expediency in this field; it had no difficulty in, for instance, resurrecting an unpaid vendor's lien over a house that had long been putatively paid off in order to protect the building society whose mortgage on the property, granted by the buyer, turned out to be invalid.[10]

---

5   Eg where a landlord is liable to repair his tenant's premises but does not, and a third party discharges his obligation in order to protect the tenant's amenity.
6   In particular A cannot normally validly discharge B's debt to C merely by paying it: see P. Birks & J. Beatson (1976) 92 LQR 188.
7   *Orakpo v Manson Investments Ltd* [1978] AC 95 at 104, [1977] 3 All ER 1 at 7; cf *L Lucas Ltd v Export Credits Guarantee Department* [1974] 2 All ER 889, [1974] 1 WLR 909.
8   The French term for certain kinds of assignment, *subrogation conventionelle*, neatly illustrates this point.
9   See Lord Denning MR's judgment in *Morris v Ford Motor Co* [1973] QB 792, [1973] 2 All ER 1084.
10 See *Thurstan v Nottingham Permanent Benefit Building Society* [1902] 1 Ch 1, 71 LJCh 83; affd [1903] AC 6, 72 LJCh 134.

Chapter 17

Enforcement of obligations[1]

We have hitherto referred to X being 'liable' for damage, or to return unjustified enrichment; and to contracts being 'enforceable', without much further thought. It is the object of this chapter to go behind these words, and to explain how the law enforces obligations that it has found to exist.

Now, the means of enforcement of obligations divide effectively into four. First, there are *pecuniary* remedies, involving the forced payment of money by the defendant to the plaintiff; either in the form of payment of a debt, or as damages for a wrong or compensation for unjustified enrichment. Secondly there are *specific* remedies, where a court orders the defendant to carry out his obligation, or reverse the effects of a wrong, *in specie* rather than merely mulcting him for a financial equivalent. Injunctions and orders of specific performance are the best examples of such remedies.[2] Thirdly a remedy may be *proprietary*, enforcing an obligation by declaring the plaintiff owner of something in the defendant's hands; for instance, giving a cohabitee contributing to the price of a house an interest in the house. Fourthly there is *self-help*, allowing an obligee in certain cases on his own initiative, without the intervention of the court, to take steps to ensure fulfilment of the obligation. Examples include the right peaceably to retake one's own property, and the right to self-defence.

In general, obligations and the means available to enforce them are clearly separate. The sellers' duty to deliver goods is primary; he is liable in damages if he does not, but that liability is secondary to his main duty. But the distinction is not absolute. A promise to pay £1,000 in the event of a breach of contract is analytically a primary obligation, like any other debt; yet it is treated as a remedy in that the obligee cannot enforce it beyond his actual interest in performance of the main contract (the doctrine of 'penalty clauses', dealt with below). Again, the right to cancel a contract for breach by the other party often, at

---

1 See generally F. H. Lawson, *Remedies of English Law*, 2nd edn, 1980.
2 Strictly speaking, the enforcement of a debt is a specific remedy as well as a pecuniary one. Nevertheless it is more convenient to treat it as pecuniary, since it shares many of the characteristics of pecuniary remedies and few of those of specific ones.

least in practice, amounts to a drastic remedy for breach rather than merely a condition placed on one's own obligation.

1. Pecuniary enforcement

The subject of pecuniary enforcement divides effectively into three: liquidated claims for debts (for instance, for the price of goods sold); unliquidated claims for damages for a wrong, such as breach of contract; and claims for sums to neutralise unjustified enrichment.

(a) LIQUIDATED CLAIMS FOR DEBTS

These are straightforward claims with few complications; those complications that do exist largely concern the extent to which the ability to claim the price of performing a contract is conditional on full performance, and were dealt with in Ch 11. With these claims there is no room for argument over the amount. It does not matter that the plaintiff himself has no interest in receiving the amount – he may, for instance, be obliged to hand it over on receipt to a third person, but that does not reduce his claim. Nor is it relevant whether a debt was reasonably or unreasonably incurred; as we saw in Ch 11, a contractor may perform and sue for the price of performance even though he knew the performance was unwanted and unnecessary and ought reasonably to have abandoned the contract and paid damages.[3]

(b) UNLIQUIDATED DAMAGES FOR WRONGS

Damages are not only *a* remedy for wrongs, such as torts and breaches of contract, in English law; they are the *primary* remedy. Rather oddly, specific remedies, where a court tells a defendant to carry out his legal obligations, are regarded as exceptional and discretionary.[4] Thus although there may be obligations enforceable pecuniarily but not specifically, there cannot – a few special cases apart – be an obligation enforceable specifically but not pecuniarily.[5]

Apart from being concerned with money, pecuniary remedies have two general features (though neither is universal). First, they lie only against the person actually subject to the obligation; hence they are sometimes called 'personal'. Thus if A agrees to sell a thing to B but then sells it to C, A is liable to B in damages but C is not. Secondly, they

3 *White & Carter (Councils) Ltd v Macgregor* [1962] AC 413, [1961] 3 All ER 1178.
4 Not all systems hold this view; German law, at least on principle, regards an order to perform a contract as the primary remedy for its breach.
5 *Garden Cottage Foods Ltd v Milk Marketing Board* [1983] 2 All ER 770 at 777 f, [1983] 3 WLR 143 at 152.

abate in insolvency, unless within a specific – normally statutory – exception; to protect himself the obligee must normally take security. Specific, and proprietary, remedies, by contrast, often apply against third parties not connected with the initial obligation (thus a specifically enforceable contract for the sale of land may be enforced not only against the vendor but also against other purchasers of it); and they normally do not abate in insolvency.

(i) Quantification of damages
We start with the quantification of damages for wrongs. Torts and breaches of contract here observe different principles, so we deal with each separately.

A. TORTS. In the absence of a more specific rule, damages in tort should, as far as possible, put the plaintiff in the financial position he would have been in had the tort not been committed. This means first of all that the law mistrusts their use for other, punitive, purposes. Thus English law limits such use effectively to two such cases;[6] the deliberate tort committed in the hope that profits will exceed damages (as with the publication of a clearly libellous best-seller), and – to express constitutional outrage rather than for any better reason – where public authorities deliberately exceed their powers (as with, say, a deliberate unprovoked assault by a policeman).

However, while tort damages may not *punish*, this does not mean that they can never compensate beyond actual money losses; quite the contrary. Defamation, for instance, protects the purely moral interest in reputation, and does so generously (besides, like any tort, compensating actual money loss suffered). Assault, false imprisonment and trespass to land similarly provide damages beyond, and in the absence of, financial loss (indeed, the non-pecuniary aspect of these torts is emphasised figuratively in their being 'actionable per se'; a plaintiff proving their commission is entitled as of right to some, albeit perhaps nominal, damages). Even damages for deprivation of property can go beyond actual loss,[7] as can damages for personal injury representing loss of amenity and pain and suffering, and damages in negligence generally for loss of managerial time.[8] With deliberate torts, moreover, damages may vary according to how unacceptably the

---

6   Listed, with others less important, by Lord Devlin in *Rookes v Barnard* [1964] AC 1129 at 1221, [1964] 1 All ER 367 at 407 f.
7   'Supposing a person took a chair out of my room, could anybody say you had a right to diminish the damages by showing I did not usually sit in that chair . . .?' – Lord Halsbury in *The Mediana* [1900] AC 113 at 117. But cf *Brandeis Goldschmidt & Co Ltd v Western Transport Ltd* [1981] QB 864, [1982] 1 All ER 28.
8   For the latter see *Tate & Lyle Food and Distribution Ltd v Greater London Council* [1981] 3 All ER 716, [1982] 2 WLR 149.

defendant acted; blatant or high-handed trespass or libel may engender 'aggravated' damages, on the argument that insult adds to injury.[9]

Damages for personal injury. Though detailed coverage of damages for different torts is outside the scope of this book, it would be incomplete without some account of how damages for personal injury are computed. The award starts, straightforwardly, with financial loss; medical expenses and loss of earnings during the plaintiff's life. More tendentiously, if life expectation has been shortened by the defendant's act, claims are allowed for the money that would have been earned in the intervening period (the 'lost years').[10] The formal justification these awards is the desperate one that most people consider the wages of the dead who would otherwise be alive to represent a genuine loss to those who would have earned them; the practical one, that the money is expected in practice to go to the injured person's dependants, who unless he were killed relatively quickly would have had no claim at all. All claims for future earnings are discounted against possible hypothetical death or disablement; claims in respect of 'lost years' additionally for what the victim in that time would have spent uselessly rather than saved.

As regards moral damage, pain and suffering and loss of amenity (such as the loss of ability to play football) are compensated on a fairly generous scale.

On principle, any gain resulting from injury is deducted; in practice this rule is not very important because there are so many exceptions to it. Thus charitable gifts, occupational pensions and insurance proceeds are ignored (the first for sentimental reasons, the other two on the not entirely convincing ground that, having been 'paid for', the injured should not lose the benefit of them[11]). As for State benefits, some are deducted, some are not and some are partly deducted; a bewildering array of rules we cannot go into here.

Wrongful death raises different problems. At common law dependants had no claim either for loss of visible support or for bereavement; but by ss 1 and 1A of the Fatal Accidents Act 1976 (which extend earlier legislation dating back to 1846) they now have a cause of action for both. This right is independent of any right of the deceased, but the deceased's acts are 'identified' with his relatives' claim (so if the deceased was contributorily negligent or consented to run the risk his relatives' claim is accordingly reduced or annulled). The action for support is what it sounds: for loss of the gain the relatives would otherwise have had from the deceased by way of support (and not, for example, by way of business relationship).

---

9   Eg *Jolliffe v Willmett & Co* [1971] 1 All ER 478.
10   *Pickett v British Rail Engineering* [1980] AC 136, [1979] 1 All ER 774.
11   See per Lord Reid in *Parry v Cleaver* [1970] AC 1 at 14, [1969] 1 All ER 555 at 558.

In addition, certain claims of the deceased in respect of an accident will pass to his estate (often his relatives) if he dies as a result of it; for instance, claims for pain and suffering suffered before he died. Lastly a note on children. The death of a child generally causes little tangible loss to parents, since parents are rarely dependent on their children. Yet to overcome revulsion at a nil award of damages for the death of a child, parents have a statutory right to a standard – and not inconsiderable – sum to cover bereavement here.[12]

Remoteness of loss, and related topics. For obvious reasons, where X has committed a tort, there must be some limit to the losses he is liable for. With negligence, much of the work of limitation is, as we saw in Ch 7, done by limiting the persons and the damage in respect of which a duty of care is owed. Nevertheless, limitations based on pure remoteness still play a part. For instance, even if X is liable to Y for damage to his property, he is liable only for the loss that would be suffered by a normal person in Y's position; he is not liable for extra loss suffered because Y was (say) already in serious financial difficulty.[13] The concept of remoteness is used haphazardly, but if anything less sparingly, in other torts; being utilised, for instance, to justify the rule that one cannot claim for personal injury or shock resulting from defamation.[14]

Connected with remoteness of loss is the rule that one cannot recover in tort to the extent that one's loss results from one's own act, or from one's failure to act reasonably to mitigate damage one has suffered. If, for instance, a car is damaged beyond economic repair its owner is limited to the cost of replacement,[15] not the cost of repairs. Nevertheless, reasonableness, given that the plaintiff did not choose to be in relationship with the defendant, is widely construed; a householder whose house is demolished can normally claim the cost of rebuilding it, rather than being told he ought to sell the site and buy another home somewhere else.[16]

B. DAMAGES FOR BREACH OF CONTRACT. As in tort, damages for breach of contract exist on principle to reflect the plaintiff's interest in the contract being performed, and not to punish the defendant for not performing. Hence, in an interesting parallel with its attitude to punitive damages in tort, the law invalidates attempts to misuse damages for

---

12 Fatal Accidents Act 1976, s 1A. The sum in 1982 was £3500.
13 *Liesbosch (Owners) v Edison (Owners), The Edison* [1933] AC 449, 102 LJP 73, HL. But this does not apply if the plaintiff merely has ordinary financial problems such as others have – *Dodd Properties (Kent) Ltd v Canterbury City Council* [1980] 1 All ER 928, [1980] 1 WLR 433.
14 See *Wheeler v Somerfield* [1966] 2 All ER 305 at 309, per Lord Denning MR.
15 *Darbishire v Warran* [1963] 3 All ER 310, [1963] 1 WLR 1067.
16 *Philips v Ward* [1956] 1 All ER 874 at 876, [1956] 1 WLR 471 at 473, per Denning LJ.

breach of contract as levers to terrorise contractors into performing. A promise to pay an exorbitant sum, beyond any 'genuine pre-estimate of damage', in the event of a breach of contract will not be enforced.[17] This rule thus exists essentially to prevent the abuse of the institution of damages, rather than (as one might have thought) to protect the improvident, as is shown by three interesting features of it. First, the prohibition on penalty clauses does not depend on unfairness; excessive damage stipulations are unenforceable even if commercially negotiated. Secondly, there is no parallel preclusion of absurdly low stipulations of damages. Thirdly, for a doctrine whose raison d'être is restriction on contractual freedom, it can be evaded astoundingly easily; if the event triggering the obligation to pay is redefined by the parties as not a breach of contract but as the exercise of a right (such as to cancel the contract) the control ceases to apply.[18]

Contract having once been considered more commercial than tort, no damages for non-pecuniary interests used to be available; but with realisation that contract means more than money that rule has disappeared. A travel agent providing a disastrous holiday must compensate for disappointment;[19] an employer guilty of wrongful demotion, for loss of *amour propre*.[20]

The plaintiff's interest. To return, however, to the plaintiff's interest in seeing the contract performed. This subject is more complicated than it looks, since the plaintiff in fact has two entirely separate interests in seeing the contract performed. First, he can recover any gain he stood to make had the contract been performed; sometimes called his 'expectation interest'. On a gratuitous promise to pay £5,000 this would be £5,000; on a promise to sell a thing worth £150 for £100, £50. Secondly, the plaintiff can recover any loss he suffered by relying on the contract being kept which he would otherwise have recouped (sometimes called his 'reliance interest'); for example, expenses incurred in going to collect a cargo that was, in breach of contract, not delivered.

If a contract is broken, prima facie both expectation and reliance interests may give rise to damages. If A sells B a thing guaranteed to be worth £80 for £60, and it turns out worth only £50, B can recover £30; £20 loss of expectation (putative profit) and £10 reliance (the amount he is out of pocket). Of course one cannot claim the same loss twice over; a

---

17 *Dunlop Pneumatic Tyre Co Ltd v New Garage and Motor Co Ltd* [1915] AC 79, 83 LJKB 1574, HL.
18 *Associated Distributors Ltd v Hall* [1938] 2 KB 83, [1938] 1 All ER 511; cf *Bridge v Campbell Discount Co Ltd* [1961] 1 QB 445, [1961] 2 All ER 97, (revsd on other grounds [1962] AC 600, [1962] 1 All ER 385).
19 *Jarvis v Swans Tours Ltd* [1973] QB 233, [1973] 1 All ER 71.
20 *Cox v Philips Industries Ltd* [1976] 3 All ER 161, [1976] 1 WLR 638. How far the authority of *Addis v Gramophone Co Ltd* [1909] AC 48, 78 LJKB 112, HL, denying such damages for wrongful dismissal, goes today must remain doubtful.

seller failing to deliver a cargo is not liable both for the buyer's expenditure wasted in going to fetch it and also for the buyer's profit on the cargo, since the former would have gone to reduce the latter anyway.[21] But such cases aside, there is no objection to both reliance and expectation interest being available in the same case.

Whether this rule is entirely desirable in all cases is doubtful. Arguably some sorts of promise ought only to give rise to claims based on wasted expenditure but not any others; with exceptions, such a concept is impossible in English law. More important, where a contract is defective there is strong argument for allowing some recoupment of expenditure even if the contract is not enforced in full. For instance, when goods are 'sold' which, unknown to both parties, do not exist, arguably the buyer should have no claim to putative profits on those goods but (especially if the seller were at fault) should recover his wasted expenditure in going to fetch them. Yet the law denies this possibility; either a contract is valid and its breach allows all sorts of damages, or it is invalid and no compenstion is available to anyone.[1]

In a few anomalous cases a contract may give rise to only one kind of damages. A seller of a house, for instance, who innocently fails to make title to it, is not liable for anything but the buyer's wasted conveyancing expenses.[2]

The problem of indirect loss. A contract breaker may be liable as much for indirect as for direct loss. Assume breach of a contract to redecorate a house in lamentable taste; or a building erected in breach of a covenant not to build on land next to the plaintiff's, which building nevertheless does not depreciate his land. In neither case is there any *direct* loss; nevertheless the defendant is liable in the first case for the cost of doing the decorating and in the second for what the plaintiff might reasonably have demanded for release from the covenant.[3] Such reasoning, indeed, might have alleviated the problem of privity of contract; breach by A of a promise to B to pay C £100 arguably engenders an indirect loss to B of a benefit worth £100. Perhaps unfortunately, the House of Lords has discountenanced such a development, holding instead that B here can recover no more than nominal damages.[4]

Reduction of loss. It goes without saying that one can claim in contract only loss actually suffered; anything going to reduce that loss must be in

---

21 This seems the best explanation of *C & P Haulage (a firm) v Middleton* [1983] 1 All ER 94.
1 Cf *McRae v Commonwealth Disposals Commission* (1951) 84 CLR 377, and the Sale of Goods Act 1979, s 6.
2 *Bain v Fothergill* (1874) LR 7 HL 158, 43 LJEx 243.
3 Cf *Radford v De Froberville* [1978] 1 All ER 33, [1977] 1 WLR 1262; *Wrotham Park Estate Co v Parkside Homes Ltd* [1974] 2 All ER 321, [1974] 1 WLR 798.
4 *Woodar Investment Development Ltd v Wimpey Construction (UK) Ltd* [1980] 1 All ER 571, [1980] 1 WLR 277.

account. Damages for loss of income, for instance, are reduced to the extent that that income would have been taxed in the hands of the recipient.

Remoteness of loss. A contract breaker may be liable for damages; he is not liable for all the loss resulting to the other party merely on that account. The classic authority, *Hadley v Baxendale*,[5] makes him liable only if one of two conditions is met; the loss must either have been known to him as likely to happen when he contracted, or it must have been likely 'in the normal course of events.' The first ground of liability is straightforward. The second is infinitely interpretable, but has been taken to comport a substantial degree of likelihood – rather greater, it is said, than the risk sufficing to establish liability in tort.[6] How serious this difference is, is in fact doubtful; in particular, where the same act is both a breach of contract and a tort, the idea of different tests of remoteness has been castigated as 'absurd'.[7]

Confusingly, while *remoteness* of loss may preclude recovery for it, its *extent* will not. Assume a contract to supply a machine to an industrialist, who stands to gain a very lucrative contract with X by using it. If he does not know of that contract the supplier will not be liable if he breaks the contract for the loss of it;[8] but if he does know of it, he will be liable even if the loss of it is more catastrophic than he could have foreseen.[9]

Loss the result of the plaintiff's act. In contract, as in tort, one cannot recover for that part of a loss that is one's own fault. A plaintiff, that is, must mitigate his damage;[10] if goods are not delivered, by buying or hiring a substitute, if he is dismissed, by finding another job, and so on. If he does not mitigate his loss, he will be liable to claim damages only on the footing that he has. The principle equally applies where a plaintiff positively, but unreasonably, increases his loss. If a builder, in breach of contract, builds foundations 3 ft instead of 4 ft deep but just as safely, the house owner will not be able to sue him for the vast expense of employing another builder to deepen the foundations to the agreed depth.

Slightly less obviously, one cannot claim for a loss that one has reduced or eliminated by one's own act. Assume A promises, under

5   (1854) 9 Exch 341, 23 LJEx 179.
6   See generally *Koufos v Czarnikow, The Heron II* [1969] 1 AC 350 at 385, [1967] 3 All ER 686 at 691–692, per Lord Reid.
7   *H Parsons (Livestock) Ltd v Uttley Ingham & Co Ltd* [1978] QB 791 at 806–807, [1978] 1 All ER 525 at 535–536, per Scarman LJ.
8   *Victoria Laundry (Windsor) Ltd v Newman Industries Ltd* [1949] 2 KB 528, [1949] 1 All ER 997.
9   *H Parsons (Livestock) Ltd v Uttley Ingham & Co Ltd* [1978] QB 791, [1978] 1 All ER 525.
10 *Payzu Ltd v Saunders* [1919] 2 KB 581, 89 LJKB 17.

seal, to transfer shares to B on trust for C, but never does. It might seem that B could sue A for damages for breach of contract, which damages he would then hold on trust for C. However, the law takes the view that, since B himself suffers no loss by A's failure to perform, he can claim no more than nominal damages from A.[11]

C. COMPENSATION FOR BREACH OF TRUST. A trustee's duties are surprisingly like those of a contracting party; a mixture of promissory obligation (to do as the trust instrument tells him, for instance concerning the retention and sale of assets); strict liability (for disposing of assets in breach of trust, for example); and fault liability (to take reasonable care in looking after the trust property). As a result, damages[12] for breach of trust are computed rather like those for breach of contract; broadly the beneficiary is to be put in the same position as if the trust had been carried out. This is not, of course, invariable; courts of equity retain a general discretion in the matter, and do not necessarily apply all the rules relating to contractual damages.[13] There are specific exceptions too. Strict liability, and the liability of one trustee for concurring in a breach of trust by another, are mitigated by s 1 of the Trustee Act 1925, allowing the court discretion to exonerate a trustee wholly or partly if he acted 'honestly and reasonably' (though this power is sparingly exercised[14]). The fact that most breaches of trust involve, in essense, multiple plaintiffs (since most trusts have more than one beneficiary) gives rise to two slightly odd rules. First, one beneficiary who consents (in writing) to a breach of trust, or encourages it, not only loses his right to complain of it on orthodox grounds, but must indemnify the trustee out of his own interest in the trust for the latter's liability to the other beneficiaries as a result of s 62 of the Trustee Act 1925. Secondly, the trustee's duty is owed to a mythical entity called the 'trust fund', and not directly to the beneficiaries themselves. Hence, since income tax is paid by the beneficiaries but not by a trust itself, it is irrelevant to a trustee's liability that what the beneficiary is being compensated for the loss of, would have borne tax in his hands;[15] a startling contrast to the rule of damages in breach of contract.

---

11   This best explains cases such as *Re Price* [1928] Ch 579, 97 LJCh 423 and *Re Kay's Settlement, Broadbent v Macnab* [1939] Ch 329, [1939] 1 All ER 245.

12   Often called, not damages, but 'compensation' or 'restitution', by equity lawyers, to emphasise both the doctrinal separateness of equity and the independence of the rules of assessment of equitable compensation from those used to quantify damages at common law.

13   For instance, it appears that in equity losses cannot be too remote to be claimed, provided they result from a breach of trust: *Re Dawson Union Fidelity Trustee Co Ltd v Perpetual Trustee Co Ltd* [1966] 2 NSWLR 211 at 214 f, per Street J.

14   Eg *Re Stuart, Smith v Stuart* [1897] 2 Ch 583, 66 LJCh 780.

15   Compare *British Transport Commission v Gourley* [1956] AC 185, [1955] 3 All ER 796, with *Bartlett v Barclays Bank Trust Co Ltd (No 2)* [1980] Ch 539, [1980] 2 All ER 92.

(c) RECOVERY IN RESPECT OF UNJUSTIFIED ENRICHMENT

The essence of pecuniary recovery for unjustified enrichment is the amount by which the defendant is better off after a particular transaction than before it. But, like most general rules, this one requires exegesis.

Enrichment need not be *directly* pecuniary; as will have appeared in Ch 10, services not increasing one's net financial worth nevertheless may ground recovery – if, for instance, one requested them. This is perhaps the nearest analogy in unjustified enrichment to the rule that one can recover in tort for loss not expressible in pure financial terms. Nor, of course, need enrichment be positive; discharging a debt of £100 owed by X enriches him as much as giving him £100 directly.

There is also, it is suggested, a parallel to the rule that damages for breach of contract or tort must not be too remote; the enrichment must not only result from some unjustified cause, but must do reasonably proximately. The fire brigade which, in *Upton-on-Severn RDC v Powell*,[16] was held to have a claim for putting out a fire on the defendant's land, would have had the same claim (the 'value' of its services) whether the value of the defendant's property saved was £10,000 or £100,000; such values may represent the defendant's actual enrichment, but they are too remote to form the subject of a claim. Similarly, the misuser of another's trade name must pay over profits thus gained; but not profits that, although they would not have been made but for the offending trading, really represent other sources, such as the defendant's own business exertions.[17]

2. Specific remedies

Specific remedies, as we said, involve a court ordering a defendant to perform his obligations, and – at least in English law – threatening to punish him if he does not for the crime of contempt of court. A logical legal system would give the courts general power to make such orders, and then go on to describe when it could be exercised. English law, however, grew up pragmatically rather than logically; and it provides three different kinds of orders, each subject to its own special rules: specific performance, injunction and mandatory injunction. (It also provides a fourth, mandamus, to enforce obligations of an essentially public nature; but that is outside our scope).

(a) SPECIFIC PERFORMANCE

This remedy exists to enforce positive contractual obligations and a few

16   [1942] 1 All ER 220.
17   *My Kinda Town Ltd v Soll* [1982] FSR 147 is instructive.

other similar duties.[18] Most commonly used in respect of contracts relating to land, in principle it can be used to enforce any contractual obligation. Importantly, this even includes contracts in which the plaintiff himself has no interest except as promisee; thus, if A promises B for consideration to pay C £100, although (as we have seen) B cannot recover substantial damages if A fails to do so, he can get an order of specific performance to make him.[19]

Reflecting the secondary nature of specific remedies, in general the courts have jurisdiction to grant specific performance only where damages would also be available for breach of the duty concerned. In a few cases, however, mainly concerning trusts and other equitable rights, specific performance is available as a remedy in its own right. For instance, if A promises in consideration of C's marriage to transfer property to B on trust for C, C can obtain specific performance against A,[20] even though – not being party to the contract between A and B – he could not have got damages for breach of it. Conversely, a few kinds of contract cannot be specifically enforced. One is gratuitous contracts under seal; although damages are available for breach of them in the normal way, the maxim 'equity will not assist a volunteer' precludes their specific enforcement by the equitable remedy of specific performance (with what justification is not entirely clear). Again, contracts of employment, for obvious reasons, be enforced specifically against the employee.[1]

More importantly, though, specific performance is an equitable remedy and thus discretionary; and the discretion is illiberally exercised. Some bars to it are understandable. Contracts requiring temperamental skills (such as to paint a picture); personal trust (including most contracts to provide services or, conversely, to employ[2]); or excessive supervision of performance cannot be specifically enforced for practical reasons. Less defensibly, A is not permitted, as a matter of the discretion, to enforce specifically a contract against B that B could not have enforced specifically against A (the requirement of 'mutuality'). But the most important limit on the remedy is that it is not granted unless damages are shown to be inadequate. And in practice, damages are generally regarded as adequate except in narrow classes of contract: contracts concerning land, for instance, or unique chattels, or shares in a private company. Whether this limitation is desirable is doubtful; there is much to be said for effectively reversing the presumption against specific enforcement and allowing specific performance unless there is good reason to refuse it.

18 Eg a duty to convey land based on estoppel arising out of the rule in *Dillwyn v Llewellyn* (1862) 4 De G F & J 517, 8 Jur NS 1068; above, p 132 f.
19 *Beswick v Beswick* [1968] AC 58, [1967] 2 All ER 1197.
20 See, eg, *Macdonald v Scott* [1893] AC 642 at 650.
1   Trade Union and Labour Relations Act 1974, s 16.
2   But cf *Hill v C.A. Parsons Ltd* [1972] Ch 305, [1971] 3 All ER 1345.

(b) INJUNCTIONS

Specific performance deals with positive contractual obligations; injunctions with negative obligations, whatever their source – contract, tort, breach of trust or otherwise. Although a court may ostensibly grant an injunction whenever it is 'just and convenient',[3] in fact the injunction must enforce a specific obligation; a judge cannot decide that what X is doing is undesirable, though not illegal, and then award an injunction merely because it is just and convenient to stop him. The injunctive jurisdiction seems to divide into four cases. First, injunctions are available to enforce purely equitable rights, such as to prevent breach of confidence – understandably, since the jurisdiction to award an injunction is equitable in any case. Secondly, they may prevent an act, such as a breach of contract or tort, which, if committed, would found an action in damages. Thirdly, the Attorney-General, but no-one else, can prevent the commission of a crime.[4] Lastly there are a few exceptional cases. In family law, for instance, a party to a divorce can be preventing from subverting orders as to custody by improper communication with the child;[5] similarly the police may apparently prevent disposal of stolen property;[6] even though in such cases no action for damages would lie.

These cases, it now seems, are exhaustive. Both the Court of Appeal and the House of Lords have discountenanced attempts to argue that they are not.[7] (This supplants an earlier, more easy-going, view that acts illegitimate or, in a very broad sense, illegal – such as the commission of a crime or the telling of untruth – could be restrained by injunction by anyone suffering special damage, whatever the position as to damages. That view, for all its attractiveness, is irreconcileable with the dogma that specific remedies are secondary).

So much for when injunctions *can* be granted; more important, in the light of their being secondary remedies, available only by discretion, is when they *will*. Doubtless because orders not to do something are less intrusive and less difficult to police than those requiring positive action, they are much easier to get than orders of specific performance. Indeed, effectively injunctions are available to enforce any negative contractual stipulation (such as not to compete, or not to build on a given piece of land), or to prevent a large number of torts (such as nuisance) unless

3   Supreme Court Act 1981, s 37(1).
4   Compare *A-G v Harris* [1961] 1 QB 74, [1960] 3 All ER 207, with *Gouriet v Union of Post Office Workers* [1978] AC 435, [1977] 3 All ER 70.
5   *R v R & I* [1961] 3 All ER 461, [1961] 1 WLR 1334.
6   *Chief Constable of Kent v V* [1983] QB 34, [1982] 3 All ER 36. Sed quaere?
7   *Lonrho Ltd v Shell Petroleum Co Ltd* [1982] AC 173, [1981] 2 All ER 456; *Garden Cottage Foods Ltd v Milk Marketing Board* [1983] 2 All ER 770, *RCA Corpn v Pollard* [1983] Ch 135, [1982] 3 All ER 771, CA.

there is a good reason to the contrary.[8] What counts as a good reason is, moreover, limited. It includes the fact that the plaintiff has misbehaved (as by deceiving the court), or that his complaint is trivial, or that the injunction will do him no good anyway because he will continue to suffer the same damage from other sources;[9] but, significantly, not either that the plaintiff is acting for an ulterior motive, or even (within reason) that he is exercising his rights in a socially harmful way. I can prevent you infringing my right to light merely with the intent to extort as much as I can for the release of that right;[10] again, I can vindicate my right to peace and quiet, or unpolluted water, even if as a result popular sports are curtailed or sewage disposal badly hampered.[11]

This generous attitude to injunctions is, however, curtailed in one case. If ordering a contractor not to break a contract in effect forces him positively to perform it (ordering a skilled employee of A, for instance, not to work for A's competitors may effectively force him to work for A or not at all), then if the contract is one that would not be directly specifically enforced, the court will refuse an injunction to prevent the same thing happening indirectly.[12]

(c) MANDATORY INJUNCTIONS

There is no reason in logic to distinguish a mandatory injunction, which orders a person to do a positive act, from an order of specific performance, which orders him positively to perform his contract; the difference merely reflects a long mental separation of contractual and other obligations.[13] Mandatory injunctions are used for two purposes. One is where a person is obliged, non-contractually, to do some positive act (for instance, a landowner must remove erections blocking his neighbour's right to light; and a possessor of another's thing may have to return it to the owner). The other occasional function is the neutralisation of the effects of wrongful acts. If A, for instance, contracts with B not to convey certain land to C but does so, B may obtain an injunction telling C (at least if he knew the facts) to reconvey the land to A.[14]

For the same reasons as apply to specific performance, and also since

8   See *Doherty v Allman* (1878) 3 App Cas 709 at 720, per Lord Cairns.
9   *Wood v Sutcliffe* (1851) 2 Sim NS 163, 21 LJCh 253.
10 *Cowper v Laidler* [1903] 2 Ch 337, 72 LJCh 578.
11 See *Kennaway v Thompson* [1981] QB 88, [1980] 3 All ER 329; and *Pride of Derby and Derbyshire Angling Association Ltd v British Celanese Ltd* [1953] Ch 149, [1953] 1 All ER 179.
12 *Page One Records Ltd v Britton* [1967] 3 All ER 822, [1968] 1 WLR 157.
13 A separation not in any case absolute. In *Puddephatt v Leith* [1916] 1 Ch 200, 85 LJCh 185, a contract was enforced by mandatory injunction.
14 *Esso Petroleum Co Ltd v Kingswood Motors (Addlestone) Ltd* [1974] QB 142, [1973] 3 All ER 1057.

the effects of a mandatory injunction may well be drastic in terms of expense or otherwise (by requiring demolition of a house, or execution of works whose costs are disproportionate to their benefit[15]) mandatory injunctions are very sparingly granted.

(d) GENERAL FEATURES OF SPECIFIC REMEDIES

Besides providing the plaintiff with what he wants rather than a substituted remedy in money, two general features distinguish specific remedies in general; the effect of the defendant's insolvency, and (a related matter) their effect on third parties.

On insolvency, the rule is simple: specific remedies prevail in full, while substitutionary remedies in damages – not to mention debts – do not. If a prepaid seller of goods becomes insolvent, the buyer can prima facie only prove in the insolvency to recover what he has paid;[16] but if the contract is specifically enforceable, then the buyer obtains his goods in specie and thus prevails. Admittedly this case is often explained on the ground that the buyer under a specifically enforceable contract is 'owner' in equity as soon as the contract is made, and thus that we are in the realms of property and not obligation. But this is not convincing. Specific remedies sometimes prevail in insolvency even though no conceivable element of property is involved. Few would suggest, for instance, that an employee could not be restrained from revealing his employer's trade secrets merely because he happened to be insolvent at the time the action was brought; yet that would follow from the proposition that only proprietary rights, as against specifically enforceable ones, could prevail in in insolvency.

Secondly, at least in certain cases, specifically enforceable obligations relating to property can be enforced against others than the obligor. Thus a contract of sale (or lease) of land can be enforced a transferee from the contractor who first agreed to convey the land (assuming that the contract was registered under the Land Registration Act 1925 or the Land Charges Act 1972). Admittedly, as with insolvency, this is traditionally explained by invoking property, and saying that the buyer's rights under a specifically enforceable contract of sale can be enforced against third parties only because the buyer is owner in equity as soon as the contract is made. But here too this explanation is unconvincing. Not only does a bare trust of property bear many of the characteristics of an obligation to transfer it in future, as we have observed; more to the point, the 'trust' created by an enforceable contract for the sale of land has few of the features of an

---

15   As in *Redland Bricks Ltd v Morris* [1970] AC 652, [1969] 2 All ER 576, HL.
16   See *Re Wait* [1927] Ch 606, 96 LJCh 179; compare *Freevale Ltd v Metrostore (Holdings) Ltd* [1984] 1 All ER 495.

orthodox trust except the name, and the fact that it can be enforced against third parties.[17] To say it is a proprietary right is thus at best to encapsulate the form without the substance.

(e) DAMAGES IN LIEU OF EQUITABLE RELIEF

By the Chancery Amendment Act 1858, the courts were given what seems rather an odd power to substitute an award of damages for specific relief; to make, wherever an injunction or order of specific performance was available, a monetary award instead. The effect of this power, at first sight otiose (since normally injunctions and specific performance are available only when damages are anyway), is in fact twofold. First, it allows obligations originally enforceable only in equity, such as the duty not to misuse confidential information, to be enforced by damages. Secondly, specific remedies ex hypothesi deal with future breaches of obligation, damages with past ones. But what of the plaintiff faced with the defendant determined to continue committing (say) a minor nuisance, which the court will not restrain by injunction? To tell him to sue periodically for damages is unsatisfactory; to give him a sum in lieu of the injunction he has not got which can cover, for once and for all, both past and future loss, is rather better.

It used to be thought that damages in lieu of specific relief, where they paralleled a power to award damages at common law (for instance, if they were in lieu of specific performance) might be awarded on different principles. But recently any such differences have practically disappeared; in general, a plaintiff with concurrent rights to damages in equity and at common law will have little advantage in suing for one rather than the other.[18]

3. Self-help

Within strict limits, a person may take private action to enforce certain obligations; notably, to protect his rights to property and payment of debts. The right to exercise reasonable force in self-defence is a rather specialised application of the same principle.

(a) SELF-HELP IN PROTECTING PROPERTY RIGHTS

As far as the law of obligations is concerned, a person with the right to possession of land can use reasonable force to get it back from whoever

---

17 D. Waters, *The Constructive Trust,* 87 f.
18 See in particular *Wroth v Tyler* [1974] Ch 30, [1973] 1 All ER 897 and *Johnson v Agnew* [1980] AC 367, [1979] 1 All ER 883.

has it. If he does so he is liable for neither trespass nor assault. But this right is not very significant, at least where non-residential land is concerned, since s 6 of the Criminal Law Act 1977 makes it an offence to take back such land by force even though one is the owner of it.

Chattels, however, are a different matter. An owner of a chattel may use reasonable force to recover it from a wrongful possessor, even an innocent one; a woman can thus forcibly recover her hand bag either from the thief who snatched it or from the person who bought it innocently from him.[19]

A landowner may protect his land from damage or encroachment resulting from the state of neighbouring land. He can thus cut off roots and branches from trees impinging on his property;[20] and indeed, it seems he can use reasonable force to abate any state of affairs amounting to a nuisance, even if it involves going on to his neighbour's land to do so. (Though, obviously, forcibly abating some nuisances would be so drastic that it would automatically be unreasonable. One would hardly be justified in demolishing an office block that happened to infringe one's right to light.)

Lastly, a landowner may keep pending satisfaction (though oddly enough it appears he may not sell) any chattel[1] on his land which was the instrument of damage for which someone was liable; for example a ball, carelessly thrown, that has just broken his window.[2] The owner of the chattel himself need not be the one liable in damages; he must pay what is owed to get his thing back, and then proceed as best he can, in tort or on the basis of unjustified enrichment, against the real wrongdoer.

(b) SELF-HELP TO ENFORCE CONSENSUAL OBLIGATIONS

If you owe me £100 I cannot forcibly seize property of yours worth £100 and hold it until you pay me. Nevertheless, there are various devices an obligee can use to secure payment.

First, he can make obligations of his own conditional on payment. A ship may be chartered for two years at a monthly rate, but the owner given by contract the right to withdraw the vessel if the charterer fails to pay or pays late.[3] Especially if the charterer has a good bargain, this power gives the owner a potent weapon; particularly since it is now clear that the courts refuse to control its exercise in any way.[4]

---

19   Cf *Blades v Higgs* (1861) 10 CB(NS) 713, 30 LJCP 347; subsequent proceedings (1865) 11 HLCas 621, 34 LJCP 286.
20   *Lemmon v Webb* [1895] AC 1, 64 LJCh 205.
 1   If the chattel is an animal, though, his rights are governed by a specific statutory code: Animals Act 1971, s 7.
 2   See the odd Canadian case of *R v Howson* [1966] 2 OR 63, 55 DLR (2d) 582, CA.
 3   Which, being a right exercisable independently of court action, is essentially a right of self-help.
 4   *Scandinavian Trading Tanker Co AB v Flota Petrolera Eucatoriana, The Scaptrade* [1983] 2 All ER 763, [1983] 3 WLR 203.

A related device is the deposit. A contracting party may deposit a sum of money on terms that if he breaks his contract in any respect, or does not pay any sum owing under it, he forfeits what he has deposited. Although a *promise* to pay a sum out of all proportion to the consequences of a breach of contract is unenforceable, authority suggests – at least in commercial contracts not relating to land – that no similar rule applies to deposits, which may be forfeited without control, according simply to the terms of the contract.[5]

Uncontrolled 'do-it-yourself' contractual remedies can be criticised, not only because on principle remedies for breach of obligation should be at least supervised by the courts,[6] but on the more general ground that using the general law of contract to obtain disproportionate redress smacks of abuse in the same way as stipulating for an excessive sum to be paid in the event of a breach. Lack of control, however, can be defended pragmatically. It reduces litigation, increases certainty, and seems to do little harm in practice. Moreover, promises to pay large sums by way of 'damages' can perhaps be differentiated from actual deposits of such large sums on the ground that foolish payments are less common than rash promises, and thus give rise to a smaller need for protection.

Liens. Lastly, there is the device of the lien. Where A is in possession of B's thing, as with a garage repairing a car, he can stipulate for a right to keep it pending payment of anything owing to him by B. Certain relationships, indeed, give rise to such a right by implication; thus stockbrokers, solicitors, and innkeepers are given liens by implication, as are all those who repair or work on and improve others' property (such as garages, or jewellers cutting uncut diamonds): though, oddly enough not those, such as warehousemen, who merely store and preserve others' property.[7] But even outside these cases, parties can, and frequently do, stipulate for a lien.

There is no reason why a lien over A's property should not secure money owed by B, and indeed this is sometimes the case; an owner of a car, for instance, who hires it out impliedly consents to the hirer creating repairers' liens over it, and is bound by such liens if the hirer fails to pay for the repairs concerned.[8] But these cases are exceptional because in general one is bound by a lien over one's property created

---

5 See *Galbraith v Mitchenall Estates Ltd* [1965] 2 QB 473, [1964] 2 All ER 653. For contracts relating to land, however, cases such as *Steedman v Drinkle* [1916] 1 AC 275, 85 LJPC 79, suggest a different result.

6 French law begins from the position that a contract may be rescinded only by court intervention, even though in practice the rule is easily sidestepped.

7 *Hatton v Car Maintenance Ltd* [1915] 1 Ch 621, 84 LJCh 847. In practice most such bailees stipulate specifically for such a lien, so the rule matters little in practice.

8 See *Tappenden v Artus* [1964] 2 QB 185, [1963] 3 All ER 213, CA, where, however, permission to create the lien was inferred on the facts.

by someone else only if one expressly or impliedly consented to its creation. Only in very rare cases can liens be created without any consent of the owner, for instance by a thief; the most important is the case of the innkeeper.[9]

4. Proprietary remedies

We mentioned in Ch 10 that English law not infrequently does by the law of property what other systems do by the law of obligations; thus I can recover property I transfer by mistake, not because the recipient is unjustifiably enriched by receiving it, but because title to it never passes in any case.[10] Again, we have mentioned that if I pay money by mistake, ownership of that money remains in me in equity and I can get it back therefore, not as owed to me, but as mine.[11] The difference is significant, since proprietary rights share two features of specifically enforceable rights; they prevail in insolvency, and they prevail against third parties. Thus I can recover property transferred under a contract avoided for mistake from innocent third partes as well as from the actual transferee; similarly, if I am owner in equity of money paid by mistake, it follows that, provided the payee still has it, I obtain preference in his insolvency.

The chief form of proprietary remedy dealt with here is the 'constructive trust'; an institution whereby, in certain cases, property legally owned by A is impressed with a trust in favour of B and thus becomes B's in equity in order to give effect to some obligation of A's. Not that this is a remedy available to enforce obligations in general, still less to do abstract justice between the parties in the absence of any other form of obligation;[12] on the contrary, it is a means of enforcing a limited number of specific obligations. (By contrast, American jurisdictions have in many cases come to regard the constructive trust as generally available to enforce any obligation based on unjustified enrichment, and indeed on occasion to be imposed whenever it seems fair to do so; the criterion being whether it is thought just in the individual case that a remedy should be given that prevails over general creditors.[13] Hitherto, this idea has found little welcome in England – though times may change.)

The obligations thus enforced by English law split effectively into three. First, there are conditional transfers of land. As mentioned in Ch 11,

9   *Marsh v Metropolitan Police Comr* [1945] KB 43, [1944] 2 All ER 392.
10 Eg *Hardman v Booth* (1863) 1 H & C 803, 32 LJEx 105.
11 *Chase Manhattan Bank, NA v Israel-British Bank (London) Ltd* [1981] Ch 105, [1979] 3 All ER 1025.
12 *Burns v Burns* [1984] 1 All ER 244, makes the point well.
13 See, eg, Scott (1955) 71 LQR 39, for discussion and advocacy of the American position.

where A transfers land to B on the basis of B's undertaking to let A himself or a third party, C, have some rights in it, B is deemed, to the extent of A's or C's rights, to hold the land on constructive trust to effectuate them.[14]

Secondly, there is the doctrine of secret trusts (together with its offshoot, that of mutual wills). As with a conditional transfer of land, so with a conditional transfer by will; if A leaves property by will to B on the faith of B's promise to let C have it, then even though B's promise is unattested and not enforceable as part of the will, and even though it is unenforceable as a matter of contract because made in favour of a third party, it is enforced by the device of making B hold on trust for C.[15]

Thirdly, a constructive trust is available to enforce certain obligations based on unjustified enrichment. Where money or property is transferred because of mistake, undue influence or (doubtless) duress, then that property is held by the recipient on constructive trust for the transferor, who therefore, as we have mentioned, will take precedence in the recipient's insolvency if the latter still has what was transferred.[16] (The transferor, of course, also retains his personal right to recover it back.) The same apparently applies where a criminal seeks to benefit from his crime. If I murder my uncle, I can make no claim to inherit under his will if I am detected before his estate is distributed; if I am found out later, having inherited, it seems I hold what I received on trust for his residuary estate. Whether this principle extends to other examples of unjustified enrichment, not involving property transferred subject to defective consent, or attempts by a wrongdoer to profit from his own wrong, is doubtful. It has certainly been doubted, for instance, whether the principle applies where it is sought to strip a fiduciary of his profit. Thus in *Lister v Stubbs*,[17] where the matter was discussed, an agent receiving a bribe was held to owe the amount of it to his principal, but not to hold the actual bribe on trust for him. Despite criticisms of *Lister v Stubbs*, it is submitted that this is the better answer. The question is effectively whether claimants in unjustified enrichment cases ought to be paid in full when faced with insolvent defendants; and it is suggested that there is no reason why they should, any more than claimants relying on breach of contract or tort. To say, as some have, that a person's general creditors should not benefit from property the insolvent should never have had because it represents his unjustified enrichment, is beside the point; they have no more moral right to benefit from money that he ought to have paid over in damages for breach of contract or tort, yet we do not for that reason make contract and tort claimants preferential creditors in insolvency.

14 See *Bannister v Bannister* [1948] 2 All ER 133, CA; *Binions v Evans* [1972] Ch 359, [1972] 2 All ER 70.
15 *Dufour v Pereira* (1769) 1 Dick 419.
16 *Chase Manhattan Bank NA v Israel-British Bank (London) Ltd* [1981] Ch 105, [1975] 3 All ER 1025.
17 (1890) 45 Ch D 1, 59 LJCh 570, CA.

Fourthly, as we mentioned in Ch 10, the constructive trust is the means by which those, such as cohabitees, who contribute to others' property on the basis that they are to get an interest in it, are protected. The net result, of course, of using this device to protect such contributors is to give them an extensive right protected from alienees of the property (because it is itself proprietary),[18] and also from the general creditors of the original owners of it. Whether one approves of such development is, of course, a matter of social, rather than legal, policy.

---

18   *Williams & Glyns Bank Ltd v Boland* [1981] AC 487, [1980] 2 All ER 408.

Index

Acceptance
contract, as ingredient of, 126, 127
Accident
compensation for, generally, 72–75
Advertisement
invitation to treat, as, 126
Agency
acts of agent, generally, 153
authority in, 158–161
limitation of agent's authority, 161
nature of, 158
necessity, of, 172
ostensible authority, 159
ratification of agent's acts, 160
undisclosed principal, doctrine of, 160, 161
vicarious liability distinguished, 158
Agreement
consent distinguished, 188
defective, 193, 194
enrichment justified by, 123
equitable estoppel, 189, 190
falling short of contract, 189
Amenity
land, of, damage to, 21
Animals
dangerous, 43, 44
dog damaging livestock, 43
farm animals, damage by, 43
statutory provisions as to, 43
Arrest
powers and liabilities, 29
Assault
fear and distress, causing, 26, 27
tort of, 25
Assignment
equitable—
contract, by way of, 202
generally, 204
significance of, 204, 205
trust, by declaration of, 203, 204
holder in due course, 206
rights of assignee, 205, 206
statutory, 202

Assignment—*continued*
subrogation distinguished, 210
third party rights, 206, 207
Auction
mistake at sale, 168
stolen goods sold by, 15

Bailment
bailor and bailee, liabilities, 61–63
borrower of goods, position of, 15
involuntary bailee, 15
Banker
customer, relation with, 58, 59
Bankruptcy
reputed ownership, 206
Battery
examples, 25, 26
generally, 25
interference without injury, 26
meaning, 25, 26
surgeon, liability of, 26
Benefit and burden
doctrine of, 120, 121
Bill of exchange
holder in due course, 206

Care
duty of—
bailor and bailee, 61, 62
company officers, 65
contracting parties, 60, 61
extent—
generally, 49–51
limits on recovery, 51, 52
omission, liability for, 52–54
land occupation—
adjoining premises, 56, 57
outsiders, 55, 56
trespassers, 55
visitors, 54, 55
misstatement, negligent, 57–60
principle from which arising, 49
sources of, 49
specific duties, 54 et seq.
trustee and beneficiaries, 63–65

Nervous shock
injury through, 25, 26
Noise
nuisance caused by, 20
Non est factum
principle of, 168
Novus actus interveniens
doctrine of, 197
Nuisance
amenity, damage to, 21
existing, plaintiff coming to, 22
generally, 20–22
highway, obstruction of, 27
noise, 20
noxious activity, 40, 41
public, 96
smell, fumes and smoke, 20–22

Obligation
aspects, 1, 2
assignment of, 202–207
benefit and burden, doctrine of, 120, 121
concurrent, 162–164
criminal law compared to law of, 4–6
death, transmission on, 207
enforcement—
damages in lieu of equitable relief, 225
general features of specific remedies, 224, 225
generally, 211, 212
injunction, 220–224
pecuniary—
generally, 212
liquidated claims for debts, 212
unjustified enrichment, recovery in respect of, 220
unliquidated damages for wrongs, 212–219
proprietary remedies, 228–230
self-help, 225–228
specific performance, 220, 221
extinction and modification, 183 et seq.
factors negativing—
duress, 171
illegality, 175–178
impossibility, 173
minority, 174, 175
mistake, 165–170
necessity, 171–173
plaintiff's own act, 181, 182
public policy, 178–181
joint and several liability, 163
meaning, 1
non-tortious, liability for others in, 157. 158

Obligation—*continued*
participation in breach of, 83–85
parties to, rights and duties, 2, 3
primary and secondary, 3
promissory, 124 et seq.
See also PROMISE
property, relating to, 6, 7
remedy distinguished, 3
sources of, 3, 4
transfer of, 199 et seq.
Occupation
land, of, duties arising from. *See* LAND
Occupier
adjoining premises, liability for damage to, 56, 57
care, duty of, 54
defective premises, of, 55, 57
obligations to others—
passers-by, 56, 57
trespassers, 55
visitors, 54, 55
Offer
acceptance of, 126, 127
contract, as ingredient of, 126
withdrawal of, 126
Omission
liability for, 52–54

Passing off
generally, 80, 81
Performance
extinction of obligation by, 183
tender of, 183
Person
interference with. *See* INTERFERENCE
Plaintiff
damage by own act, 181, 182
Privilege
absolute, 35
defamation, generally, 35, 36
qualified, 35, 36
reports, 36, 37
Promise
act in certain way, to, 143–147
bilateral, 125
breach of, 133
coupled with fault, 134, 135
categories of, 129
conditional, 141 et seq.
enforceable, form of—
certainty, requirement of, 128, 129
consideration, 129–132
expression of promise, form of, 127, 128
gratuitous promises, 135